DATE DUE

MY 29 '97			
MY 28 '98			
NO 27 00			

DEMCO 38-296

THE UN AND THE BRETTON WOODS INSTITUTIONS

The UN and the Bretton Woods Institutions

New Challenges for the Twenty-First Century

Edited by

Mahbub ul Haq
Special Adviser to UNDP Administrator
New York

Richard Jolly
Deputy Executive Director
UNICEF

Paul Streeten
Emeritus Professor
Boston University

and

Khadija Haq
Executive Director
North South Roundtable
New York

St. Martin's Press   New York

© North South Roundtable 1995

HG 205 .U54 1995

The UN and the Bretton Woods in 1995
institutions

ISBN 0–312–12449–X (cloth)
ISBN 0–312–12450–3 (pbk.)

Library of Congress Cataloging-in-Publication Data
The UN and the Bretton Woods institutions : new challenges
for the twenty-first century / edited by Mahbub ul Haq . . . [et al.].
p. cm. .
Includes index.
ISBN 0–312–12449–X. — ISBN 0–312–12450–3 (pbk.)
1. International finance—Congresses. 2. International economic
relations—Congresses. 3. World Bank—Congresses. 4. International
Monetary Fund—Congresses. 5. Economic history—1990– —Congresses.
6. United Nations Monetary and Financial Conference (1944 : Bretton
Woods, N.H.)—Congresses. I. Haq, Mahbub ul, 1934– .
HG205.U54 1995
332'.042—dc20
                                                        94–36892
                                                          CIP

Contents

Preface

With the end of the cold war, the United Nations is experiencing a new lease on life. In political and peace-keeping matters, it has often been thrust to centre-stage. However, in economic and social development, the United Nations continues much as before, with most of the finance and much of the action concentrated on the Bretton Woods institutions.

This book explores why this is unsatisfactory and how it can be changed. It presents the papers and conclusions prepared for and reviewed by two meetings of the North–South Roundtable of the Society for International Development, in April and September 1993, on the eve of the fiftieth anniversary of the conference in Bretton Woods which laid the basis for the institutions which bear that name.

Earlier meetings of the North–South Roundtable had considered measures to strengthen the United Nations for the 1990s. Other reports, notably the series of reports under the Nordic Project, reviewed changes of policy and actions needed to reform the United Nations. But most of these took only marginal account of the Bretton Woods institutions, and discussions of the need for reforms of the Bretton Woods institutions have so far concentrated on measures to improve internal effectiveness with no fundamental questioning of their basic objectives and roles in relation to the world economy of the next century.

The papers in this volume consider reform of global economic governance from a perspective given by four concerns:

- An integral view of the United Nations and the Bretton Woods institutions taken together;
- A priority for human development, including gender awareness, not just economic and financial concerns;
- A long-term perspective, looking to global issues of the twenty-first century, not merely problems of the 1990s;
- Perspectives given by needs and concerns in the South as well as the North, taking account also of regional perspectives in Asia, Africa, Latin America and the Middle East.

Forty-five eminent personalities from different backgrounds, nationalities and expertise participated in the discussions of these papers organized by the North–South Roundtable meeting in Bretton Woods. The participants are listed on pp. x–xi. About half have worked in the United

Nations at different times and about one-quarter in the Bretton Woods institutions. Nine have served as ministers in their own countries and most have at one time or another been members or advisers of governments and the international agencies. Thus, although most had reputations as academics or analysts, the wealth of practical experience was also considerable.

Part I of the volume presents an overview of the main themes and conclusions of the discussion. This summary has been prepared by a small team consisting of Mahbub ul Haq, Khadija Haq, Lal Jayawardena and Richard Jolly and was published as a summary report of the Bretton Woods meeting. Part II analyses the Bretton Woods system in the light of the original vision of the founders. Two regional perspectives, African and West European, are also presented here. Part III offers some proposals for reform. Part IV sets out the priority areas for global governance for the next century.

The fiftieth anniversary of the Bretton Woods institutions took place in 1994; the fiftieth anniversary of the United Nations will take place in 1995. Both events mark the need for fundamental rethinking of these institutions in relation to the needs and challenges of the final part of the twentieth century and the opening years of the next. It is hoped that this book will provide a stimulus and challenge to the new thinking and perspectives required for this task.

New York
March 1994

Mahbub ul Haq, Richard Jolly,
Paul Streeten and Khadija Haq

List of Abbreviations

ASEAN	Association of South-East Asian Nations
ECA	Economic Commission for Africa
ECOSOC	Economic and Social Council of the UN
FAO	Food and Agriculture Organisation of the United Nations
GATT	General Agreement on Tariffs and Trade
GNP	Gross national product
IBRD	International Bank for Reconstruction and Development
IDA	International Development Association
IFAD	International Fund for Agricultural Development
ILO	International Labour Organisation
IMF	International Monetary Fund
INSTRAW	United Nations International Research and Training Institute for the Advancement of Women
LPA	Lagos Plan of Action
NAFTA	North American Free Trade Agreement
NGO	Non-governmental organisation
OAU	Organisation for African Unity
OECD	Organisation for Economic Cooperation and Development
OPEC	Organisation of Petroleum Exporting Countries
SAARC	South Asian Association for Regional Cooperation
SAP	Structural Adjustment Programmes
SDR	Special drawing rights of IMF
UNCTAD	United Nations Conference on Trade and Development
UNDP	United Nations Development Programme
UNESCO	United Nations Educational, Scientific and Cultural Organisation
UNFPA	United Nations Population Fund
UNICEF	United Nations Children's Fund
UNIFEM	United Nations Development Fund for Women
WHO	World Health Organisation

Conference Participants and Contributors

All participants attended in their personal capacities. Participants' affiliations given here are those at the time of the meeting and not necessarily their present affiliations. An asterisk (*) before a name indicates a contributor to this volume.

Ismail Sabri Abdalla, Chairman, Third World Forum, Cairo
Jim Adams, Director, Operations Policy, The World Bank, Washington, DC
*Adebayo Adedeji, Former Executive Director of ECA, Nigeria
Lourdes Arizpe, Director, Institute of Anthropological Research, Mexico
Princess Basma, Q.A. Jordan Social Welfare Fund, Jordan
*Andrea Boltho, Fellow, Magdalen College, Oxford University, UK
Margaret Catley-Carlson, President, Population Council, New York
James P. Grant, Executive Director, UNICEF, New York
*Stephany Griffith-Jones, Institute of Development Studies, Sussex, UK
*Catherine Gwin, Vice-President, Overseas Development Council, Washington, DC
Peter Hansen, Secretary-General, Commission on Global Governance, Geneva
*Khadija Haq, Executive Director, North–South Roundtable, New York
*Mahbub ul Haq, Special Adviser to the Administrator, UNDP, New York
Gerry Helleiner, Professor of Economics, University of Toronto, Canada
Eveline Herfkens, Executive Director of the World Bank, Washington, DC
Ryokichi Hirono, Faculty of Economics, Seikei University, Japan
Enrique Iglesias, President, Inter-American Development Bank, Washington, DC
  (Represented by *Nora Marulanda*, Senior Advisor, Inter-American Development Bank)
Shafiqul Islam, Senior Fellow, Council on Foreign Relations, New York
*Lal Jayawardena, Former Director of WIDER, Sri Lanka
*Richard Jolly, Chairman, North–South Roundtable, UNICEF, New York
Alexander Love, Chairman, DAC, Paris
Carlos Massad, Deputy Executive Secretary of ECLAC
Solita Monsod, Professor of Economics, University of the Philippines, Quezon City
Philip Ndegwa, Chairman First Chartered Securities Ltd, Nairobi

I. G. Patel, Former Director, London School of Economics, India

Jan Pronk, Minister for Development Cooperation, The Netherlands

Shridath Ramphal, Co-Chairman, United Nations Commission on Global Governance, Geneva

Gustav Ranis, Professor of Economics, Yale University, New Haven

Nafis Sadik, Executive Director, UNFPA, New York

Horst Schulmann, President, Landeszentral Bank, Frankfurt, Germany

*Alexander Shakow, Director, External Relations, The World Bank, Washington, DC

Alexander Shokhin, Vice Prime Minister, Russia
(Represented by *Edward Kudryavtsev*, Deputy Permanent Representative, Russian Mission to the United Nations)

*H. W. Singer, Institute of Development Studies, Sussex, England

Anoop Singh, Senior Advisor, Policy Development and Review Department. IMF, Washington, DC

Joel Spiro, Director, Office of Technical Specialised Agencies, US Department of State, Washington, DC

*Frances Stewart, Institute of Commonwealth Studies, Oxford, UK

*Paul Streeten, Consultant, UNDP Human Development Report

*Maurice Williams, President, Society for International Development, Washington, DC

*John Williamson, Institute of International Economics, Washington, DC

Part I

Overview

Two major issues dominated the creative period of international rethinking during and just after the Second World War. One was to avoid another catastrophic war. The other was to avoid another global economic depression and to ensure universal economic and social well-being. The first preoccupation was with military security; the second with human security – and the link between the two was never forgotten. Unfortunately, with the start of the cold war between the superpowers, the first component of security often dominated the second. But it is good to remind ourselves that human security was an essential part of the original vision.

A good place to start is with the Charter of the United Nations itself:

> With a view to the creation of conditions of stability and well-being which are necessary for peaceful and friendly relations among nations...all members pledge themselves to take joint and separate action in cooperation with the organization for *promoting higher standards of living, full employment, and conditions of economic and social progress and development.* (Chapter IX).[1]

What is even more revealing is the foresight of the founders of the United Nations. The US Secretary of State, in his Report to the President on the results of the San Francisco Conference, had this to say on 26 June 1945:

> The battle of peace has to be fought on two fronts. The first is the security front where victory spells freedom from fear. The second is the economic and social front where victory means freedom from want. Only victory on both fronts can assure the world of an enduring peace.[2]

THE KEYNESIAN VISION

The economic and social security aspects of human survival were dealt with primarily by Lord Keynes in his intellectually powerful writings in the 1940s. There were at least three cornerstones of his analysis:

- Advocacy of full employment policies in an expanding world economy;
- Implicit faith in the need for government action to redress the shortfalls of the markets;
- Tremendous confidence in building new global institutions to manage an increasingly interdependent global economy.

Each of these became important themes of mainstream national and international policy for the first two decades of the postwar world. And for 25 years or so, they underpinned an unprecedented period of world economic growth, with unprecedented stability and low unemployment in most of the industrialised countries.

But the three pillars of the new approach were never as strong as needed, and over time, each was weakened rather than strengthened. Full employment goals receded in their importance. Free working of the market took over as an economic ideology, reducing the role of the state. And private market flows came to assume more importance than official flows.

THE BRETTON WOODS INSTITUTIONS

It appears that international institutions have weakened precisely at a time when global interdependence has increased. The Keynesian vision was already considerably diluted in the actual emergence of the Bretton Woods institutions. Over time, their role has been undermined further as global economic decision-making shifted increasingly to smaller groups like the G-7 or to the workings of the international private capital markets. It is instructive to view the gap between the original vision and the present reality.

IMF is no longer the global monetary manager that it was supposed to be:

- Keynes proposed a Fund equal to one-half of world imports. In actual practice, the IMF today controls liquidity equal to 2 per cent of world imports.
- Keynes envisioned the IMF as a world central bank, issuing its own reserve currency (the 'bancors'). Keynes's concept was never accepted at the time, and even the later attempt of the IMF to create SDRs in the 1970s proved to be stillborn because of the persistent US trade deficits. SDRs constitute less than 3 per cent of global liquidity today.
- Keynes placed the burden of adjustment on *both* surplus and deficit nations, envisaging a penal interest rate of 1 per cent a month on outstanding trade surpluses. In actual practice, deficit nations (mainly developing countries) have had to bear the principal burden of adjustment.
- The heart of the global monetary system was fixed exchange rates: this disappeared in 1971 with the introduction of floating exchange rates and consequent currency instability.
- The IMF by now exercises some monetary discipline only on developing countries, responsible for less than 10 per cent of global liquidity.

Similar erosion has taken place in the role of the World Bank, which was supposed to stand in between the global capital markets and the developing countries and recycle resources to poor nations both by using its own creditworthiness and by gradually building up the creditworthiness of its clients. The reality is long removed from the original vision:

● While there was a global surplus of $180 billion in 1990, the World Bank recycled only *minus* $1.7 billion to developing countries.[3] Private capital markets did most of the recycling towards a handful of already better-off creditworthy nations.
● While the number of absolute poor has been going up, the real IDA resources per poor person have been going down – underscoring the disturbing reality that the resource profile of the Bank and the poverty profile of the developing world are completely out of sync.
● The World Bank does not possess the policy instruments to deal with the debt problem of the developing countries. Since it refuses to reschedule its own debts, it is ending up owning a major part of the debts of its recipients. By now, it is beginning to recycle its own debts rather than real resources.

The third pillar of the Bretton Woods system – GATT, even with the later addition of UNCTAD – has proved to be even more marginal:

● Keynes envisioned an International Trade Organisation (ITO), which would not only maintain free trade but also help stabilise world commodity prices. That is why he linked the value of his world currency (the bancors) with the average price of 30 primary commodities, including gold and oil. In actual practice, GATT excluded primary commodities altogether and a belated effort was made to include them in the Uruguay Round of trade negotiations. In the meantime, commodity prices have hit their lowest level since the Great Depression.
● The marginal role of GATT in policing world trade is revealed by a startling statistic: only 7 per cent of the world production entering trade markets is presently subject to GATT rules – excluding as it does agricultural commodities, tropical products, textiles, services, capital flows, labour flows, intellectual property resources, etc.

THE UNITED NATIONS SYSTEM

The fourth pillar of the global economic system was supposed to be the role of the United Nations agencies in social and human fields – though Keynes hardly ever mentioned this fact in his writings. But the mandate for such a role clearly existed in the United Nations Charter, and many United

Nations agencies were created to implement the concern for the second economic and social (security) front where victory means 'freedom from want' – in fields as diverse as education, health, food and nutrition, labour and employment, children and women, drug control, humanitarian assistance, the environment and human development.

The United Nations agencies, though often starting with vision, usually failed to develop the expertise or influence required to make a major impact on the pattern of world development, even in developing countries. Resources remained limited, relative either to bilateral agencies or to the Bretton Woods institutions and the regional development banks.

There were some exceptions: the leadership of WHO in mobilising worldwide action for the eradication of smallpox; the creation by FAO of an early warning and monitoring network for food production; the leadership of UNESCO in drawing up regional plans for educational expansion in the 1960s and 1970s; the ILO world employment programme in the 1970s.

There are also the steady but quiet achievements of the small, specialised agencies like the World Meteorological Organisation, the International Civil Aviation Organisation, the Universal Postal Union and, first to be established (in 1865), the International Telecommunication Union. Several of these have truly global perspectives underlying their work, regulate important aspects of the global system and provide technical assistance to the poorer or weaker countries to enable their fuller participation in the system.

At times also, the United Nations has provided important intellectual leadership through its analytical work. It was the United Nations Statistical Office and specialised agencies that first helped build up many of the statistical systems we rely on to track world economic and social developments, including the SNA, the standardised system of national accounts underlying the statistics of GNP production, consumption, trade and transfers throughout the world.

Notwithstanding these positive examples, many gaps in the international systems existed from the beginning and, especially after the 1960s, the inadequacies of the system grew more apparent while the need for international action grew. Many of the priority needs were identified in a series of international conferences in the 1970s and 1980s – on women, population, food and nutrition, employment, human settlements, science and technology, energy, etc. But follow-up action was weak and the United Nations system failed to generate the focus, organization or resources needed to support accelerated national action.

Nonetheless, the international system functioned for 25 years with remarkable effectiveness. The quarter-century from the late 1940s to the early 1970s was economically and socially a golden age, certainly by the standards of any previous quarter-century since the Industrial Revolution. The rate of world economic growth was double that of any previous 25-year period; unemployment in the industrialised countries was kept to an unprecedentedly low level; and though fluctuations continued, cyclical movements were more limited than ever before. Structural change in the Third World was also unprecedented: several score of countries had come to independence. A Development Decade was launched in the 1960s; economic growth in the developing countries accelerated with the achievement of an average of 5 per cent growth by all developing countries, together with rapid expansion of education and major improvements in health, life expectancy and infant and child mortality.

Of course, this was far from meeting all the basic human needs, let alone other economic and political aspirations. But economically and socially, the international system functioned remarkably well by previous standards and helped underpin much of this achievement, country by country. Globally, perhaps the most obvious weakness from the Third World was the failure to provide adequate support for primary producing and low-income developing countries, which, while making accelerated progress, still slipped further behind relative to other parts of the world.

In the early 1970s, however, contradictions and inadequacies in this international system began to appear. The US deficit became unsustainable, leading to the abandonment of the dollar–gold exchange at $35; two years later, oil prices rose three to four times, reflecting not only the creation of OPEC but more causally the long, previous decline of oil prices. Following this, the next quarter-century has been a rocky road. The 1970s were a period of greater fluctuations and rising unemployment with greater imbalances between different countries and regions of the world.

Regional differentiation became extreme in the 1980s, especially with the adoption of free market policies in many parts of the world and the abandonment of central planning and the command system in most former socialist economies. For Africa and much of Latin America, the 1980s became a lost decade, with sharp declines in per capita income, rising debt and declines in commodity prices to the lowest levels since the 1930s. All this was notwithstanding severe stabilisation and adjustment programmes, the main benefits of which are still to appear. In contrast, South-East Asia and increasingly South Asia, including China and India, have shown accelerated growth and have become the most dynamic part of the world economy.

The North–South Roundtable discussed at least briefly how much of the economic difficulties of the last 25 years might have been avoided if the original vision of Bretton Woods had been put in place and had remained there. Key elements would have included requirements for reciprocal action by surplus countries, measures to stabilise commodity prices, the creation of sufficient liquidity internationally and adequate finance and reliance on an effective United Nations. No simple answer is possible, and other major changes in the basic structure of the world economy would have required important adaptations – to the growing role of transnational corporations, growing rates of inflation and the shift from hegemony to a world in which political and military power was increasingly separate from economic power and both ever more distributed in a multipolar world.

This brought the Roundtable to the world of today and the challenges of the future. The Roundtable tried to concentrate on a limited number of key and central proposals, while recognizing that within and around them many specific details would need to be developed and elaborated.

AN OVERALL POLICY FRAMEWORK

The deliberations of the Roundtable identified many components of an overall policy framework to guide human action in the coming decades:

- A new concept of human security emerged, which focused on people security, not just territorial security; which valued security of each individual, not only security of nations; which advanced security through development, not through arms. It was felt that future conflicts may well be more between people rather than between nations, and that such situations required socio-economic reforms, not soldiers in uniform.

- It was agreed that the time was ripe for reform and there was both the need and the possibility of reform in the international system. Fundamental changes within the United Nations were already under way – though, so far, primarily concentrated on issues of politics and peace-keeping. The Secretary-General's *Agenda for Peace* had set out measures to broaden United Nations functions in peace-keeping to encompass conflict prevention, peace-making and peace-building. New international approaches to human rights, crossing the boundaries of traditional sovereignty, were already under debate, but far from agreed upon. Nevertheless, the level of involvement of the United Nations system in these areas was obviously and dramatically in advance of the situation ten or more years ago. *An Agenda for Peace* should now be supplemented by an *Agenda of Development*.

- In the areas of human development, the beginnings of new approaches could be traced. These needed to be strengthened and advanced. UNDP's *Human Development Report* had set out a new philosophy, increasingly accepted as a consensus for action. Goals for the year 2000, endorsed politically at the World Summit for Children and at the United Nations Conference for Environment and Development, provided an agenda for national and international action in key areas of sustainable human development. Increasingly, agencies like UNICEF, UNFPA and WHO were adopting specific goals as practical guidelines for country support and mobilization, more specifically than in earlier periods. What was still missing was coherence between these different objectives and initiatives and their fuller integration into systems of management of the world economy.
- To achieve greater coherence and support, all four pillars of the international economic and social system needed to be strengthened. This would involve strengthening the capacity, efficiency and effectiveness of the IMF, the World Bank, GATT and UNCTAD, as well as the relevant economic and social agencies of the United Nations system. Functionally, it meant strengthening institutional support and international management in the areas of finance, trade, capital flows and investment, as well as economic and social policy-making and support.
- Public opinion, including the continuing strong support for humanitarian action, needed to be built upon and extended – to focus on eradicating the worst aspects of poverty and moving to acceptable patterns and lifestyles of sustainable human development. Communications had to be strengthened to encourage a sense of human solidarity. Links with Parliamentarians, NGOs and other institutions of civil society were absolutely vital. This was an area where experimentation was needed – to reach out to people's organizations in a way that helped democratise the United Nations and made its relevance to human action more real to citizens throughout the world.

A DOUBLE AGENDA FOR ACTION

Within this broad policy framework, the Roundtable concentrated on a limited number of key proposals, while recognising that many specific details would need to be developed within and around these proposals. The agenda focused on the following five proposals:

1. *A World Social Charter* It was agreed that a World Social Charter must be drawn up to give concrete shape to the emerging concept of global

human security. Just as social contracts emerged at the national level in the 1940s, following the Beveridge Plan in Britain and the New Deal in the US, social contracts must now be constructed at the international level in recognition of growing global interdependence. A number of specific steps must be taken for this purpose:

● The specific commitments in economic and social fields, already endorsed by world leaders in various summits and international forums, should all be brought together in a single social Charter. Any notable missing items should be added to this Charter. The main objective of the Charter should be to lead towards a global civil society.

● There should be a realistic costing of various global commitments.

● A concrete timetable should be prepared to establish priorities among various components of the Charter and to indicate a time sequence in which they could be implemented.

● The World Social Charter should be backed up by specific national development strategies that incorporate the main targets of the overall Charter in accordance with the priorities and resources of each country.

● A specific financial plan should be prepared to implement the World Social Charter, both by reallocating priorities in existing budgets and by raising additional resources (discussed in item 3, below). The burden of financing should be shared equitably between developing and developed countries.

● The responsibility for preparing such a specific World Social Charter and for monitoring its implementation should be given to a strengthened United Nations system (see item 4, below), specifically to a New Development Security Council within the United Nations (see item 2, below).

● One of the major tasks of the forthcoming World Social Summit in March 1995 should be to approve such a World Social Charter and to mandate specific steps for its orderly implementation.

2. *A Development Security Council*   In order to provide a decision-making forum at the highest level to ensure global human security, it is proposed that a Development Security Council be set up within the United Nations to review critical social and economic threats to people all over the globe and to reach political agreements on specific policy responses. The Development Security Council will deal with such basic issues as global poverty, unemployment, food security, ecological security, drug-trafficking, migration, humanitarian assistance, and a new framework for sustainable human development. Such a Development Security Council needs to incorporate the following six elements:

- The focus should lie clearly on economic and human development issues as distinct from political and peace-keeping matters.
- Membership should be small, for example, comprising 11 permanent members from the main industrialised countries and larger developing economies and rotating membership of, say, 12 countries drawn from smaller countries in regional groupings.
- Voting needs to involve certain protections, such as a requirement that all decisions be ratified by a majority of both developed and developing groups in addition to an overall majority.
- A small but high-quality professional secretariat is needed, led by a Deputy Secretary-General, to prepare various policy options for consideration of the Council.
- Participation should be by nationals with economic and financial expertise, with occasional high-level sessions at the ministerial level, incorporating Ministers of Finance and Planning, and at annual sessions at the heads of state/government level.
- The umbrella of the Development Security Council must extend not only to the actions by member states and by the United Nations agencies but also to actions by the Bretton Woods institutions and other regional economic bodies like OECD, the European Community, ASEAN, SAARC, NAFTA, etc.

3. *A New Framework of Development Cooperation* To meet the emerging requirements of global human security, there must be a fundamental change in the present framework of development cooperation. It must be based on mutual interests, not charity; on greater cooperation between nations, not increased confrontation; on a more equitable sharing of global market opportunities, not greater protection; on growing internationalism, not increasing national isolation. Such a new framework of development cooperation should include at least the following six components:

- A new motivation for aid, based on fighting the growing threat of global poverty rather than the receding threat of the cold war;
- Continued pressure to reduce global military expenditures, to phase out arms build-up from the Third World as well, and to link the emerging peace dividend with the unfinished social agenda;
- A practical '20-20 compact' to implement an essential human agenda over the next 10 years, by earmarking an average of 20 per cent share in existing developing country budgets and aid allocations for human priority concerns of basic education, primary health care, safe drinking water and family planning services;

- An automatic mobilization of resources for the common objectives of global human survival, particularly to ensure ecological security, through innovative devices such as an international tax on non-renewable sources of energy, international trading permits in carbon emissions, or a tax on speculative movements of capital across international borders;
- A broadening of the concept of development cooperation to include all international flows, including trade, investment, technology and labour flows;
- A new policy dialogue based on persuasion, not coercion; on two-way contracts, not one-way transfers; and on balancing human lives, not just balancing financial budgets.

4. *Restructuring and Strengthening of Existing Institutions*   The Round-table discussed many new initiatives that may need to be taken to fit the needs of the twenty-first century – including a World Central Bank, an International Investment Trust, a Multilateral Trade Organisation, a Human Development Agency, and an Anti-Monopoly Law Authority. There was a consensus, however, that the most immediate task must be to restructure and strengthen the existing international institutions as a basis of any future dialogue. It was agreed that the following six proposals offered a promising area of reform:

- The IMF can be strengthened by reviving the issue of SDRs now that global inflation is at an all-time low level and the US budget deficit may be coming under greater control. The current interest rate on SDRs should be greatly lowered, as the new creation of SDRs should be regarded as an international public good. These SDRs can be used to provide supplemental foreign exchange reserves to poor nations. A special SDR issue can also be used to cancel the debts of the poorest nations, especially in sub-Saharan Africa, including debts to multilateral institutions.
- The role of the World Bank in recycling international surpluses to developing countries can be increased significantly by persuading the major surplus countries, particularly Japan and Germany, to recycle some of their surplus funds through a third window of the Bank. This new window should establish intermediate terms in between the IBRD and IDA terms (say, an interest rate of 4 per cent with a repayment period of 25 years). It should focus its lending on graduating economies in South Asia, like China, and on some middle-income developing countries. The management board of the new window should be reshaped to reflect the influence of the major contributors: in fact, it should be based on a simi-

lar composition as that suggested for the Development Security Council, to try out a fresh management initiative within the Bretton Woods institutions.

● The resource base and the development mandate of the regional development banks should be considerably strengthened and their policy dialogue brought closer to the realities in their respective regions.

● GATT should be strengthened by concluding the Uruguay Round of multilateral negotiations before the end of 1993 and by taking up some of the remaining issues in new trade talks, which should also embrace the emerging reality of regional trade groupings like NAFTA, the European Common Market, Pacific-rim trade collaboration, etc.

● The United Nations system must be strengthened as the principal vehicle for sustainable human development. For this purpose, the policy frameworks of the main funding mechanisms within the United Nations (UNDP, UNICEF, UNFPA, WFP, IFAD) and other specialised agencies need to be more effectively brought together and, at country level, the agencies need to work together under the resident coordinator in support of poverty eradication and human development. The country strategy notes currently being prepared in some 40 countries can provide a useful framework. The proposed '20-20 compact' should be made a clear focus of the consultative group and roundtable meetings.

● Special measures need to be developed for Africa and least developed countries outside Africa. In principle, new mechanisms for international trade are needed. But if these prove impossible to create, a major increase of resources and support must be found for the poorest countries in other ways: through debt relief, reform of aid, special measures of international support or concession. Guidelines must be created to establish minimum rates of economic growth and minimum targets for the reduction of poverty and the achievement of human development in the poorest countries. Extreme imbalance within the global economy must be recognised as incompatible with political stability, environmental sustainability and human solidarity in both ethical and practical terms.

5. *A United Nations Agency for Advancement of Women* Some practical steps must be taken to protect the vital interests of the neglected majority on this planet – women – and to rescue the present institutional efforts from the legitimate charge of mere 'tokenism'. The time has come to establish a highly visible, integrated United Nations Agency for the Advancement of Women (UNAAW). Such an agency should be based on the following premises:

- Its main objective should be to elevate women's empowerment to the top of the national and international policy agendas, to monitor the specific achievements and failures in this field on a regular basis, and to provide a coordinated policy framework to galvanise the energies and the efforts throughout the international system, including the United Nations system.
- The focus of the new agency will be on policy issues, not on implementation of specific projects, which will continue to be the responsibility of national governments and relevant international institutions.
- The new agency can be quite cost-effective: it can emerge by integrating UNIFEM, INSTRAW and other scattered efforts throughout the international system, as well as by a few supplemental resources of a highly competent professional staff under the guidance of an outstanding leader.
- The forthcoming World Social Summit should mandate such an agency to gradually reduce, and finally eliminate, existing male–female disparities in social services and in jobs, according to an internationally agreed timetable; to improve the status of women in the legal, political and economic spheres; and to empower women to play their legitimate roles at home, in the community, within the country and on the international stage. The advancement of true equality between men and women in all spheres of life by the year 2000 should be the guiding light of the new agency.

The Roundtable concluded that the ultimate aim of all our efforts must be to build a new global civil society where people matter, where development models are woven around people rather than people around development models, where a new concept of global human security is adopted by the entire international community, where a new framework of development cooperation is designed step by step between nations and between people, and where global governance puts people at the very centre of its many concerns. Reforms in global institutions are only a means. People must remain their ultimate end.

NOTES

1. Emphasis added.
2. Emphasis added.
3. UNDP, *Human Development Report, 1992* (Oxford: Oxford University Press).

Part II

The Bretton Woods System

1 An Historical Perspective
H. W. Singer

It is customary to date the origin of the Bretton Woods system back to 1942 when Keynes, and his associates in London, prepared the three famous memoranda on the International Clearing Union, on Commodity Buffer Stocks and Plans for Relief and Reconstruction. To these three memoranda we may add the Beveridge Report, which appeared in the same year. Keynes had taken a great interest in the Beveridge Report and this model of a national social welfare state was readily capable of international extension and application.

However, in this historical perspective we may well go a little further back. The Great Depression of the 1930s had shown that in the absence of multilateral agreements and multilateral institutions the economic system was in danger of degenerating into beggar-my-neighbour policies leading to general immiserisation. The World Economic Conference of 1931 had been a first attempt to create an international economic order to prevent this from continuing. Although this attempt ended in failure, the ideas then brought forward had continued to reverberate in Keynes's mind. His vision underlying the 1942 documents was governed by the overarching principle of 'never again!' – never again back to the conditions of the 1930s which were seen as having brought about not only mass misery and mass unemployment but also Hitlerism and war. Also never again a failure like that of the 1931 World Economic Conference.

We may then move forward to 1940. Hitler was triumphant and his Minister of Economics and President of the Reichbank, Walter Funk, proclaimed in Berlin a 'new order' under which Europe with its colonies and indeed the world would be unified under German leadership. This was treated as a big propaganda item by the Germans and the British Minister of Information, worried about the propaganda effect of Funk's new order, asked Keynes to prepare a broadcast to counteract and discredit the German propaganda. At that point Keynes became convinced that the most effective counter-move would be to prepare a valid counter-proposal rather than attack Funk's 'fraudulent offer' as he called it. From then on Keynes's mind turned to such a constructive counter-proposal, a genuine new international system. In that sense the Bretton Woods system can be considered as a case of good coming out of evil.

The structure envisaged by Keynes, arising from his belief in the possibility and sustainability of full employment through active government policy – later expanded by Harrod and Domar to full employment growth – and embodied in the 1942 memoranda rested on four pillars. The first pillar was that of global macroeconomic monetary and financial management. The original bold idea was of a world central bank which would maintain full employment equilibrium and provide the liquidity required for this purpose by expanding the supply of bancors (his proposed world currency). This would mainly serve to finance the balance of payments deficit countries: quite logically, they were to be supported; they were the 'good boys' who created additional net employment in the rest of the world. By contrast, the balance of payments surplus countries were the 'bad boys' exporting unemployment to the rest of the world. In fact, at one stage Keynes proposed an international tax on balance of payments surpluses at the rate of 1 per cent a month, partly to finance the deficits, partly to finance international commodity buffer stocks and partly to give an incentive to balance of payments surplus countries to reduce their surpluses by following more expansive policies. While this is an over-simplified picture of 1942 thinking, there is sufficient truth in it to bring home to us the startling contrast to the current orthodoxy when balance of payments equilibrium or surpluses are considered to be the result of virtue and deficits are a symptom of vice.

Even in 1942, in his Proposals for an International Clearing Union, when ideas of a world currency and world central bank were beginning to recede, Keynes had written: 'We need a system possessed of an internal stabilising mechanism, by which pressure is exercised on any country whose balance of payments with the rest of the world is departing from equilibrium *in either direction*, so as to prevent movements which must create for its neighbours an equal but opposite want of balance.' (Note that the italics are in Keynes' own Proposals). Some traces of this original vision are still visible today in the somewhat shadowy so-called 'surveillance' of industrial countries by the IMF, as well as demands that structural adjustment enforced by the Bretton Woods institutions should be more 'symmetrical'. In essence, however, the task of global macroeconomic management has been removed from the multilateral system and is now undertaken – in theory at least – by the G-5 and G-7, in combination with 'privatised liquidity creation' through the commercial banks.

Keynes had already given a great deal of thought to what emerged as one of the key controversies surrounding the IMF, i.e. the question of conditionality. He objected to a 'grandmotherly' Fund. Today the Fund as well as the Bank have become worse than grandmotherly – grandmothers are supposed to have a human face! When he had to accept the idea of conditionality, he did so on the basis and assumption of a very large Fund. He proposed a Fund equal to half of annual world imports and on that basis was willing to concede conditionality. The American side (Harry Dexter White) proposed a much smaller Fund – one-sixth of annual world imports – and on that basis was ready to relax the criteria for conditionality. In the upshot what we got instead of a trade-off between size of the Fund and degree of conditionality was the worst of all possible worlds – a small Fund with tough conditionality. Today's Fund is only 2 per cent of annual world imports. Perhaps the difference between Keynes's originally proposed 50 per cent and the actual 2 per cent is a measure of the degree to which our vision of international economic management has shrunk.

The second pillar was what ultimately emerged as the World Bank, or International Bank for Reconstruction and Development. The historical origin of this lies in the proposed European Reconstruction Fund – a natural answer to Funk. In the 1942 relevant memorandum this had developed into an investment fund for relief and reconstruction – hence the often-quoted statement that originally the IMF was supposed to be a bank (i.e. a world central bank), while the World Bank was supposed to be a fund (i.e. the investment fund proposed in 1942). The reconstruction task proved to be less important for the new institution than was visualised in 1942, partly because of the Marshall Plan and the large US loan to the UK negotiated by Keynes towards the end of his life, and partly because some of the intended functions were taken over by the newly-created UN Relief and Rehabilitation Administration (UNRRA). On the other hand, the development function for poor countries was given additional emphasis at Bretton Woods as a result of the presence of delegations from these countries (mainly Latin American but also including a British and Indian delegation in the transition to independence). Originally in 1942 not much attention had been paid to development problems. Most of the countries involved, especially the Latin American countries, were assumed to do quite well during the war as a result of high prices and high demand for their raw materials, and also the protection afforded to their nascent industries as a result of reduced competition from the belligerent industrial countries. In fact, Argentina emerged at the end of the war as one of the richest countries in the world in terms of per capita GNP. Most of the rest of the Third World had not yet emerged into independence and was not considered to be in urgent need of external support. Many, like India, were accumulating large external surpluses – the sterling balances – and the problem seemed to be more one of help for the UK in clearing these sterling balances than of external aid for India.

It is fair to say that originally the British side – in other words, Keynes – was much more interested in the Fund than in the Bank. By contrast, the preparatory moves on the US side had been much more centred on what became the Bank. The first major move in US thinking about the postwar International Order was the commissioned report of a study group of the US Council of Foreign Relations (led by Jacob Viner and Alvin Hansen). This proposed an International Development Board to study and prepare development projects throughout the world. The shape of a future project-oriented World Bank can be clearly seen to emerge from this report. Given this initial concentration of the British side on the Fund or International Clearing Union and the US initial concentration on the Bank, it is somewhat ironic that at Bretton Woods itself it was the Americans (in the person of Harry Dexter White) who chaired and organised the discussions of the Fund in Commission I, while the British (in the person of Keynes) chaired the discussions on the Bank in Commission II. By that time, in 1944, the work in the US Treasury on the Fund had, of course, strongly developed, while Keynes's interest in the Bank had steadily increased. However, perhaps even more important in his thinking was the establishment of an international organisation to stabilise primary commodity prices. That was the third pillar of the system he envisaged, to which we will turn later.

The World Bank was set up on a project basis without a mandate to make lending conditional on the overall macroeconomic policies of the recipient government, nor even on its general micro or supply-side policies. However, in so far as more general policies or quality of governance affected the rate of return from projects, this was of course a legitimate factor in World Bank lending; so it entered in this indirect way. The limitation to project lending was not thought to be a serious constraint. It was assumed that, given the scarcity of capital in poorer countries, the marginal productivity of capital there must be high; it was also assumed that there must be an abundance of potential high-yielding projects only waiting to be designed, financed and implemented. Why then did the Bank move into programme lending and adopt policy conditionality?

There are a number of reasons which may be listed as follows:

(1) While the Bank acquired tremendous and unchallenged competence in project design, project analysis, cost–benefit calculations, monitoring of projects, etc., this very competence was acquired at the expense of devoting considerable staff resources to these functions. This meant that the total volume of lending which could be 'pushed out' while maintaining this high quality of project work was rather limited. When Mr McNamara became President of the Bank – he had

been used to handling much larger budgets as US Secretary of Defence – he understandably was impatient with the small sums pushed out by the project-based system. He wanted to continue to play a larger part on the world scene than that, and the addition of programme lending seemed to open a door to such a larger role.

(2) The academic analysts had pointed out at an early stage that there was a fallacy involved in project lending.[1] If the project was in fact a high-yielding top-priority project it would be carried out with the government's own resources. The World Bank financing would then merely set free government resources which would go into another marginal – and possibly low-yielding – project. Thus in effect the Bank's money would serve to finance projects which it had not examined and was not even aware of. This principle of 'fungibility' would thus provide an obvious argument for examining the overall investment programme of the government, to make sure that the marginal projects were still sound and creditworthy. Mr McNamara readily adopted this academic fig-leaf for his ambitions!

(3) It became increasingly clear that the success of individual projects depended as much (or more) on the efficiency of policies and institutions in the recipient countries as on the design of the project itself. This became particularly clear as the Bank adopted objectives such as poverty alleviation and moved into social sectors such as health, education, etc.[2]

(4) The shift to programme lending was also related to a marked shift in power and self-confidence between recipient governments and the World Bank. In the earlier period, the governments were supposed to be the Platonic guardians and best judges of national interests and the World Bank a UN organisation designed to serve them. As late as 1971, in his David Owen Memorial Lecture on *The Evolution of Foreign Aid*, Arthur Lewis took it for granted that there could be no policy conditionality in foreign aid since the developing countries would consider this as an enfringement of their sovereignty and would never accept it.[3] More recently, there has been a remarkable reversal of this relationship: now the governments are depicted as centres of corruption, policy failures, rent-seeking, ignorance, etc., while the Bank has acquired a self-confident position of being in possession of the Holy Grail of good policies and an ability to sort out the 'good boys' from the 'bad boys'. The debt burden has also been instrumental in reducing the power and bargaining status of the recipient governments while enhancing that of the Bank. It has also helped to give the Bank a focus and target for structural adjustment,

i.e. to achieve a balance of payments position enabling them to service debts. All this, while strengthening the Bank's position *vis-à-vis* the governments, has weakened its position *vis-à-vis* the Fund which has the unquestioned mandate to concern itself with government policies which the Bank lacks.

The third pillar was the International Trade Organisation (ITO). Keynes had been a long-term advocate of stabilising primary commodity prices, particularly in his article on 'The Policy of Government Storage of Food-Stuffs and Raw Materials' in *The Economic Journal*, 1938. Predictably he incorporated this idea in his proposals for Bretton Woods, linking it in an early version with his proposed International Clearing Union by suggesting a world currency based not on the dollar, gold, bancor, or SDRs, but on the average price of thirty primary commodities (including gold and oil). This would automatically have stabilised the average price of these commodities without ruling out fluctuations of individual commodity prices. The main idea was to prevent the collapse of primary commodity prices, which had been a marked feature – and in Keynes's view, a contributory factor – of the Great Depression of the 1930s.

Such bold ideas cut little ice with Henry Morgenthau, the Secretary of the US Treasury, and in fact were quickly subdued even in the London preparatory group. What remained was the proposal to set up an ITO which would have among other objectives that of stabilising primary commodity prices by buffer stocks, commodity agreements and direct intervention. The establishment of the ITO was firmly decided at Bretton Woods and when Keynes left the conference with everybody standing up in his honour and singing 'For he's a jolly good fellow', it was in the firm belief that the achievements of Bretton Woods included the creation of this favourite brain-child of his.

Alas, the ITO was never created. Although it was quite smoothly negotiated in Havana and accepted there by all concerned, the mood in the US Congress by the time it was presented for ratification had begun to swing against the UN and international institutions. The internationalist Roosevelt/Truman era was coming to an end and the McCarthy era was beginning to cast its shadows. The ITO charter was not brought to the US Congress in time to catch the favourable tide. By the time it was brought to the US Congress, ratification had become hopeless and the ITO was abandoned even without a vote. The other countries were all set to ratify but had waited for the US Congress to ratify first. Thus the Bretton Woods system was incomplete from the beginning, lacking its intended third pillar. GATT did not fill the gap since it had no functions relating to the stabilisation of commodity prices or regulation of commodity markets.

One can engage in a number of counter-factual speculations. If Keynes had suspected that the ITO would not be created, would he still have advocated acceptance of the agreement concerning the Bank and the Fund? We do not know – by the time it was clear that the ITO would not be established, Keynes was dead. My own guess is to answer this hypothetical question with a 'no' – but there is no way of proving it (or for that matter of disproving it). Another counter-factual speculation is that if the real price of oil – together with practically all other primary commodities – had not deteriorated from the 1950s to 1973, would the OPEC countries still have engaged in their dramatic quadrupling of oil prices in 1973 and then again multiplied them in 1979? It is often forgotten that the 1973 action did little more than restore the real price of oil in terms of manufactures to what it had been before. Without the OPEC action in 1973 the Bretton Woods system might not have collapsed and might have recovered from the abandonment of the fixed exchange rate between gold and dollar by President Nixon in 1971. Also, if the non-oil primary commodity prices had been maintained and stabilised between the 1950s and 1973, the rise in oil prices would not have created the balance of payments crisis and subsequent debt crisis among the developing countries. Yet another speculation: if the Havana ITO Charter had been brought more speedily to Congress for ratification and had been more firmly supported by the US Administration, the ITO might well have come into existence. History as it might have been is always a fascinating business.

The fourth pillar of the system was meant to be a soft aid programme linked more directly with the United Nations. It is noteworthy that the first draft proposal for the World Bank prepared at the US Treasury under the direction of Harry Dexter White was entitled 'A Bank for Reconstruction and Development of the United and Associated Nations'. At that time, of course, it was still visualised that the two Bretton Woods institutions would be a firm and integral part of the United Nations system, which had still to be created during the year or two following upon Bretton Woods. Indeed, legally and technically, the Fund and Bank are specialised agencies of the United Nations and their guidance by the UN General Assembly and UN Economic and Social Council are still embodied in their respective charters – but we all know what the reality is. Today, the Secretary-General of the United Nations is not even allowed to address the annual meetings of the Fund and Bank!

The aid programme within the United Nations was meant to be different from World Bank lending in being on a grant or highly concessional basis, and also not limited to a project basis. The attempt to create such a mechanism within the United Nations centred on the proposal for UNEDA (United

Nations Economic Development Administration). This was originally proposed by V. K. R. V. Rao in his capacity as Chairman of the UN Sub-Commission for Economic Development and in a simultaneous UN Secretariat Report on *Methods of Financing Economic Development in Underdeveloped Countries*. This was then continued in the negotiations for SUNFED (Special United Nations Fund for Economic Development). In the uncongenial climate for the UN of the early and mid-fifties, this – like the ITO – was doomed to failure. SUNFED remained UNFED – its original and unfortunate acronym.[4] However, in the happier climate of the late fifties and early sixties (the Kennedy era), there was at least a partially satisfactory outcome. The soft aid fund was created, but it was attached to the Bank rather than to the United Nations, in the form of IDA. The United Nations obtained two valuable consolation prizes: the UNDP (technical assistance had always been a strong feature of UNEDA and SUNFED) and the World Food Programme. While this 'Grand Compromise' of 1959–61 was more satisfactory than could have been hoped for some years earlier, it laid the foundation for an unfortunate division between financial aid on the one hand and food aid and technical assistance on the other. It also helped to confirm an even broader cleavage: the UN was not to be trusted with the 'hard' instruments of development such as finance and macroeconomic policy-making – that was to be the preserve of the Bretton Woods institutions with their system of weighted voting and firm control by the Western industrial countries. The UN was to be put in charge of the 'soft' instruments, such as food aid, technical assistance, children, women, social policy, and more recently the environment. We will not here discuss the justification and viability of such a division of functions.[5] All this would not matter too much if there were really a unified UN system – this remains a hope for the future.

Thus in overview the original vision of a system resting on four pillars has remained unfulfilled. Some pillars are missing altogether, and some are constructed in a way quite different from the original plans. All the same, the system proved an immense benefit to the world for the 25 years or so until its collapse in 1971 and 1973. Our task is to recreate a genuine system with the same vision as that shown in 1942. It would not of course be the same system: times have changed and we should have learnt some lessons from past experience; but, all the same, the original ideas have still much to teach us if we can only recapture the spirit of 1942.

NOTES

1. See H. W. Singer: 'External aid: for plans or projects?', *Economic Journal*, Vol. 75, September 1965.
2. This point has been quite recently emphasised by the World Bank's Portfolio Management Task Force: *Effective Implementation; Key to Development Impact* (the Wapenhans Report), World Bank, 1992. In this report an increasing percentage of unsatisfactory results over the last decade was attributed to a failure to appreciate the importance of policy and institutional factors in determining the rate of return on projects. The report did not make the point – at least not explicitly – that this deterioration could also have something to do with the diversion of attention and staff resources to structural adjustment lending in the service of debt collection.
3. Sir W. Arthur Lewis, *The Evolution of Foreign Aid* (Cardiff: University College, 1971).
4. For further detail see H. W. Singer 'The Terms of Trade Controversy and the Evolution of Soft Financing: Early Years in the U.N.', in *Pioneers in Development*, ed. Gerald M. Meier and Dudley Seers (World Bank/Oxford University Press, 1984).
5. See *International Governance* by Paul Streeten, Louis Emmerij, Carlos Fortin and with an introduction by H. W. Singer, IDS Silver Jubilee Papers Nos 1, 2 and 3, Institute of Development Studies, 1992.

2 The Vision and the Reality

Mahbub ul Haq

The Keynesian vision for the Bretton Woods institutions has not survived. First, the vision was greatly diluted in its actual implementation – as the IMF, the World Bank and GATT emerged through several compromises with the Realpolitik of the time. And, second, the original role of the Bretton Woods institutions has changed beyond recognition in the last five decades of their operation.

It is instructive to contrast the vision and the reality.

First, Keynes's objective was full employment in a global setting. He believed in the role of the state to regulate the excesses of the market. Unfortunately, the employment objective greatly receded in its policy importance, particularly in the 1980s, and a new theology of the markets, rather than social purpose, guiding the economic systems, took over during this period – with disastrous consequences, as we find now. Only recently, full employment is again moving to the top of the national and global policy agendas as industrial countries are confronting the 'joys' of jobless growth: while total output has doubled since 1975, total employment has declined. The regulatory as well as the compassionate role of the nation state (as well as of global institutions) is also witnessing a reluctant revival.

THE INTERNATIONAL MONETARY FUND

Second, the IMF in its present form is a mere caricature of Keynes's, original vision. Consider the following contrasts:

- Keynes proposed a Fund equal to one-half of world imports. (Even the more conservative White proposal suggested global liquidity equal to one-sixth of global imports.) In actual practice, the IMF today controls liquidity equal to 2 per cent of world imports. It is too insignificant to exercise much of a global monetary discipline at a time when speculative private capital movements of over $1 trillion cross international borders every 24 hours at the push of computer buttons in response to the slightest changes in currency and interest rates – capital movements which are currently playing havoc with the stability of most economies.

26

- Keynes envisioned IMF as a world central bank, issuing its own reserve currency (the 'bancors') and creating sufficient international reserves wherever needed. The IMF was authorised in the 1970s to create SDRs but the experiment was stillborn because of the persistent US trade deficits which were creating global liquidity, and since the US was content to finance its deficits by issuing its own currency rather than to adjust. The SDRs were further made unattractive to hold by raising their interest rate nearer to market rate during the course of the 1970s. By now, SDRs constitute only 3 per cent of global liquidity. For the world monetary system, the actions of the heads of the US Federal Reserve Board and the German Bundesbank are far more important than the actions of the Managing Director of the IMF – a long distance from the Keynesian vision.

- Keynes regarded balance of payments deficits as a virtue – as they sustained global effective demand and created more employment – and surpluses as a vice. This led him to advocate a penal interest rate of 1 per cent a month on outstanding trade surpluses. Consider the real situation: deficit nations, particularly in the developing world, come under a tremendous pressure for real adjustment. There is no symmetry for surplus nations. Even the deficit industrial nations can borrow endlessly to finance their deficits rather than to adjust, especially the US, which has the unique privilege of borrowing in its own currency.

- In the Keynesian vision, there would be no persistent debt problem as surpluses would be used by the IMF to finance deficits. No separate International Debt Refinancing Facility[1] was needed. Neither were the poor nations going to be obliged to provide a reverse transfer of resources to the rich nations (as they are doing now) to earn their legitimate requirement of growing international reserves: these reserves would have been provided by the international currency issued by the Fund. An automatic mechanism for meeting the liquidity requirements of developing countries has been replaced in actual practice by punitive measures for debt problems and for prudent international reserve requirements.

- The heart of the global monetary system was fixed exchange rates. That died in the early 1970s with the delinking of the US dollar from gold and with the introduction of floating exchange rates. All attempts to introduce a modicum of stability in the volatility of exchange rates have proved futile since then (e.g. through ERM).

- The IMF, therefore, has become largely irrelevant to the global monetary discipline. It has not much of a role *vis-à-vis* the rich nations. It may be characterised as a somewhat harsh and overzealous policeman for the poor nations. But these poor nations are responsible for less than

10 per cent of global liquidity. Isn't it rather charitable to call a 10 per cent money manager an *international* monetary fund?

THE WORLD BANK

Third, the World Bank was supposed to stand between the global capital markets and the developing countries and recycle resources to poor nations both by using its own creditworthiness and by gradually building up the creditworthiness of these nations over time. The reality is again a long way from the original vision.

- In 1990, there was a global surplus of $180 billion – half of it contributed by Japan. Most of it was recycled by the private capital markets, principally to the US and other richer nations. And what was the role of the World Bank as an International Investment Trust – a role Paul Streeten[2] would like the Bank to assume? The Bank recycled *minus* $1.7 billion to the developing countries: its receipts of interest and principal from past loans exceeded its fresh disbursements. In fact, the Bank is by now recycling its own debt rather than new resources. This shows how marginal its role is in global capital movements or in international net transfer of resources. The Bank was supposed to build up the creditworthiness of individual developing countries and enable them to walk off with confidence into private capital markets. Except for South Korea, the Bank does not have too many successes to boast of. Most of its clients emerged with reduced creditworthiness in the late 1980s compared to what they enjoyed in the 1970s – thanks to a severe global debt problem which the Bank did not even have the professional honesty to acknowledge as a general problem but which it kept treating on a case-by-case basis. The disastrous decision of President Clausen to link the IBRD lending rate to the private capital market rate in 1982 further compounded the debt problem as, instead of cushioning the developing countries against the high market interest rates, it only gave institutional blessing to these rates.
- The resource profile of the Bank and the poverty profile of the developing world are completely out of sync. According to the Bank's own estimates, the number of absolute poor has been increasing in the developing world. Yet real IDA availability per poor person has been shrinking. This is not a fault of the Bank management but of its donors, who have refused to see the implications of such an imbalance. No wonder India acquired commercial debts of $50 billion in the 1980s – as

its IDA allocations were rationed – and it acquired a Latin-type of debt problem at a per capita income of only $260.

● The sources of fresh creativity are missing in the World Bank. After the innovation of IDA in 1960, the Bank bureaucracy has quietly gone to sleep, unable to innovate in response to the changing global requirements. For instance, the emergence of OPEC surpluses in the 1970s and Japanese surpluses in the 1980s required a new intermediate window in between IDA and IBRD – maybe with 4 per cent interest rate and 25 years' repayment period. This would have enabled the Bank to phase South Asia out of IDA and into the new window while concentrating IDA resources primarily on Sub-Saharan Africa. But the Bank management made only one half-hearted attempt in 1974 to set up a 'third window' with OPEC financial surpluses (which lasted only a year as the Bank's traditional contributors refused to give any enhanced role to OPEC nations in the management of this new window even as they accepted their financial resources).

GATT

Fourth, the third pillar of the Bretton Woods system – GATT – has been even further removed from the original Keynesian vision than the IMF and the World Bank.

● Keynes envisioned an International Trade Organisation (ITO), which would not only maintain free trade but also help stabilise world commodity prices. That is why he linked the value of his world currency (the bancors) with the average price of 30 primary commodities, including gold and oil. In actual practice, GATT excluded primary commodities altogether and only belatedly an effort was made in the Uruguay Round of Negotiations to include agriculture and tropical products in the global trade package. In the meantime, the commodity prices have hit their lowest levels since the Great Depression: Africa alone has lost $50 billion in reduced earnings in the 1980s as a result of declining commodity prices. And an oil crisis exploded in the 1970s.

● The actual operations of the GATT system reflect the same disparity in global power structure as the two other Bretton Woods institutions. The South and the former socialist bloc are opening up their markets: the North, according to an OECD study, has been restricting its markets in the 1980s. GATT does not have the mandate or the political clout to bring parity in the current trade liberalisation efforts or to impose penalties for growing trade protectionism in the OECD nations. It will be too far-fetched to suggest that it should have been able to demand even compensatory action by the rich nations to open up greater trade opportunities as they impose greater migration barriers – though, logically, there is no reason that this should not happen since the only alternatives left for the poor nations will be to encourage out-migration of their people if more trade is not allowed.

● One indicator of the irrelevance of GATT is that its jurisdiction excludes textile manufactures, primary commodities, services, capital flows, labour flows, intellectual property resources, etc. The recently concluded Uruguay Round of Multilateral Trade Negotiations may, however, change this situation.

GROWING IRRELEVANCE OF BRETTON WOODS INSTITUTIONs

This summary review of the international financial institutions brings out one stark reality: the Bretton Woods institutions have become largely *irrelevant* in the global picture. Many critics have faulted their policy conditionality, their non-democratic decision-making structures, their seeming arrogance. But that is yet another issue. The real issue is the *irrelevance* of these institutions to manage the global system they were supposed to manage. That task of management has quietly passed on to the *ad hoc* improvisations of the G-7. Such a situation is in the long-term self-interest neither of the rich nations nor of the poor nations.

Some observers of this scene are willing to throw in the towel. For instance, even as perceptive and shrewd an analyst as John Williamson argues:[3]

If one accepts that the development of capital mobility is irreversible, the idea of controlling the world economy by developing the IMF into a world central bank is no longer within the realm of technical feasibility.

This is like arguing that if private speculators have taken over the domestic capital markets, let us fold up the regulatory role of the national central banks. No vision is ever born out of such defeatism.

To discuss and to construct a new vision for international institutions for the next fifty years is the challenge we face in the North–South Roundtable. The Keynesian version is only a starting point, not an inflexible model. The world has changed. So should our perceptions.

There are, I believe, some major compulsions for a new institutional order:

- Global financial power is more diffused now than it was after the Second World War. The US was contributing over 50 per cent of global output at that time: its share has declined to 20 per cent. Germany, Japan and OPEC nations have emerged with considerable financial clout.

- The dollar is likely to be replaced as an international currency and reserve asset by the end of this century – either through the emerging ECU or an international currency unit.

- The US is beginning to address its deficit and debt problems – and, as such, may be more likely to accept additional global liquidity emerging from a world central bank.

- There is going to be increasing concern with world capital movements disrupting national economies and sabotaging full employment policies. Jobs, in particular, are going to become the rallying-cry of the 1990s.

- New concepts of human security are likely to dominate global thinking – not just security for land, but security for people. As poverty is globalised and begins to travel in unpleasant forms – drugs, pollution, new diseases, migration, terrorism, political instability – it will be the rich nations, even more than the poor nations, which will be reaching out to design new international institutions or to strengthen the existing ones to meet these unprecedented threats to their lifestyles.

NEW INSTITUTIONS FOR THE TWENTY-FIRST CENTURY

It is time that a blueprint was prepared for the new global institutions that will be needed in the next century and that a feasible strategy was formulated to evolve such institutions, step by step, either by broadening the mandate of the existing institutions, or by creating entirely new mechanisms. In a way, it is quite likely that the institutional evolution we have already experienced at the national level will be followed at the global level, only a few crises and a few decades removed: an international central bank, an international investment trust, a progressive world income tax, and many other institutions of a global civil society. It is worthwhile to focus on some of the more important innovations.

(a) A World Central Bank

As Paul Streeten has pointed out, the present international monetary system, or non-system, is not satisfactory. It is a mixture of fixed and fluctuating exchange rates. It is buffeted by massive movements of private capital every day. Its global liquidity depends on the national policies of the US rather than on international requirements. An international central bank is needed to provide sufficient liquid resources for world transactions, to be a lender of the last resort, and to maintain the financial stability of the global economic system. Of course, the IMF is the primary candidate for such a role. As a first step, the IMF and the central banks of the major trading countries could form a coordinating committee to manage world liquidity.[4] As the role of the IMF in providing world liquidity increases, its regulatory function would have to grow with it. The role of the SDRs could grow as a substitution account is established. But as Paul Streeten concludes:[5] 'Whether countries are ready to coordinate their fiscal and monetary policies, and to permit the freer movements of goods, capital and labour that would be called for by a global central bank, and, to go one step further (as recommended by Keynes), by a single world currency, is, to say the least, an open question.'

(b) An International Investment Trust

There is a need for an institution that would recycle the current account surpluses of persistent surplus countries (Japan and Germany at present) to developing countries in need of capital. Presently, these surpluses are being recycled mainly by private capital markets and often towards the richer countries (US) or some better-off developing countries (mostly in East Asia and Latin America). As Paul Streeten points out:[6]

> The purpose of (such a) proposal is to bring together, to mutual benefit, three now grossly underutilized pools of resources: the current account surpluses of Japan (and Germany), in search of safe returns; the underutilized industrial capacity and skilled unemployed of the OECD countries, on whose exports some of the recycled loans will be spent; and the vast idle or underemployed unskilled and semi-skilled manpower of the South, hungry for capital. And all this in the service of a growing world economy.

The World Bank is an obvious candidate to graduate into this larger role. The main dilemmas are: how to convert private surpluses into public transfers? And how to subsidise some of the flows to match the limited creditworthiness of many developing country borrowers?

(c) Global Taxation

In a world of such glaring and widening income disparities and such growing interdependence, it is only a matter of time for a battle-cry to go up for a progressive world income tax. If the future threats to the lifestyles of the rich nations arise from the travel of global poverty across international frontiers (in the form of drugs, pollution, migration and terrorism), it is not unlikely that the rich nations themselves will think of global social safety-nets to contain poverty within national borders. Perhaps the beginning of a global taxation system may arise out of taxes on global pollution – with polluting nations obliged to pay heavy penalties. The main principle of such global taxation will be to move towards a system of automatic collection of revenue, but not automatic disbursements. Disbursements must be guided both by the evidence of poverty and the existence of good performance.

Several other institutional innovations are possible:[7] a Global Energy Agency, a Global Anti-Monopoly Agency, an Economic Security Council in the UN, an Agency for Transnational Corporations. Moreover, many new institutions of a global civil society may need to be created or the existing ones strengthened, to monitor human rights, corruption, drug money or gender discrimination.

The NSRT meeting needs to review the global institutional requirements of an increasingly shrinking planet and to identify some imaginative proposals for the twenty-first century, even if they appear somewhat idealistic today.

NOTES

1. Mahbub ul Haq, *An International Debt Refinancing Facility*, Speech to the ECOSOC Session in Geneva in July 1984.
2. Paul Streeten, 'Global Governance for Human Development', in *International Governance*, Institute of Development Studies, 1992.
3. John Williamson, 'International Monetary Reform and the Prospects for Economic Development', a paper presented to the Forum on Debt and Development, The Hague, 9–10 June 1992.
4. A. W. Mullineux, 'Do we Need a World Central Bank?', *Royal Bank of Scotland Review*, No. 160, December 1988, pp. 23–35; Michael Lipton and Stephany Griffith-Jones,'International Lenders of Last Resort: Are Changes Required?', *Midland Bank Occasional Paper in International Trade and Finance*, March 1984.
5. Paul Streeten, 'Global Governance for Human Development', *Occasional Paper No. 4*, Human Development Report Office, UNDP, p. 14.
6. Streeten, ibid, p. 11.
7. Streeten, ibid, pp. 17–18.

3 A Changing Institution in a Changing World

Alexander Shakow

A CHANGING WORLD

The world is at a turning-point. With the end of the cold war and superpower competition, multipolar politics have replaced the bipolar world of the past. Events as diverse as famine in Somalia, ethnic conflict in the former Yugoslavia, and political crises in parts of the former Soviet Union suggest that the very concept of the nation-state may be at risk.[1]

Other factors are also contributing to the breakdown of traditional thinking about national borders:

- The movement toward creating 'regional' trading blocs, for example, in Western Europe (EEC), North America (NAFTA), and Asia (ASEAN).
- Environmental problems transcending national boundaries – global warming and ozone depletion, biodiversity loss, air and water pollution.
- People increasingly migrating across borders – with already some 27 million political and economic refugees on the move.
- Diseases and illegal drugs spreading across national boundaries.
- Information moving instantaneously around the world via CNN, the fax machine and electronic mail.

Economic relations too, are being rapidly transformed. Computer-driven transactions across continents are forcing the reinvention of financial and trading systems. Some US$3 trillion of capital circulates the globe every day – sometimes overwhelming traditional central bank interventions. Technology is revolutionising industry and agriculture – and shrinking time and distance.

It had been envisaged that the end of the cold war would release supplemental resources for development – the 'peace dividend'. Yet, even some of the strongest proponents of development assistance – the Nordic countries, for example – are *reducing* their aid budgets due to domestic fiscal pressures.[2]

This is one sign of the apparent tendency for countries to turn inward even, paradoxically, as the world becomes more interconnected.

Against this backdrop of change and preoccupation with national, as opposed to global interests, the role of international institutions takes on added importance. There is a whole set of issues – political, economic, ecological and social – which only international institutions can handle effectively.

UN Secretary-General Boutros-Ghali has set forth an ambitious agenda for reform of the UN system in his *Agenda for Peace*. Conflict resolution and peace-keeping, clearly, are areas where the United Nations has a unique role – and the renewed interest in strengthening the UN to play this role is greatly welcomed, for the magnitude of the task is enormous, especially in those places where ethnic conflicts are dominant. But in the long run, many of the conflicts, the economic dislocations, and the environmental degradation will only be resolved by *development* – by improving people's living standards and offering them hope of a better future.[3]

Those institutions concerned with development – including the UN and the Bretton Woods institutions in particular – therefore have a special responsibility in the new era. They are needed more than ever before. But at the same time, they must show themselves to be more effective than ever before in getting results.

CHANGING VIEW OF DEVELOPMENT

Just as traditional political and economic relationships are changing, thinking on development is changing too. The development universe has been transformed. Thinking of the Third World as a single group of countries – poor, backward, dependent on foreign aid – was never a fully accurate description. Today, it is an irrelevant concept:

● The countries of *East Asia* (Thailand, Malaysia, Korea, China, Indonesia) are growing rapidly. They are increasingly sophisticated economies, able to access public capital markets and to attract private investment. Between 1970 and 1990, these countries reduced the number of people in poverty from 30 per cent to 10 per cent of the population. Complete poverty-eradication is within sight within the next generation.[4]

● The countries of *Latin America* have refined their objectives for economic management, are redefining the role of government, have decided to rely on the private sector for growth and have, by and large, put the debt crisis behind them. In many countries, growth has been restored (1991–92: Chile 7.3 per cent; Argentina 5.8 per cent; Mexico 3.2 per cent; Venezuela 7.6 per cent) as has access to international capital markets and investment opportunities. The region attracted about $60 billion in total private capital flows last year – the highest level in history.

- The countries of *Eastern Europe* and the *former Soviet Union* should not be considered 'developing' countries at all. They have an educated labour force, advanced industrial and technological capacity, and comprehensive social services. Their problems of transition are immense and costly; but they are fundamentally problems of redesign and reconstruction of their economies, not of 'development' in the traditional sense – although there are many more people living below the poverty-line than had been previously thought (some 50 million, or a third of the population, in Russia alone). As Anatoli Chubais, the deputy prime minister of Russia, recently stated: 'Never before has so large a country attempted to recreate itself over so short a time, and there is no use understating the scale of the upheaval or the enormity of the challenge.'[5]

- Finally, *Africa*, and the low-income countries of *South Asia* remain the most basic development challenge. They are the poorest nations (50 per cent of the population in both regions), with the weakest institutions, fragile health and education services, and limited prospects for growth in the near term. Sub-Saharan Africa is the *only* region of the world where poverty is projected to increase – by about 100 million people – by the year 2000. These poor regions remain almost totally dependent on concessional assistance – *aid*.

As well as this increasingly differentiated development universe, the diversity of development issues has also multiplied. In the case of the World Bank, for example, this is represented by the increasing demand for assistance on a broad spectrum of issues:

- from mobilising support for economic reform in the poorest African nations through the Special Programme of Assistance, to encouraging private sector investment in the more sophisticated economies of East Asia and Latin America;
- from coordinating international agricultural research (through the Consultative Group on International Agricultural Research) to help meet the needs of an additional four billion people by the year 2030, to helping address global warming and other international environmental issues through the Global Environment Facility;

● from contributing economic analysis to the peace process in the Middle East, to investing in education, health and family planning in Bangladesh and many other countries.

In addition, of course, the Bank remains the world's single largest source of development aid. The Bank's concessional affiliate, the International Development Association (IDA) is of special importance for the world's poorest countries – and a recent replenishment of IDA's resources (IDA-10) was achieved at a level of US$18 billion.

Three issues in particular have emerged over the last several years which have heavily influenced the Bank and, indeed, the global development agenda:

1. *Market-friendly approach* There has been a revolution in economic thinking – the switch to 'market-friendly' approaches. It would be difficult to overstate the scope of this 'revolution'. Everywhere, rapid growth is now associated with the removal of restrictions on trade and private investment. There is a widespread recognition that the past heavy reliance on government to invest in the productive sectors, to protect domestic producers against international competition, to allocate capital, to control prices, and to decide on investments was not an efficient or productive system – financially or economically.

Broadly, governments have recognised that these kinds of past practices were inconsistent with the requirements of today's increasingly competitive and integrated international economy – and inconsistent with the requirements of the twenty-first century. Redefinitions of the roles of the private and public sector are taking place in many countries – most obviously in Eastern Europe and the former Soviet Union, but also in India, Morocco, Pakistan and Egypt and even in the poorest countries of Africa. A greater emphasis on economic stability, reduction of direct and indirect subsidies, recognition that the private sector is a more efficient producer, that market signals are a better guide to demand and new investments – these are now commonly accepted propositions.

At the same time, there is a recognition that markets *alone* are not enough. Governments must also play a positive role, making the tangible and intangible investments that underpin rapid growth and a healthy private sector – and that ensure social and economic justice. Governments must intervene to establish legal and regulatory frameworks and to provide essential public services: social safety-nets, investment in infrastructure and environmental protection. Thus, a better balance between the role of the state and markets is now being achieved throughout the world.[6]

2. *Environmental Protection*   The second major issue to emerge over the last decade is the urgent need to ensure that development is sustainable: environmental protection. The Earth Summit in Rio in the summer of 1992 gave this issue added impetus. More than a hundred world leaders made a commitment to sustainable development and endorsed *Agenda 21*.

The consensus that emerged from Rio was very important: first, that promoting development is the best way to protect the environment – and vice versa. Policies that make economic sense often make environmental sense. A second point of consensus was the critical need to tackle climate change, loss of biodiversity, and other global issues. The two conventions signed made clear that the rich countries must play a primary role in addressing these problems. Third, the Earth Summit recognised that not enough attention has been given to the most serious environmental problems which affect large numbers of the world's poorest people: unclean water, inadequate sanitation, air pollution and soil depletion (a billion people are without safe drinking-water; 1.3 billion are exposed to indoor pollution caused by soot and smoke; 1.7 billion have inadequate sanitation).[7] These environmental problems are poverty problems – and they are today's most urgent priorities.

A fourth major point of agreement in Rio was the importance of partnership: within governments – finance ministries and environmental ministries need to cooperate in order to operationalise the commitments their leaders made in Brazil. And among international institutions – making the most effective use of comparative advantages, including the special skills of NGOs.

Partnership between the rich and poor nations is also crucial. The developed world must help the poor countries help themselves: by increasing the flow of concessional resources for poverty reduction and environmental protection; and by improving the international economic climate. It is inconsistent, for example, to claim a concern for the environment but not to support the Uruguay Round, which could generate tremendous resources for sustainable development – especially in the developing countries.

3. *Governance*   The third issue that has emerged as a major influence on development in recent years is really a set of problems – the efficiency and effectiveness of development expenditures, government and donor accountability, levels of openness and participation in development, the rule of law in economic life. These are often folded under the general rubric of 'governance'.

The 1980s witnessed political reforms and shifts to participatory forms of government in many parts of the world. In recently published work, scholars and policy-makers have placed greater stress on personal freedom and pluralist government, not only as values in their own right, but also as factors that are associated with development. Today, fairness and pluralism loom ever larger in donor governments' consideration of aid effectiveness and aid priorities.

'Good governance' is interpreted by the World Bank as being syn-onymous with sound development management. The Bank's experience has shown that the programmes and projects it helps finance may be technically sound, but fail to deliver anticipated results for reasons connected to the quality of government action. Legal reforms, however urgent, may come to naught if the new laws are not enforced consistently or there are severe delays in implementation. Efforts to develop privatized production and encourage market-led growth may not succeed unless investors face clear rules and institutions that reduce uncertainty about future government action. Vital reforms of public expenditure may founder if accounting systems are so weak that budgetary policies cannot be implemented or monitored, or if poor procurement systems encourage corruption and distort public investment priorities. Failure to involve beneficiaries and others affected in the design and implementation of projects can substantially erode their sustainability.[8] Broad participation in development is essential to its effectiveness.

These examples illustrate a broader point: 'good governance' is central to creating and sustaining an environment which fosters strong and equitable development.

A CHANGING INSTITUTION: THE WORLD BANK

How is the World Bank changing in response to these changing global circumstances and the changing perspective on development? How is it responding – and how is it going to respond – to the increasing number of borrower countries, the increasing expectations of its shareholders, and the diversity of issues on which it is asked for assistance?

It is important, first, to clarify that in the context of the global development process, the Bank can in most cases play only a modest role. Second, it is equally important to be realistic about what the Bank actually can do, given the political, social and economic complexity referred to earlier. Third, the impact of the Bank's work is often slow to appear. Structural economic changes do not yield positive results overnight. The benefits from investing in people take a long time to harvest. No blueprints, no quick fixes, exist for the borrower when it comes to changing the course of development. There is no single strategy that the Bank can – or should –

define for all its customers. In short, the role of the Bank must be kept in perspective.

Moreover, whatever the Bank does or does not do, the main responsibility for undertaking necessary changes to improve peoples' living standards rests with the borrowing countries themselves. Peoples and governments have the deciding voice in shaping their future. The Bank is only a *partner* in this endeavour.

(a) Poverty-reduction

The Bank's fundamental objective, now and for the future, remains poverty-reduction. As the Bank's President, Lewis T. Preston, has stated: 'Poverty reduction is the benchmark by which our performance as a development institution will be measured.'

Bank/IDA lending of over $20 billion a year supports our borrower countries in their economic reform efforts and with investment in virtually every major area of development. All of the Bank's lending and advisory work, however, is focused on achieving the fundamental objective of helping our borrowers reduce poverty.

Bank policies in this area have recently been strengthened significantly. For example, detailed, policy-oriented poverty assessments in the Bank's client countries have been initiated. These assessments help to measure the magnitude of a country's poverty problems; a government's commitment to addressing them; and the Bank's impact in helping to reduce them. Specific country programmes are designed accordingly and the volume of Bank lending to a country will be responsive, *inter alia*, to the strength of a government's efforts to reduce poverty.

The Bank has long been committed to poverty reduction. But these new approaches, and particularly the performance measures, will enable it to better achieve the goal – by focusing on policies which promote a pattern of growth and poverty-reduction; and by setting indicative targets for poverty-reduction as reflected by key social indicators such as child mortality and malnutrition, the latter based on UNICEF targets as set forth at the Summit for Children.[9]

In its dialogue with borrowers, the Bank is encouraging policies that increase opportunities for the poor and help them to participate in growth through economy-wide and sectoral policies that stimulate rural development and urban employment; and through policies to increase the access of the poor to land, credit, public infrastructure and services. The Bank supports these policies through support for reform efforts (about 25 per cent of the annual lending programme) and through finance for infrastructure, agriculture, industry and other sectors (about 75 per cent of total lending).

The social sectors are particularly important in the fight against poverty. The Bank has thus increased its economic and sector work in these areas as a base for expanded lending in the years ahead. For IDA – whose resources go to the countries where over 80 per cent of the world's poor live – the proportion of population, health and nutrition (PHN) lending rose from 3.4 per cent in fiscal years 1987–89 to 10.8 per cent in fiscal year 1990–92. For IBRD and IDA combined, lending for PHN grew from 1.6 per cent to over 5.3 per cent in the same periods.

The Bank also has become the largest single external source of funding for education in developing countries. IDA lending for education increased from 7.2 per cent in fiscal years 1987–90 to 12.4 per cent in fiscal year 1992. For both IBRD and IDA combined, lending expanded from 3.9 per cent to 8.6 per cent, or nearly US$2 billion a year over the last three years.

A key component of the poverty-reduction strategy is to greatly strengthen the involvement of women. There is a proven correlation between a mother's education and the general health and well-being of her family. In addition, higher levels of female education result in increased family planning and lower fertility. Women also account for at least half the food produced in the developing world and for one-third of the wage labour force. Their access to education and training is likely to raise productivity in all sectors. In short, promoting the role of women is key to maximizing investment in people – and reducing poverty.[10]

The Bank's 'refocus' on poverty has been dramatic in recent years – beginning with the 1990 World Development Report.[11] The changes might not be all that visible from the outside; but through new policy directives, increased levels of lending and research work, there has been a radical shift toward focusing on direct or indirect poverty-related issues. That focus will be intensified in the years to come.

(b) Environmental Protection

There has also been an increasing awareness of environmental concerns at the Bank over the last five years or so – and a major effort to integrate them into its work.

● A system for environmental assessment is now in place for the projects which the Bank helps finance.
● The Bank supports member countries with their National Environmental Action Plans. IDA plays a key role in this area – incorporating in these

Action Plans issues of policy and institutional reform, sectoral linkages, participation and financing.

- The Bank is already assisting over 40 countries with specific environmental management projects – from pollution control in Beijing and Mexico City, to land management in Uganda.

- The Bank is also expanding support for investments that are good for poverty-reduction and for the environment: support for clean water and sanitation is projected to double over the next three years; investment in education, health, nutrition and family planning should rise by two-thirds.

- The Bank is giving increased priority to the crucial role of women as managers of natural resources – through targeted extension, training and credit programmes, and through educational reforms. Fifty per cent of agricultural projects, and two-thirds of education projects, now include specific measures to help women.

- Finally, the Bank is maintaining its support for research on environmental technologies. The Consultative Group on International Agricultural Research (CGIAR) – chaired by the Bank and supported by other donors – holds great potential to improve both agricultural productivity and environmental sustainability.

On global issues, the Bank is working with UNEP, UNDP and our other partners through the Global Environment Facility (GEF). The comparative advantage of the GEF is that it can help mobilise resources and coordinate actions – without creating yet another international bureaucracy.

The future challenge for the Bank in this particular area is to keep up with the environmental demand from borrowers at all stages of development. Even those in the midst of economic crisis – like the nations of Eastern Europe and the former Soviet Union – have asked for the Bank's assistance to clean up their environment (including, in the case of the former Soviet Union, helping to identify alternative energy sources to nuclear power). At the same time, countries which have had some success in restructuring their economies – such as Chile, Indonesia and Mexico – are asking for help in giving increased priority to the environment.

The *World Development Report 1992* made it clear that any serious effort to reduce poverty must go hand-in-hand with an equally serious effort to protect the environment. The Bank has recently undertaken a reorganisation which includes the establishment of new Vice Presidencies for Environmentally Sustainable Development, and Human Resource Development. A major effort to recruit the necessary staff and develop the skills to meet the challenge of sustainable development is underway.

In terms of future environmental issues, there are four challenges that are crucial if real progress is to be made. These are challenges not just for the Bank, but for all concerned with sustainable development.

- First, follow up and implement the specific commitments made in Rio – including the international conventions and the promises made to provide additional concessional resources for the environment.
- Second, support the developing countries as they strengthen their environmental policies and institutions – by helping them prepare and, even more importantly, implement National Environmental Action Plans.
- Third, attack the local environmental problems which hurt the poor the most – especially unclean water, inadequate sanitation and soil degradation.
- Fourth, increase the focus on slowing global population growth, which poses a major threat to environmental sustainability. Central to this effort is accelerated development and, particularly, increasing access to education for girls in the developing world.

(c) An Enabling Environment

In order to have the resources to reduce poverty and protect the environment, there must be growth – and that must remain a priority for the developing countries. The Bank, therefore, will continue to support borrower countries in shaping and implementing the sound policies that are required to ensure growth:

- *Supporting the climate for enterprise*. Governments need to reduce their interventions in industrial and agricultural pricing, create a regulatory and legal environment conducive to entrepreneurship, and focus on ensuring adequate infrastructure and institutions.
- *Opening economies to international trade and investment*. This calls for a reduction in non-tariff barriers to trade, substantially lower tariffs, and policies that encourage investment.
- *Economic policy reforms and adjustment programmes*. These are required to establish the conditions for growth and long-term development.

The 1991 *World Development Report* staked out a pragmatic approach to policies aimed at encouraging 'market-friendly' development – and the complementary roles of government and the private sector. But striking the right balance in each country requires – and will continue to require – adjustment of economic policies.

We have all learned from experience. Adjustment programmes have evolved considerably in recent years. For example, the 'second generation' programmes of the later 1980s have gone well beyond issues of stabilisation and fiscal balance. There is more concentration on sectoral policies which underpin the macroeconomic framework, and more attention to the pacing of reforms. The complementarity between financing for adjustment and investment is emphasised, with particular focus on stimulating a private sector response.

The impact of adjustment on the poor has rightly become a major priority, with UNICEF's efforts to flag this concern having had a major influence. In the medium-to-long term, economic restructuring is essential to help the poor by providing an improved climate for productivity and increased earnings. In the short run, however, the poor can be negatively affected by policies aimed at reducing subsidies and rationalising public expenditures. During the transition period, therefore, adjustment programmes must include specific measures to protect the poor.

Since the mid-1980s, increased attention has been given to the protection of vulnerable groups during adjustment – through the creation of safety-nets and other special programmes. Moreover, adjustment programmes are now being increasingly focused on supporting a pattern of growth which enables the poor to participate through their labour and which promotes poverty-reduction. This focus on a pro-poor 'pattern' of growth enables the poor to participate through their labour and is central to future strategies.

At the same time, it is now universally recognised that growth, by itself, is not sufficient to achieve sustainable development and poverty reduction. Investment in human capital, in people, is of equal importance – and is an essential component of the overall enabling environment for growth and poverty reduction. Human development is a priority on which the World Bank and the UN agencies are agreed – and on which they are working closely together.

To maintain necessary investment in human resource development, particularly during times of economic crisis, additional resources are required. The issue, however, is not simply one of additional funding, but of better allocation and targeting. For recipient countries, this means a rigorous focus on priorities within public expenditure programmes.

A sensitive issue in this context is that of military expenditures. In the developing countries in general, military outlays quintupled, in constant dollars, between 1960 and 1988. This was twice the rate of per capita income and almost equal to total expenditures for health and education. As the UNDP and IMF have so often and so forcefully stressed, military expenditure, therefore, is a prime target for reallocation to more productive purposes. This is also true, of course, for the industrial countries. It has been estimated, for example, that a 10 per cent cut in defence spending by the NATO countries could finance a doubling of aid.

These issues are related to the whole question of governance and its integral role in creating the enabling environment for development.

It must be stressed (a) that good governance is not synonymous with any particular form of government; and (b) good governance is a 'two-way street' – donors must also hold themselves accountable for their policies and actions. Other factors to be considered include:

Time horizon Institutional development cannot be accomplished overnight. Assistance must, therefore, be designed with a long time horizon, assuring the recipient sustained support at a pace consistent with its capacity to absorb and learn. This involves a major overhaul of bilateral and multilateral donor practices in technical cooperation along the lines reflected in the DAC Principles of Technical Cooperation.

Country-specificity Assistance needs to be highly differentiated, taking account of cultural, social, political and institutional traditions of the country. This can only be accomplished with a high degree of involvement by beneficiaries in the design and implementation of assistance programmes.

Limits Donors need to lower expectations about what outsiders can achieve in this area. Reforms are unlikely to be effective if there is not a genuine public demand for them and a public awareness of the issue. Good governance must be driven by internal rather than external imperatives.

CHANGING APPROACHES

Making progress in achieving sustainable development in the 1990s is, if anything, going to be more difficult in the post-cold war era than ever before. There is a whole array of new challenges and the demise of the old geopolitical order may actually lead to a net reduction, rather than an increase, in resources for development – an unacceptable result.

While there is considerable room for IBRD lending to grow, from about US$16 billion to about US$26 billion annually, given current resources, the ODA 'pie' at the end of the cold war is under tremendous pressure – from newly eligible recipients and the exceptional needs of the reforming socialist economies, as well as financing requirements for addressing international relief, peace-keeping and environmental concerns. Already, between 1981 and 1991, aid flows have fallen as a percentage of donor GNP (from 0.29 per cent to 0.26 per cent).

A commonly cited aid target is 0.7 per cent of GNP, which was endorsed at the first meeting of UNCTAD, some 25 years ago. Some countries continue to subscribe to this target; others have never accepted it.

Being realistic, the prospect in the 1990s is for a more limited aid pie in real terms – even though three categories of countries appear as new claimants. First, countries that are now able to support only concessional borrowing (e.g. Angola, Mongolia). Second, countries that are potentially reactivated aid recipients, following poor economic performance and exceptional factors such as war (e.g. Afghanistan, Cambodia, Vietnam). Third, the republics of the former Soviet Union and the formerly socialist economies of Eastern Europe.

Clearly, donor countries and international institutions need to explore new ways to augment the slow or non-existent growth in aid flows of recent years – and to ensure that what aid is available is concentrated on the poorest countries (much more easily said than done, given the record over many years!). Recipient countries must demonstrate a capacity to use aid effectively – through both sound economic policy and effective governance – or risk losing it.

But the World Bank – and the United Nations and all other institutions committed to development – also face the challenge of being as efficient and effective as possible. There are three key areas where improvement is urgently required:

● *Better results* In an age when there is increasing scepticism about all aid programmes, and fewer resources available, development institutions must focus on results – on effective implementation. This means more rigorous self-evaluation, openness to criticism and responsiveness to change. The Bank has recently undertaken a comprehensive evaluation of its entire portfolio – and has published the results. The imperatives of ownership, commitment and increased beneficiary participation are clear.[12] This kind of rigorous reexamination is a healthy exercise for every institution – and the principal beneficiaries will be those we are trying to help. Honesty in assessing the performance of development institutions is the first step toward improving their effectiveness.

● *Focus* Given the diversity of development problems and the new challenges – in the former Soviet Union, for example – all development institutions run the risk of strategic overstretch. The focus on poverty-reduction – helping to improve the lives of the more than a billion people who live on less than a dollar a day – must not be diluted or lost. As previously indicated, the World Bank has recently restated its commitment to the overarching objective of poverty-reduction.

● *Partnership* Directly related to the issues of improved results and focus is the question of partnership. No single institution has all the answers nor all the resources to meet the needs of the world's poorest people. Development institutions – multilateral, bilateral and non-governmental – simply *must* do a better job of recognising each other's comparative advantages and working together.

The World Bank is determined to work even more closely with its partners to this end. The Bank's relationships with the UN agencies is particularly important – and ties are already deep. There is collaboration on human development, on drought relief in Southern Africa, and the Global Environment Facility; partnerships on riverblindness and capacity-building in Africa; combined work on water and sanitation all over the world; and joint efforts to combat AIDS. In fact, in almost every sphere of development, the Bank and the UN agencies are in close collaboration.

Nevertheless, there remains considerable potential for increased positive synergies between the sectoral agencies of the United Nations and the Bretton Woods institutions. What is needed is a candid assessment of where we wish to be five years from now in terms of sharing the burden among development agencies. Our common shareholders will presumably insist upon some greater reliance on comparative advantage, and if the Bank is to be able to play its role effectively, it will need to concentrate somewhat more then it is now able to do. And yet the functions performed by the Bank are all necessary. Is it possible that a strengthened set of UN agencies will be able to share some of the burden to a greater degree? At some point an effort to plan ahead in this fashion might be productive.

We must tap this potential aggressively, as we work together to achieve our shared objective: a better life and a brighter future for those most in need.

NOTES

1. James Schlesinger, 'Quest for a Post-Cold War Foreign Policy', *Foreign Affairs* (The Year Ahead), 1993.
2. A recent example of unexpected budget stringency was Sweden which, in late 1992, was buffeted by the currency crisis in the European exchange rate mechanism (ERM) and was forced to cut its aid budget.
3. Lewis T. Preston, 'The Priority of Development In The Post-Cold War Era and the Role of the World Bank', Address to the US Foreign Policy Association, New York City, 25 March 1993.
4. The World Bank, *Sustaining Rapid Development in East Asia and the Pacific* (Washington DC: The World Bank, March 1993).
5. *The Financial Times*, 2 April, 1993.

6.   The World Bank, *World Development Report 1991: The Challenge of Development* (Washington DC: The World Bank, 1991).
7.   The World Bank, *World Development Report 1992: Development and the Environment* (Washington DC: The World Bank, 1992).
8.   The World Bank, *Governance and Development* (1992).
9.   Sven Sandstrom, *An Effective Strategy for Poverty Reduction* (address to the International Development Conference, Washington DC, 12 January 1993) and see UNICEF, *State of the World's Children*, 1993, p. 59.
10.   Lawrence H. Summers, *Investing in All the People: Educating Women In Developing Countries* (Washington, DC: The World Bank, 1991).
11.   The World Bank, *World Development Report 1990: Poverty* (Washington, DC: The World Bank, 1990).
12.   *The World Bank, Effective Implementation: Key to Development Impact:* Report of the World Bank's Portfolio Management Task Force (1992).

4 The Keynesian Vision and the Developing Countries

Lal Jayawardena

This chapter seeks to examine the vision which inspired Keynes in putting forward his design for the postwar world which was eventually finalised at Bretton Woods. It asks two specific questions: (1) Was that vision adequate to the circumstances of the time from the standpoint of both developed and developing countries? (2) How well has the developing world been served by the structure of institutions that eventually emerged at Bretton Woods?

(1) The underlying concern of Keynes and his associates in London who worked on the seminal papers prepared in 1941–42, underpinning the Bretton Woods Conference, was to safeguard the postwar world against any relapse into the harsh experiences of the thirties. The Great Depression had shown, that in the absence of multilateral agreements and institutions, the economic system could rapidly degenerate into 'beggar-my-neighbor' policies culminating in generalised deflation, mass unemployment, and general immiserisation. The World Economic Conference of 1933, called in an attempt to create an international economic order, had ended in failure.

Keynes's more immediate concern in building a set of effective postwar international economic institutions was rooted in a preoccupation with what would happen in Britain if the attempt failed. There would then be no prospect of 'abolishing economic want and of providing continuous good employment at a high standard of life'. Beyond this, failure would 'result ... in social disorders'.[1] If the attempt succeeded, then it followed that the benefits would spread beyond Britain and be broadcast throughout the world. In this sense Keynes's vision may be said to have been adequate to the circumstances of the time.

This vision was based on the assumption that all that was necessary was to bridge the trade gaps associated with high levels of employment, by devising the necessary financing mechanism – the International Clearing Union. For Britain in particular it was clear to Keynes that the imports necessary for full employment, especially of food and raw materials from the primary producing countries, could not be financed out of her sharply diminished postwar export revenues, both visible and invisible. The system

49

he designed would work asymmetrically with a distinct bias in favour of deficit countries, the major burden of adjustment being placed on the surplus countries. As Keynes defined the task in his first draft of the International Clearing Union proposal dated 8 September 1941,

> the objective of the new system must be to require the chief initiative from the creditor countries, while maintaining enough discipline on the debtor countries to prevent them from exploiting the new ease allowed them in living profligately beyond their means.[2]

Deficit countries would be permitted to run deficits with the Union up to a ceiling set by the 'index-quota' allotted to it which was generously set at one–half the sum of its total imports and exports over the average of the previous five years. A further check to profligate behaviour on the part of deficit countries would come from their being put under gentle pressure to devalue their currencies by no more than 5 per cent a year, once their debit balance with the Union exceeded half their 'index-quota'. The devaluation, however, was by no means compulsory, and was only an action which 'might' be required.

Surplus countries, on the other hand, were under much stronger mandatory pressures to revalue their currencies. Since in the aggregate, deficits were the counterpart of their surpluses, it followed that deficits were not solely the result of countries living beyond their means, and that surplus countries must assume some share of the responsibility for deficits. Accordingly, a surplus country was obliged to revalue its currency by 5 per cent, if it had a credit balance with the Union exceeding half its 'index quota' for more than a year, with a mandatory further 5 per cent revaluation being required whenever additions to its credit balance exceeded a further 10 per cent of its 'index-quota'. An upper limit, also equivalent to its 'index-quota', was set for any annual credit balance which a surplus country could enjoy with the Union, to be enforced in successive drafts of the plan by varying penalties. In Keynes's first draft, the entire excess credit balance was to be confiscated and transferred to the Reserve Fund of the Union, with less stringent proposals including a 1 per cent monthly tax on excess balances being introduced in later versions.

In summary, the plan envisaged swings in either direction around balance-of-payments equilibrium up to a limit set by the country's generous 'index-quota'. The deficit countries were the good boys of the system, creating and exporting employment, who were to be encouraged, though within distinct limits, while the surplus countries were the villains of the piece, whose excesses were to be punished in various ways.[3]

The developing countries entered the picture in two ways. First, they were to become the beneficiary of chronic surpluses run by countries in excess of their quotas. In Keynes's second draft, dated 18 November 1941, a provision was made for the transfer of credit balances in excess of quotas, to the International Investment Board – the World Bank in embryo – proposals for which were being developed by Professors Hansen and Gulick.[4] In the third draft, dated 15 December 1941, the notion of a cciling on the credit balance of a surplus country was abandoned, and replaced by an obligation of that country to discuss with the Governing Board of the Union appropriate measures for restoring its balance-of-payments equilibrium. 'International loans for the development of backward countries' were included as the last item (d) of four such measures.[5] The others were:

(a) measures for the expansion of domestic credit and domestic demand;

(b) The appreciation of its local currency in terms of bancor, or, if preferred, an increase in money-wages;

(c) the reduction of excessive tariffs and other discouragements against imports; ....

What is significant is that this hierarchy of measures for dealing with persistent surplus positions has been carried over, in that order, into the present – fifty years after Bretton Woods – as any conventional contemporary discussion of the problem of the Japanese surplus will show. In other words, as things stand today, the G-7 coordination process seems to take the form largely of putting pressure on Japan to implement measures (a) to (c) in Keynes's listing. Little attention is given to the consideration that Japan's excess domestic savings are being absorbed by the US because US domestic savings are inadequate.

If, however, today's principal global macroeconomic problem is regarded as being the unsustainability of the US deficit, then there is evidence to suggest that priority ought to attach to Keynes's measure (d), namely loans to developing countries. The evidence is that, in terms of work done for UNU/WIDER by Professor Jeffrey Sachs of Harvard University, it turns out that recycling Japan's surplus to developing countries is five times as effective in improving the US trade balance as domestic expansion in Japan. Specifically, the simulation sought to trace the effects on the US trade balance of a US$25 billion annual recycling programme to developing countries as urged by a WIDER Study Group,[6] as contrasted with an equivalent domestic expansion package of US$25 billion. The finding was that this order of domestic expansion in Japan would improve the US trade balance by US$2 billion, while an equivalent recycling programme would improve it by US$10 billion, i.e. by a factor of five.

The developing countries came into the picture in 1941, in the second place, essentially as producers of primary products whose supplies were vital if 'continuous good employment' was to be maintained in the developed countries (such as the UK). Equally, these supplies could be financed only if primary producers purchased equivalent developed-country manufactured products, *supplemented* by the capacity of the Clearing Union to finance developed-country deficits to the extent required by full-employment considerations.

There was, however, an important area of concern with the threat to the living standards of primary producers as a result of the commodity cycle. Keynes's buffer stock scheme for stabilising commodity prices – the Council for Commodity Controls – had as an important objective the imposition of automatic export and production quotas when a commodity price fell below the level that would fail to ensure a 'reasonable standard of life' to producers defined as equivalent to the normal level of living enjoyed by three-quarters of the population of the countries affected. But the overriding objective was to ensure the smooth, as opposed to erratic, working of the commodity price mechanism, so that prices would stabilise about whatever trend was necessary to elicit the necessary continuing supplies of primary products to the developed countries. Indeed, the financing of the buffer stock was explicitly arranged in counter-cyclical fashion to bring about this result. The Clearing Union would extend a line of credit to the Council for Commodity Controls which would be drawn upon in times of slump to build up buffer stocks, raise commodity prices, and inject purchasing power into the economic system, while this line would be retired, purchasing power withdrawn, and commodity prices reduced, by selling from buffer stocks in times of boom.

But the wider issues of development economics – those of full employment growth in developing countries resulting from the adaptation of Keynesian economics by Harrod and Domar – did not preoccupy Keynes, except as already noted, in the provision for resource transfers to developing countries as a mechanism for adjusting chronic surplus positions of developed countries. It was left to the first generation of development economists of the 1950s, the most conspicuous of whom in this respect was Raoul Prebisch, to state the development problem in precisely the same terms in which Keynes perceived Britain's postwar full-employment problem in 1941. Just as Britain faced a trade-gap problem with full-employment imports exceeding postwar export earnings, the developing countries were faced, in Prebisch's view, with a structural trade-gap problem in their attempt to accelerate GDP growth.

The aggregate magnitudes of the trade gap of developing countries were first brought into focus by Prebisch in UNCTAD I in 1964. Developing countries would need to grow at a minimum of 6 per cent, in terms of GDP annually, in order to realise their minimum employment and per capita income goals, while the import capacity required to sustain this growth rate would have to exceed 6 per cent annually. Since their exports were largely composed of primary commodities, the international demand for which was relatively sluggish, export growth was projected to be at a figure well below 6 per cent annually – in the region of 4 per cent. The resulting trade gap for 1970 was estimated at US$20 billion, to bridge which a combination of trade and aid measures were proposed by the UNCTAD Secretariat which became the focus of the debate in UNCTAD I. This represented a range of issues which Keynes's vision did not explicitly comprehend in 1941 but which, as has been argued above, can be easily accommodated using the Keynesian framework by an extension of his reasoning.

The Prebisch 'trade gap' exercise has indeed been updated for the 1990s by UNU/WIDER using a very different methodology which extrapolated the results of a number of country studies. On this basis the capital needs of a minimum 5.5 per cent GDP growth rate in the developing countries during the 1990s (including provision for a degree of environmental protection) were estimated to rise from US$60 billion in the early 1990s to US$140 billion in the year 2000.[7] When annual interpolations are made in this rising series, the total flow for the eight years 1993 to the year 2000 rises to US$1000 billion, or an annual average of US$125 billion. This turns out to be identical to the estimates provided to the Earth Summit in Rio by the UNCED Secretariat, using again a very different methodology.

(2) In addressing the second question, namely how well the developing world has been served as regards global economic management by the Bretton Woods framework of institutions, it is necessary to recognise the significant departure of the reality resulting from the negotiations, from Keynes's original vision. In particular, two institutions were not given birth to – the International Trade Organisation, and the Council for Commodity Controls. In the absence of the latter body, the developing countries were deprived of a mechanism for stabilising commodity prices, and therefore of access to a substantial volume of unconditional finance. In addition, the IMF, as it emerged, was not equipped to adjust changes in surplus and deficit positions as between countries, by making the necessary entries in the books of an International Clearing Union as Keynes intended;

consequently, it was unable to handle institutionally the massive shifts in international payments that resulted from the oil crisis of the 1970s, although it has been argued by Triffin that it was not beyond the wit of man to improvise an appropriate structure within the Bretton Woods institutions at the time. What is material is that the non-implementation of Keynes's Clearing Union design meant that the recycling of OPEC surpluses was left to private markets, with the result that the developing countries were bequeathed a debt problem in the 1980s from which Latin America has made a painful recovery only in the early 1990s, while Africa still awaits relief.

The result of failure, both on the commodity front and on the debt front, has been a massive deterioration in the international economic environment facing the developing countries. As Hans Singer has effectively summarised the problem:

> Even if one accepts that 'more development' is to a large extent the responsibility of the developing countries, the history of the past two decades shows only too clearly that the lack of a global compact and of effective global economic management has had a great deal to do with the setbacks to development which many developing countries have experienced. 'More development' in an unfavourable international environment is a near-impossible task.[8]

Leaving aside the question of a global compact for the moment, it is the failure of global economic management in the postwar period to prevent the emergence of an unfavourable international economic environment that requires to be documented, at least for the 1980s, as it is in this respect that the world has been inadequately served by the post-Bretton Woods framework of institutions resulting from the failure to implement Keynes's original vision.

So far as the costs to the developing countries of the debt problem is concerned, the evidence is to be found in the World Bank's 1991 Development Report. Average annual savings rates for developing countries exceeded investment rates (representing a net resource transfer from South to North) by at least one-half per cent of world GDP or nearly US$100 billion in 1989 prices, taking world GDP at nearly US$20 trillion in 1989. It is this perverse transfer which must, in significant measure, explain the fact that the average annual GDP growth rates in sub-Saharan Africa and Latin America dropped by about 2.5 percentage points between 1973–80 and 1980–89. For the developing countries as a whole, taking their 1989 GDP as US$3.1 trillion, this net resource transfer amounted to an uncompensated annual external shock of 3 per cent of GDP. It is scarcely surprising that their growth rates slowed and that the 1980s became 'lost for development'. This is in no way intended to suggest that inadequate domestic policies in developing countries had no bearing upon the débâcle of the 1980s. The contention rather is that no degree of feasible domestic economic reform would have survived an annual external shock of this magnitude.

In regard to non-oil primary commodities, the history both of the postwar trends in commodity prices, and of fluctuations about these trends, would surely have been significantly different had Keynes's commodity stabilisation plan been in existence. As it was, the experience of the 1980s contrasted sharply with that of previous postwar decades. In earlier decades, the principal characteristic of the commodity market situation was the relatively large short-term price instability of prices, while the general trend of commodity prices was gently downward (in terms of the prices of manufactures exported by developed countries). In the period since the early 1980s, by contrast, the dominant feature has been a sharply deteriorating real price trend, and a greatly reduced degree of short-term price instability. Real commodity prices recovered somewhat during the short-lived recovery of 1983 and 1984, but thereafter there has been a rapid deterioration, the real price index declining by 1990 to 65 per cent of the 1980 level.

This deterioration in the trend of real commodity prices has involved a massive loss in export earnings of developing countries. It has been estimated that over the period 1980–88, this loss amounted, on a cumulative basis, to US$128 billion at 1980 prices, equivalent to almost 120 per cent of the developing countries' commodity exports in 1980.[9]

An update of this estimate yields a total cumulative loss for the decade 1981–90 of US$219 billion, or double the total value of commodity exports in 1980 as indicated in Table 4.1. During the first half of the 1980s, the terms of trade loss was entirely due to the fall in commodity prices, the effects of which were partly offset by a decline in manufactures prices during the recession. In the later 1980s, however, the prices of manufactures rose appreciably in terms of US dollars, and added substantially to the terms of trade loss. On an annual average basis, this loss had been marginal (US$6 billion p.a.) over the first half of the 1980s but was almost US$40 billion p.a. in the latter half.

In relation to GDP, the terms of trade loss was much greater for Africa than for the other developing regions. For 1980–88, it was equivalent to about one-sixth of Africa's total GDP in 1980 – an enormous drain on resources by any measure. For Asia and Latin America, the corresponding losses were smaller – 6 per cent for Asia (on a cumulative basis), and almost 9 per cent for Latin America. On an annual basis, the real income loss resulting from the terms of trade deterioration from 1980 to 1988

Table 4.1   The terms of trade of the developing countries, 1980–90

	Annual average			Cumulative total		
	1981–85	1986–90	1981–90	1981–85	1986–90	1981–90
Terms of trade effect due to movement in:	(US$ billion at 1980 prices)					
1. Unit value of commodity exports of developing countries	−18	−17	−35	−89	−87	−176
2. Unit value of manufactures exports of developed countries	+12	−20	−9	+58	−101	−43
Total	−6	−37	−44	−31	−188	-219

Source: Private communication from Professor Alfred Maizels

represented 1 per cent of developing countries' aggregate GDP in 1980, but the proportion for Africa was as high as 2.4 per cent. This compares with the real income loss suffered by the OECD countries as a result of the oil price rises of 1973–74 and 1978–79 of about 2 per cent of their combined GDP in each case. A given percentage real income loss involves, of course, a much greater calamity for poor countries than a similar loss for wealthy OECD countries.

The foreign exchange loss resulting from the terms of trade deterioration was evidently a major factor behind the rise in developing countries' total foreign debt, since many countries sought to borrow to offset, at least in part, the adverse terms of trade effect. It also contributed directly to a sharp liquidity squeeze and, for many countries, to a phase of 'import compression', if not of 'import strangulation'. The empirical evidence indicates that the burden of import compression was placed largely on domestic investment and social expenditures on human development, thus substantially undermining the potential of a large number of countries for longer-term development and structural change.

Against this background, global economic management failed the developing countries in another crucial respect. The scale on which unconditional resources were made available to countries in payments deficit fell considerably short of Keynes's original vision. This implied only the relatively mild conditionality attaching to borrowing from the Clearing Union that we have already noted. Keynes swallowed even this degree of conditionality only on the basis that significant resources were available in return to deficit countries – namely, a very large IMF in which, as mentioned, each country had a quota equal to half the five-year average of the sum of its imports plus exports. The US proposed a smaller IMF, equivalent to one-sixth or 16 per cent of world imports, and was prepared in exchange to relax the criteria of conditionality. What resulted, in Hans Singer's words, was 'the worst of all possible worlds' – a small IMF with tough conditionality. The IMF was already too small from Keynes's standpoint at 15 per cent of world imports when it was eventually set up. Since then IMF quota increases have fallen significantly behind the growth of world trade so that total quotas now stand at only 2 per cent of world imports.

As a result, it is hard to resist the conclusion that conditionality has been used as a device to ration available resources among claimants. This situation with the IMF has, over the last two decades, been aggravated by the stagnation of development assistance which has also adversely affected the World Bank and the Aid Groups it chairs. In particular, IDA flows within the World Bank have shrunk in real terms in relation to the growth of poverty. As a result, India's IDA allocations were rationed with the result that it acquired a massive debt problem in the 1980s of Latin American proportions – on an income of under $300 per capita.

Tough conditionality and a small IMF in effect meant that the World Bank was required to step in to supplement the IMF as a provider of programme finance and depart increasingly from its traditional project financing role. Even so, the resources available in support of adjustment by the two institutions have been inadequate and made available on too short-term a basis. As a result, where programmes have succeeded, as recently in Latin America, the successes have been achieved at a substantial social cost in terms of cutbacks in income, real wages and consumption, given the paucity of external resources provided in support of reform. In Africa, on the other hand, there is a substantial body of opinion which contends that structural adjustment programmes have failed altogether. A recent Oxfam assessment summarises this view as follows:

> Structural adjustment programmes (SAPs), implemented by African governments under the tutelage of the World Bank and the IMF, have failed to create a platform for economic recovery and even more conspicuously to address the challenge of poverty alleviation. The World Bank's own most recent review confirmed that SAPs have a particularly

bad record in terms of restoring investment, the yardstick against which recovery prospects must be measured.

In part, this can be traced to the impact of deflationary monetary policies and sweeping trade liberalisation measures under SAPs. These have exposed fragile, but potentially competitive, manufacturing industries to increased competition in the face of spiralling interest rates and rising import costs. The predictable result has been disinvestment, deindustrialisation, and mounting unemployment.

Rather than apportion blame between doctor and patient, surely it is time to recognise that both are hooked on the wrong medicine. It is time for the World Bank and IMF to surrender their dogmatic attachment to an outmoded set of economic prescriptions. What is needed is a new approach to adjustment, based on redistribution policies, selective import liberalisation, more carefully phased market reforms and above all a commitment to increased investment in human capital.[10]

NOTES

1. Donald Moggridge (ed.), *The Collected Writings of John Maynard Keynes*, Vol. XXV, p. 27.
2. Ibid., p. 30.
3. It is significant that when the Bretton Woods system as it stood collapsed in 1971, and when the shoe was on the other foot with the US being the principal deficit country, it was the US that resurrected Keynes's ideas in the attempt at negotiated international monetary reform that followed in the early 1970s – the Committee of 20. 'Symmetrical' adjustment was explicitly incorporated in the Outline of Reform that emerged from the exercise – although there was disagreement between the US and Europe as to how this might be accomplished. The US proposed explicit reserve targets with taxes on excessive reserve accumulation, while the Europeans preferred the more nebulous concept of 'graduated pressures' on countries in persistent surplus. In the event, the reform exercise of the 1970s was blown off course by the OPEC oil price increase, and the generalised recourse to floating exchange rates that ensued. Today's 'non-system' is arguably no more than the rationalisation of prevailing practice that occurred in the formal Jamaica Agreement of 1975, with a few sops to the developing countries (e.g. a Trust Fund financed by the partial sale of IMF gold) to ensure its smooth passage.
4. Moggridge (ed.), op. cit., pp. 64 and 59.
5. Ibid., p. 80.
6. Saburo Okita *et al.*, *Mobilizing International Surpluses for World Development: A WIDER Plan for a Japanese Initiative*, UNI/WIDER Study Group Series, Report No. 2, Helsinki, 1987.
7. Lal Jayawardena, *A Global Environment Compact for Sustainable Development: Resource Requirements and Mechanisms*, p. 18, Table 3. The

estimate combines external resource gap projections made by Professor Lance Taylor of MIT for UNU/WIDER on the basis of several country studies, with data on environmental protection expenditures from the World Watch Institute. See Lance Taylor, *Foreign Resource Flows and Developing Country Growth*, WIDER Research for Action, Helsinki, 1991; and Lester R. Brown *et al.*, *State of the World 1988*, W. W. Norton & Co. (for World Watch Institute), New York, 1988, p. 77, Table 10-4.

8. Letter from Professor Hans Singer to *The Financial Times*, 21 May 1992.
9. Maizels, *Commodities in Crisis*, 1992, p. 26.
10. Letter from Stewart Wallace, Overseas Director, Oxfam, to *The Financial Times*, 6 May 1993.

5 An African Perspective on Bretton Woods

Adebayo Adedeji

INTRODUCTION

If there was a referendum in Africa today, an overwhelming majority of the people would vote against their governments having anything to do with the Bretton Woods institutions, i.e. the World Bank and the International Monetary Fund (IMF). They know all too well that there has definitely been a considerable net welfare loss *to them* as a result of the way these two agencies have been operating in their countries during the past decade-and-a-half. There is no doubt that the overwhelming majority of the African people – and most African governments – would prefer to see fundamental changes in their countries' relations with the Bretton Woods institutions. There is a virtual consensus among the general public, vocally expressed in the local media, as well as among officials, who naturally prefer putting forth their views in more private settings, that the relationship between Africa and the Bretton Woods institutions has been detrimental to the continent, that far from helping it to become economically viable, these two institutions have been capitalising on, exacerbating and perpetuating Africa's crisis. Little wonder that there have been many IMF riots throughout Africa and that youth, workers and women have rebelled against structural adjustment programmes (SAP), the parade horses of the Bretton Woods institutions.

Yet, in spite of the dramatic and visible decline in living conditions for the average African and in spite of widespread popular protest against their programmes, the Bretton Woods institutions have only marginally modified their policies. Their prescriptions dominate the shape which 'national' policies take and their *de facto* power in Africa thus remains overwhelming.

Before exploring the possible future nature and scope of relations between Africa and the Bretton Woods institutions, especially the potential for a qualitative change for the better, the emergence of the current constellation requires to be looked at again. It needs to be determined which manoeuvring space there had been in the past, i.e. to what extent the actors had the choice to go one way and not another and for which reasons. Only a realistic assessment of the major underlying political and economic factors which govern Africa's relations with the North – and the costs which they entail – will allow the development of a viable future scenario.

THE DEVELOPMENT OF THE DOMINANCE OF THE BRETTON WOODS INSTITUTIONS IN AFRICA

The association of the Bretton Woods institutions with African countries predated political independence. Indeed, in many cases the first economic surveys and/or development plans and strategies of these countries were prepared by the World Bank. In the case of Nigeria, the Bank was invited in 1953 – seven years before independence – to send an economic mission. The Bank's report was published in 1954 and the 1955–60 economic programmes followed in large measure the recommendations contained in this report, entitled *The Economic Development of Nigeria.*

During the 1960s, the World Bank's region of concentration was clearly Asia, particularly India and Pakistan, for both of which it established consortia. In Africa, the Bank's involvement in the development of countries south of the Sahara concentrated on sectoral and project loans. Yet, consultative groups were also established for four countries outside Asia, two of which were in sub-Saharan Africa (Nigeria and Sudan) and one in North Africa (Tunisia). Under these consortia/consultative group arrangements, the Bank submitted to each country concerned periodic, comprehensive investigations covering the economy of the recipient country as a whole, its development possibilities and its problems and performance. The investigations also dealt with the main sectors of the country's economy with a clear indication by the Bank of the sectors deserving priority for external financing. The Bank even assisted in identifying projects and in arranging feasibility studies. And the consortia and consultative groups discussed critically and frankly the uses which the recipient country had made of all evidently available resources (domestic and foreign) before identifying the additional foreign-aid requirements of the country. The only difference between a consortium and a consultative group was that no pledges took place at the meetings of the latter. There can, therefore, be no doubt that the World Bank had been deeply involved in Africa's development even before independence.

But even as early as the 1960s, the biases of the Bank were becoming increasingly apparent. While it did not think then that investment in universal primary education in Africa was wise, it backed rather heavily large-scale infrastructural facilities such as highways and hydro dams. And while it provided some resources in support of industrialisation, it was more favourably inclined towards financing agricultural production for export.

From the beginning of its involvement, there has thus been a strong tendency on the part of the Bank to perpetuate the economic *status quo* rather than to assist African countries in the fundamental restructuring of their colonially-tainted economies. It was precisely this restructuring which would have allowed them to fulfil the promise of independence in a sustainable manner. Yet this was not to be.

The most important historical factor which makes Africa so vulnerable to external 'policy advice' is its unhealthy external dependence, which, colonially inherited, it has not been able to shed. Tragically, the failure of the very attempts to diversify its economies away from merely extracting and exporting primary commodities and to move towards a more productive and expanded agricultural sector, towards an industrial and service structure which would allow for more value-added to be captured internally, is at the very core of today's economic and social problems and has, in fact, dramatically exacerbated the dependence of African countries on external powers.

Apart from explanations having to do with the historical constellations into which newly-independent African countries were born, African governments certainly need to shoulder much of the responsibility for this process having been aborted. But there are also sufficient accounts of those responsible for policy-making in the countries, mostly only expressed in private, of very clear pressure being exerted upon them to adopt policies which they knew were detrimental to their goals and which did not correspond to their priorities.

Faced with African countries whose expectations to develop viable economies ended before they really began, which found themselves thrown back on to their classical export commodities, many of which experienced a virtual price collapse during the 1980s, which were liable for unserviceable debts and which were perennially short of foreign exchange to import crucial agricultural and industrial inputs – or even food – the Bretton Woods institutions had been able to increasingly lord it over many an African government.

The strong influence of the Bretton Woods institutions on African countries took on unprecedented and unparalleled proportions in the 1980s. It was transformed into dominance and a virtual monopoly of these institutions. As the depth of the African crisis became manifest, the major donor countries abrogated their responsibilities to them by making them the sole designers and overseers of economic policies that would command their support, the sole judges of which programmes were right and acceptable and of 'good', 'bad', 'strongly' or 'weakly' adjusting African countries.

Virtually every external support to any African country, including debt rescheduling and relief, became dependent on the award of a certificate of good behaviour by these institutions. Such an award was and is dependent upon adherence to SAP and their conditionalities. Consequently, independent policy-making and national economic management were considerably diminished and narrowed in Africa. The Bretton Woods institutions have pushed on Africa

> a dogmatic view of the 'free market' policies that are not practised in any part of the industrial world and were never practised either in the nearly 200 years of industrial capitalism.... These policies and attitudes, ennobling greed and avarice, have crippled the manufacturing and productive sectors of the economy while encouraging the 'animal spirits' of crude capitalism and fostering the worst forms of speculative finance capital which economists from Adam Smith to John Maynard Keynes have decried.[1]

Indeed, it seemed that Africa had become a laboratory for freshman economists who lacked much insight and experience as far as African economies and societies were concerned. But as the victims were weak, their voices, if heard at all, were ignored. There is no doubt that for political and economic reasons – and this also refers to the political weakness of African leadership and structures – the Bretton Woods institutions could afford to treat African countries in a much more high-handed manner than they could treat Asian and Latin American countries in comparable situations. The July 1989 issue (Vol.2, no.10) of the influential *Southern Africa Political and Economic Monthly* (SAPEM), which was devoted to the theme 'The World Bank and Africa', stated in a scathing editorial:

> The World Bank (and other financial institutions) have capitalised on the African continent and further (aggravated) the political and economic crisis ... there is no historical precedent for the extent and degree of overt policy leverage now being exerted by the World Bank (and other financial institutions) on African governments. Hence the arrogance implicit in recent words and deeds of the World Bank. The World Bank acts with impunity in Africa, establishing institutions at will, with or without the consent of African governments; a pattern which it has not been able to do in other areas of the world.[2]

These policies have devastated African countries, their populations and productive structures and have eroded private and public institutions. The extent of the damage is enormous. In a recent publication the Bank admits high failure rates in its completed projects which soared to almost two-fifths of completed projects in 1991. If this report[3] is to be believed, this was a dramatic 150 per cent increase in failures over the last ten years, i.e. from 15 per cent in 1981 and 30.5 per cent in 1989 to 37.5 per cent in 1992. In dollar terms this amounted to no less than US$ 51.75 billion.

As interesting as the total amount wasted is, however, the fact that one could have known better. Representatives of governments from half of the borrowing countries offered the following reasons for the disastrous performance record:

(a) Bank staff were taking a negotiating position not a consulting position – 'they know what they want from the outset and aren't open to hearing what the country has to say.'

(b) Bank staff were making the potential recipient feel 'psychologically pressured' to take the loan or leave it, with the country ending up with conditions it has no way of honouring and a contract that cannot be implemented.

(c) The Bank was changing its wisdom with the passage of time. 'We saw the Bank talking about import substitution in the sixties, then export substitution, then social problems and then the environment.'

(d) The Bank staff were accused of being high-handed and insensitive, insisting on designing projects according to its policies at the time, instead of consulting with the borrowers and local people.

(e) Bank staff appeared more driven by pressure to lend than a desire for successful project implementation.

(f) The Bank often insisted on international consultants with no local experience to prepare projects, resulting inevitably in poor quality.

Of the nine countries whose success rate was two-thirds or even less for completed projects, five were African. The full list is as follows: Bangladesh (66 per cent), Philippines (65.8 per cent), Algeria (58.3 per cent), Mexico (56 per cent), Brazil (55.9 per cent), Kenya (48.2 per cent), Tanzania (34.8 per cent), Nigeria (26.3 per cent) and Uganda (17.2 per cent).

As stated earlier, a large number of the projects in Africa, if not virtually all the major ones since independence have been studied, often initiated, and/or financed fully or partially by the Bank. When the disasters became ever more glaring, one could have expected a process of incisive questioning and soul-searching so that the accountability of all actors involved could have been established. Yet, it is only the African governments that are castigated for their 'white elephants'. The Bank absolves itself of any responsibility although it has been equally involved in mapping out these development strategies and projects. But when the crisis engulfed the very countries that had accepted its advice, it distanced itself from them and joined critics in putting all the blame on these countries – bad governance, high propensity for prestige projects, poor implementation, corruption, and so on. It is no doubt this kind of attitude by economic policy advisers that made Simon Jenkins lament in an article in *The Times* on 3 February 1993 that:

> It is in the nature of a novice profession (like economics) to oversell itself to politicians. It will also tend to claim that bad decisions were a perversion of its advice.... If economic advisers were members of a professional body, there would surely have been hearings and strikings off: economics shares with architecture a belief that its blunders are due to the idiocy of its clients.[4]

No one can fault the World Bank for inconsistency in this respect. Right from its very beginning when it was pure and simple the bank for reconstruction and development of war-devastated Western Europe the World Bank had manifested its

> American flavour and ideology.... The Bank's ideological bias against public ownership of manufacturing industry has... been a demonstration of the domination of the Bank by predilections and prejudices peculiar to the United States.[5]

The prejudices were so intense that in 1959, Professor Alec Cairncross in his essay on the Bank said,

> A European observer, living in a mixed economy, cannot altogether share the ideological hostility of the Bank to public enterprises in manufacturing industry, although he may recognize its imperfections.[6]

Over the years, both Bretton Woods institutions have become more, not less ideological with American influence in the ascendancy. As we have already noted, the faith of both institutions in the determination of output, employment and prices on the basis of the free interplay of market forces and the quantity theory of money seems unshakable. Hence, their near-religious belief in the effectiveness and universal applicability of structural adjustment programmes. As far as they are concerned, those programmes are as valid for the industrialised market economies as they are for the basically subsistent economies of most sub-Saharan African countries.

The fact that economic aggregates are not fully responsive to market forces in Africa and that basic structural rigidities are at the heart of Africa's persistent crisis are ignored. A satisfactory functioning of the policy instruments of SAP – exchange rate manipulation, control of levels of money supply, trade liberalisation, price deregulation, high nominal interest rates, subsidy reduction and balanced budgets through reduction in public expenditure without regard to the consequences of such measures on the human condition – is predicated upon the existence of a competitive model of production and exchange and a well-developed institutional framework. Yet one of the main features of the African economy is the fragmentation of the product and factor markets. To build a development paradigm for Africa based on the assumption that these markets are competitive and that resources are perfectly mobile and that well-developed financial institutions and money capital markets exist is to build one's house on sand. Sooner rather than later, such a structure would collapse.

Not surprisingly, therefore, SAP have not led to sustainable development in Africa nor elsewhere in the Third World, nor have they even succeeded in meeting their limited objectives of internal and external equilibrium. Yet any criticism of them is regarded as heresy. Given the background of the officials of the Bretton Woods institutions who decide on what policies and strategies are best for Africa, it is but natural for them to universalise economic mechanisms which are peculiar to industrial market economies. In fact this error is not confined to the Bretton Woods institutions. Early development economists – most of them Westerners by origin – had also developed a tendency to universalise ideas and knowledge based on the particular experiences of their societies. This ethno-centricity has done untold havoc to the discipline of development economics and, what is much worse, through the Bretton Woods institutions' virtual monopoly, to developing countries.

In such circumstances, the cleavage – if not the gulf – existing in perceptions as to the appropriate policy framework and development strategies for Africa between the Africans and the officials of Bretton Woods institutions supported by their colleagues in the donor community has dogged the path of progress in the continent and to a large measure has accounted for the persistent crisis that has engulfed it.

But can the world really allow this process of self-immunisation on the part of the Bretton Woods institutions to continue as its extremely counter-productive consequences and its soaring political and social costs, and not only for Africa, become clearer by the day?

- The continuation of 'business-as-usual' will result in the persistence – and, as the rest of the world moves on at high speed, this means regression – of Africa's economic and social condition;

- Repressible in the short run, this will create a potential for explosion the effects of which will not be limited to Africa (and will certainly affect Africa's nearest neighbour, Europe) in the medium-to-long term;
- The current lack of accountability of the Bretton Woods institutions will also continue the scandalous use of taxpayers' money in countries of the North – and likely promote political tendencies of exclusion and repulsion *vis-à-vis* the South.

Can the world afford to further tolerate, if not condone, the dominant attitude as far as the Bretton Woods institutions mandarins are concerned? It is heads they win, tails we lose.

In these days when pro-democracy movements are rightly being encouraged in Africa, do policy-makers in the North also pause to consider how the democratisation of the development process could ever take root in countries where socio-economic policies are not seen by the people to be formulated by themselves and their governments but by officials of the Bretton Woods institutions?

THE NEED FOR AN ALTERNATIVE

It was quite heartening to read from the Bank's *Poverty Reduction Handbook and Operational Directive*, published in April 1992, that sustainable poverty-reduction will once again become the overarching objective of the institution and that it will become the benchmark by which the Bank's performance as a development institution will be measured. This is a most welcome development and nurses hope that there is a recognition developing within the Bank that what sub-Saharan Africa needs is not adjustment at the margin, but fundamental structural transformation – not only of its economy, but also and no less importantly, of its society and polity.

But assuming the good will, it remains to be seen whether the Bank has the capacity and institutional dynamic and stamina to fundamentally change its basic outlook and attitude towards Africa. For the time being, business is conducted as usual and the hegemony of the Bretton Woods institutions seems unassailable. Africa's debt crisis is as serious as ever and the 1990s have so far not seen the end of adjustments, but rather a second generation, higher on social rhetoric and not so high on visible results.

Yet there is no time for further experiments, as the political temperature is rising by the day. How could genuine people's democracy take root in circumstances where socio-economic policies are imposed which not only marginalise the majority of the people but also put them under such an excruciating burden that they feel obliged to seek redress through riot and civil disturbance? Or is there a conscious but silent acceptance of despotic societies and pseudo-democracies so that SAP can continue to operate?

Is it not already beyond pardon that after three decades of 'development assistance' and a decade or more of implementation of SAP, the alleviation of poverty which is the plight of Africa is nowhere to be seen and, quite to the contrary, poverty is on the rise? A second generation of SAP would certainly exacerbate and aggravate the poverty problem of sub-Saharan Africa, which today is paying dearly for its failure to cut the umbilical cord of its unenviable colonial inheritance in the field of governance, economy and nation-building. According to the World Bank itself, while for all other regions of the developing world the proportion of people living below the poverty line is projected to fall – in many cases to a single digit (for example, in China it has already fallen from 28 per cent a decade ago to 8 per cent) – for Africa, the proportion is projected even on optimistic assumptions to remain well over 40 per cent and could easily become 50 per cent or more if the projected optimistic assumptions are not achieved.

In the face of such daunting challenges, Africa needs fundamental change and transformation, not just adjustment. The change and transformation required are not just narrow economistic and mechanical ones. They are the broader and fundamental changes that will bring about, over time, an Africa where there is development and economic justice, not just growth; where there is democracy and accountability, not despotism, authoritarianism and kleptocracy; and where the governed and their governments are moving hand-in-hand in the promotion of the common good; and, where it is the will of the people rather than the wishes of one person or a group of persons, foreign or indigenous or of institutions, foreign or indigenous, bilateral or multilateral, however powerful, that prevails.

The need to take account of the differentiations that exist between and among societies, cultures, beliefs, attitudes and responses to external impulses as well as differences in political and economic structures has led African governments and their regional institutions to search for endogenous development paradigms that will take full cognizance of their societies, polities and economies. Whatever other criticisms one may level against the African political leadership and their regional and national institutions, like ECA and OAU, they cannot be faulted for lack of persistent effort to come out with regional strategies and policy frameworks for meeting the challenges that confront their continent.

Based on their knowledge, experience and sense of responsibility, they have been consistent in their intellectual rejection of the dominant Northern paradigms propagated by the Bretton Woods institutions.

Tragically, this persistence has not been equalled by a stubbornness to stick to their guns and operationalise their own indigenous strategies. Faced with a barrage of ridicule and outright rejection by the Bretton Woods institutions which had by then monopolised the measurement of what sound or unsound, credit-worthy or unworthy policies were, most African governments succumbed to pressure and turned their backs on their own indigenous strategies.

These African blueprints,[7] beginning with the Monrovia Strategy in 1979 and the Lagos Plan of Action in 1980, had a holistic and human-centred approach in common. They are derived from a full understanding of the structures of the African economies with their inelastic supplies, mass poverty, low productivity and weak productive base, backward technology and a large non-monetized sector. These endogenous blueprints also address the exchange nature of the African economies, their excessive external dependence and their vulnerability to external shocks. They address in addition, the political and social issues – the pervasive lack of democracy and accountability, the crisis of legitimacy and the lack of political stability and security without which no development, let alone one on a sustainable basis, can take place.

Thus, the African human-centred and holistic development paradigms incorporate and build on the present African realities. They are predicated on the fundamental structural transformation of the polities, societies and economies of Africa. These paradigms assume a future that is economically viable and politically sustainable for Africa.

Unfortunately, to this point, the Northern perspective of Africa does not take for granted the feasibility of rapid economic progress on the continent. Nor does it assume politically viable solutions to be developed within Africa. Quite the contrary, the Northern perspective is negative and is a basic ideological pillar in justifying SAP. Therefore, in considering at the regional level what new relationships are to be forged between the UN and the Bretton Woods institutions,these historical and contemporary perspectives must be borne in mind.

UN/BRETTON WOODS RELATIONS

The theme of the North–South Roundtable at which the paper on which this chapter is based was originally presented – 'The Bretton Woods Institutions and the Rest of the UN' – suggests that these institutions perceive themselves as part of the UN. This is, however, not the case. Right from the very beginning, the Bretton Woods institutions were negotiated and came into being independently of the UN and its Charter. Although they have entered into an association agreement with ECOSOC under the terms of Article 57 of the UN Charter, this association is of a symbolic nature. In this connection it must be underlined that the World Bank refused in 1946 to sign an agreement, proposed by the UN, which would have been similar to those ccncluded with the specialised agencies. Thus, despite the elaborate and specific provisions both in the Bank's Articles of Agreement and the UN Charter which require the Bank to give consideration to the views and recommendations of competent international organisations, it was the Bank, fighting this battle jointly with the Fund, which won. Though an agreement was signed declaring the Bank a specialised agency of the UN, it was more a declaration of independence on the part of the World Bank than one of cooperation. As was emphasised in the text of the agreement concluded with the UN,

> By reason of the nature of its responsibilities and the terms of its Articles of Agreement the Bank is, and is required, to function as an independent international organisation.

Consequently, the Bretton Woods institutions do not subject themselves to substantive coordination by the UN either at the intergovernmental (ECOSOC) or at the Secretariat (ACC) level as specialised agencies do. Their link is limited to their chief executive officers making, from time to time, appearances before ECOSOC, to maintaining liaison offices at UN headquarters and to participating at some meetings of UN bodies. They are not bound by any decisions of the UN. Rather, they take pains to distance themselves from decisions which do not conform with their ideology and overall orientation. In fact, they see themselves as competitors of the UN in the broad field of development policy and research. Northern countries which are backing the Bretton Woods institutions tend to place greater confidence in their socio-economic analysis rather than in those emanating from the UN. One may also add that the openness which the UN displays *vis-à-vis* the Bretton Woods institutions is not being reciprocated as UN participation at Bretton Woods institutions' meetings is very much restricted.

If at the beginning the Bretton Woods institutions were seen as the

> product of English and American brains, with valuable assistance from the Canadians,[8]

as Harrod once put it, they are now seen as institutions promoting largely Northern interests in general – all the more so as they no longer play any significant role in the North, except in the former socialist countries.

The IMF, which was designed primarily to ensure stable monetary relations among the major industrial nations has, since the collapse of the fixed exchange rate regime in 1971, become a monetary institution for developing countries. Whereas the share of developing countries using IMF credits during the 1950s was an average 58 per cent of the total, it had risen to 65 per cent in the 1970s and to 100 per cent in the 1980s. Currently, the IMF has no influence whatsoever over developed countries running up deficits or surpluses – even though these imbalances have dire consequences well beyond their national borders. Similarly, the World Bank has moved from the rebuilding of war-devastated Western Europe into a funding institution which is essentially operating in developing countries. Yet, in spite of this fundamental shift in the concern of both Bretton Woods institutions, their orientation, philosophy, ideology and power base have remained intact. They see their role as primarily promoting Northern interests rather than as facilitator of development in the South.

Although both institutions were established when most developing countries were still under foreign rule, these countries took up their membership in the Bretton Woods institutions just as they became UN member States, following independence. However, while the United Nations and its Specialised Agencies provided a common forum for the small and poor countries to rub shoulders with the big, powerful and rich nations and to act collectively, the impact of the individualised and virtually voiceless Third World countries on the Bretton Woods institutions (as indeed also on GATT) has remained marginal. The control of these institutions has rested firmly in the hands of major industrial market economies, i.e. the G-7, through votes weighted by the size of contributions. This arrangement has perpetuated the overwhelming dominance of the United States over these institutions.

Those who thought that the exclusivity of the Bretton Woods institutions could, in a decade which flies the flag of 'democratisation', no longer be maintained must be even more disaffected by recent developments. Not only are the Bretton Woods institutions attempting to expand their sphere of operation by pushing for a division of labour between them and the UN – which would give them exclusive power over economic and financial matters (with trade being dealt with by GATT or MTO, if and when it is established), while the UN would limit itself to political, security, humanitarian and social affairs – they also seem to have found a willing and yielding partner in the UN itself.

The argument put forward is that the World Bank and the IMF have a comparative advantage over the UN in economic, financial and trade matters. But as the G-7 has repeatedly emphasised, the UN remains the only forum where issues of socio-economic development could be discussed, at the global level, *in conjunction with* political and security matters. It was thus the only global forum where a meaningful notion of security, going beyond a law and order notion and reflecting on causes of conflicts, was inherent to the agenda. At a time when a paradigm shift towards the primacy of the social over the economic seemed to make headway, the UN and the BWI are going out of their way to re-act the 1980s – instead of facing the challenges of the 1990s and of the next millennium. How immense will social and political costs – primarily for developing countries, but not only for them – have to be before a new vision prevails?

It is, therefore, imperative that a global agenda for a liveable planet in the twenty-first century must insist on adherence to the following fundamental principles in the UN and the BWI: full subscription to such universal values as democratisation, pluralism and self-determination at national, regional and international levels, global development, global governance and genuine universality. In this connection, democracy and universality mean not only the application of balancing principles, such as equitable geographical representation in the governing bodies and Secretariats of both Bretton Woods institutions, but also the democratisation and universalisation of policy and operational content. As far as membership is concerned, the Bretton Woods institutions have during the past three years seen a tremendous increase as nearly all the former member states of the socialist bloc have, after its collapse, joined. But this has, of course, not changed the fundamental power relationship determining the operations of these institutions as the weighted voting system still remains intact. Universality thus remains elusive. If anything, the G-7 countries have shown an increasing tendency to monopolise control over economic and monetary management, even though invariably they do not practice what they preach.

While these institutions may never become one-nation-one-vote institutions like the UN and its Specialised Agencies, there is a need for their democratisation, greater transparency and pluralism. They must universalise their perspective and establish policies, management and implementation procedures which reflect the interests of all peoples and countries. By rendering such a service, confidence among the peoples of the Third World could possibly be reestablished.

International governance – that is, the way in which the world economy and polity as well as international institutions are being governed and administered – must be of no lower standard, vision and transparency than national governance. The immobility in the North, its ambivalence in matters concerning democracy, self-determination and transparency at the international level, must be overcome. The tragedy of our time is the lack of world leadership imbued with vision and a sense of global responsibility.

This may, of course, sound idealistic. It can be argued that it is impossible to expect any transformation in the role, philosophy and approach of Bretton Woods institutions without a corresponding fundamental change in the world economic system; that the two institutions being the creations of the dominant forces within that system and having functioned for over forty years as the instruments of those forces can only be expected to move within the limits prescribed or allowed by those dominant forces. In other words, that as long as the existing North–South power relations remain, it will be 'business as usual' for the Bretton Woods institutions. Thus, in working out new relationships at international, regional and national levels, we have to choose between two principal scenarios – the historical or 'business as usual', and the normative scenario.

It must be admitted that in all the discussions over the years about the future of these institutions, proposals for reform have followed the historical-trend scenario. The North–South Roundtable and its Santiago Statement on World Monetary, Financial and Human Resources Issues[9] did not contain proposals for fundamental reform of these institutions. It took for granted the existing institutional framework and put forward proposals for addressing specific issues: adjustment process, conditionality, resource flow, and debt. Even conferences and workshops which have been specifically focused on reforming the Bretton Woods institutions have more or less taken the existing structure, philosophy, orientation and operational system for granted. They have tended to concentrate on making adjustments at the margin.

Important as these proposals are, they do not go far enough. We need to move from the historical-trend scenario into the normative one. In other words, we need a second Bretton Woods which will result in the total transformation of the two institutions from being perceived and performing as 'theirs' to becoming 'ours', in terms of attitude, philosophy and operation. Such a second Bretton Woods should not be perceived to neutralise the United Nations as a source of intellectual pluralism. On the contrary, the new relationships that are worth forging must be those that strengthen the UN in its leadership role as the powerhouse of the entire system which will now include Bretton Woods institutions, mapping out global overall development strategies as well as macro-economic framework (money, finance and trade) and sectoral strategies whose observance and implementation would be binding on all members of the system. This would be the very opposite of the proposal that has been put forward in some quarters that the issues of money, finance and trade be transferred to the Bretton Woods institutions and GATT on the basis of the so-called comparative advantage and on the grounds of avoiding duplication.

Such a proposal must be rejected as it is designed not only to silence all criticism of the working of the dominant world system but also to convert the UN into an instrument for maintaining the *status quo*. Instead, an effective mechanism must be established to link in a fundamental way the broad development principles and objectives agreed upon in the UN system with the financing operations of the multilateral development and monetary institutions. By so doing, these institutions would be prevented from having to evolve their own conceptual framework for development as a guide to their operational activities. Finally, the new relationship will be greatly facilitated if the elections of the chief executives of the two institutions are brought in line with the elections of the chief executives of the specialised agencies of the UN.

AFRICAN REGIONAL PERSPECTIVES

As far as Africa is concerned, the only way forward is the transformation of the Bretton Woods institutions along the path of the normative scenario. Anything less than this will continue to hurt and injure the region more than any other part of the globe. Without doubt, it has been the most hard-hit victim of the present system. As we have already pointed out, the record of both institutions in Africa leaves much to be desired. Their overwhelming dominance is the source of constant conflict and resentment. And the persistence of the socio-economic crisis in the region has put doubt on the integrity and good name of the Bretton Woods institutions. In fact, they are now seen, particularly the IMF, as a major source of drainage of resources out of these poor, backward countries. For example, in 1990, IMF new lending to sub-Sahara Africa was US$ 0.7 billion while repayments to it by the African countries was US$ 1.27 billion – resulting in negative net flow of US$ 0.57 billion. The corresponding figures for the World Bank are US$ 0.81 billion and US$ 1.37 billion. Only IDA showed a positive net flow of US$ 1.89 billion, new lending being US$ 2.04 billion while repayments were US$ 0.15 billion.

But even more important than the reverse flow of resources is the imperative of the Bretton Woods institutions yielding space to the people and governments of Africa in the formulation and implementation of their own development strategies and policies, however imperfect they may be in the experts' eyes. It is part of peoples' fundamental right to control their destiny. Inevitably, they will make mistakes but, more importantly, they will learn from such mistakes. To keep imposing strategies, policies and programmes on them shows nothing but contempt and lack of trust. It is also equally imperative for Bretton Woods institutions to accept fully and subscribe to the African perspective that the development paradigm that is most appropriate to our unique and peculiar circumstances must be people-centred and holistic – based on the conviction that, in spite of the current and protracted crises, Africa has a future that is economically viable and politically sustainable.

Fortunately, the United Nations New Agenda for the Development of Africa (UN–NADAF) has mapped out a development agenda in the 1990s – a development agenda that was negotiated between Africa and the international community and which was adopted unanimously by the UN General Assembly at its forty-sixth session in December 1991. This New Agenda has as its priority objectives the accelerated transformation, integration, diversification and growth of the African economies

> in order to strengthen them within the world economy, reduce their vulnerability to external shocks and increase their dynamism, internalise the process of development and enhance self-reliance. The New Agenda also accords special attention to human development and increased productive employment and promotes rapid progress towards the achievement of human-oriented goals by the year 2000 in the areas of life expectancy, integration of women in development, child and maternal mortality, nutrition, health, water and sanitation, basic education and shelter.[10]

These are precisely the goals which have been advocated in the various blueprints that Africa has worked out since 1979 and which have been consistently spurned by the Bretton Woods institutions. Will the New Agenda be similarly treated? Or will the Bretton Woods institutions assist in mobilising the international community to live up to its responsibilities under the New Agenda? These are finding a solution to the African debt problem, including debt owed to both institutions, and mobilising additional resources for achieving an annual target GDP growth rate of 6 per cent in Africa. The resources required were estimated to amount to a minimum of US$ 30 billion in 1992, with an annual average cumulative increase of 4 per cent. Will the World Bank support the diversification of the African economies away from commodity exports as advocated in the New Agenda by assisting in the establishment of an African Diversification Fund, once the feasibility for setting it up has been agreed upon by the UN General Assembly later this year? It needs to be pointed out that diversification away from primary commodity production for exports is the very antithesis of SAP. Not surprisingly therefore, neither the World Bank nor the International Finance Corporation had a single African country among its recipients of diversification-lending in the 1980s. The answers to these questions will indicate whether or not the much-desired new relations are emerging.

Last, but not least, a thorough review and appraisal must be conducted on the conditionality policy which both institutions are pursuing. This pertains in particular to their insistence on having to issue a certificate of good health and of clearance before any African country can approach donors for assistance or the Paris and London Clubs for a rescheduling of overdue debt service repayments. SAP conditionality has been particularly inimical to African interests. Therefore, it is essential and urgent to delink resource flows and debt-relief measures from the conditionality of SAP.

THE WORLD BANK

We have already argued for the restructuring of the role of the World Bank so as to enable it to play a more decisive role in international resources transfer and to become a true and genuine world development bank rather than the instrument of the powerful North over the poor and weak South. We have also argued that the present dominant position of the Bank in sub-Saharan Africa is neither good for itself nor for the continent. The strength of the Bank derives not so much from the quantum of resources it lends to these countries but from the leadership, coordinating and policing role it plays in Africa on behalf of the donor countries. Unfortunately, Africa is completely marginalised in the governance, direction and management of the institution and, therefore, has very little voice in the way its resources are used. It has been confined, pure and simple, to the status of a recipient.

This must change. Africa must be enabled to have an increasingly audible voice in the governance, direction and management of the Bank. This is an area where the Bank can draw from the experience of the United Nations and, by so doing, follow its example. It is now clear that Governors and Executive Directors representing weak and debt-ridden African countries are by the nature of things individually placed in a weak position *vis-à-vis* the management of the Bank. This is not just because of their negligible voting power but, more importantly, because of the fact that by representing countries which seek loans, grants and debt-relief and are under the yoke of SAP, they cannot afford to ask too many probing questions, to challenge established or proposed policies or to exercise effectively their constitutional rights of supervision. After all, countries tend to judge the performance of their Executive Directors by their success in attracting resources. Consequently, most of them avoid being marked down as controversial, difficult and/or uncooperative. Not only does such blacklisting mean that the countries which they represent would be starved of resources, but the individuals also run the risk of losing their job. Hence, African Executive Directors and Governors have tended to choose anonymity and collectivity in the presentation of their case through a joint memorandum which they address annually to the President of the Bank and to the Managing Director of the Fund. Since such a memorandum is usually negotiated it tends to represent the lowest common denominator. But even then, it is not unusual for individual Governors and Executive Directors to distance themselves privately from such a document if it is likely to prejudice their relations with Bretton Woods institutions and, therefore, the favourable consideration of their countries' cases before both institutions.

There is, accordingly, an urgent need to devise an institutional framework which will provide Africa, which has become the Bank's principal area of operation, with effective say in the governance, direction and management of the regional level. Drawing from the experience of the UN means that the Bank will need to establish in Africa an institution analogous to the UN regional commissions. These UN institutions have, over the years, become effective advocates of regional interests and have, through their constant interaction with Headquarters, provided indispensable inputs reflecting regional experience for thematic and general reports and studies which the UN submits to ECOSOC and the General Assembly on the world economic situation, international economic relations and development policies and strategies. In recent years, they have also become increasingly involved in operational activities. They have their own inter-governmental bodies which are, by UN charter, subsidiary organs of ECOSOC through which their proposals reach the UN General Assembly. This arrangement fosters substantial decentralisation of responsibility to the regions while, through ECOSOC, necessary coordination of policies and programmes is ensured.

Should the Bank wish to follow this example, it will not require major modification to its Statute, but mainly to move regional offices, now located in Washington, to their respective regions. These could be located in the same places as the UN regional commissions. In the case of Africa, the location of the regional offices of the World Bank for Sub-Saharan and North Africa in Addis Ababa would be a great advantage since, in addition to the Economic Commission for Africa, the Organization of African Unity also has its headquarters in that city.

The World Bank regional office for Africa, wherever located on the continent, should be given a greater degree of autonomy and authority, not only in reporting and analysing development but also in suggesting and implementing policies. Being located in Africa, this office will have no difficulty in cooperating to the fullest extent possible with OAU and ECA and, of course, with the African Development Bank (ADB). Over time, such cooperation might develop to a level where the analysis of Africa's socio-economic situation and appropriate policy framework would converge. Cooperation, rather than rivalry, would become the hallmark. The OAU, ECA and ADB have made considerable advance in this direction.

But relocation will not be enough. The World Bank regional office for Africa should have its own intergovernmental organ like the other regional institutions; fortunately, Article V, Section 10(b) of the Bank's Articles of Agreement provides that

> each regional office shall be advised by a regional council representative of the entire area and selected in such a manner as the Bank may decide.

This provision, which so far has been ignored, should be implemented in such a way as to allow all African governments and representatives of major donors full participatory membership on such a council.

Such decentralisation is likely to reduce the impact and suspicion of interference in African domestic affairs and the erosion of countries' economic and political sovereignty. It would also considerably improve the quality of the Bank's performance and make for more harmonious relations with the peoples of Africa. By living among the people whom they serve and maintaining continuous contacts with the governments, Bank officials might be better placed to understand the problems, needs and aspirations of the continent.

Finally, it is also recommended that some of the present functions of the World Bank in Africa should be devolved to the African Development Bank. Fortunately, senior World Bank officials have expressed repeatedly their confidence in ADB and their satisfaction in the operational effectiveness and managerial efficiency of the institution. The time therefore has come for a rational division of labour to be worked out between the two institutions and for the ADB to be generously endowed with resources so as to enable it to discharge the additional responsibilities.

THE IMF

Whereas Africa has a regional development bank, it does not have a regional monetary fund. In fact, it has no unified monetary system.

Consequently, individual central banks find it difficult to respond effectively to changes in the international monetary situation, and national monetary authorities work in virtual isolation from one another with very little consultation on (not to speak of coordination of) monetary policy. A related issue is the multiplicity of African currencies, which are mainly non-convertible. There is, at present, no framework within which the countries could work and harmonise their currencies and exchange control legislation and practices. Nor is there one for removing monetary obstacles to the expansion of intra-African trade.

There is, therefore, no gainsaying the fact that the continent needs a regional institution to deal with overall monetary issues and establish a common unit of account for regional and external transactions. In the absence of such an institution and of independently evolved domestic monetary policies, most African currencies have no autonomy and, therefore, had to be pegged to one or the other of the major world currencies for international transactions. The creation of a regional monetary institution which would facilitate the move towards inter-currency convertibility, monetary integration and improved monetary management would foster the socio-economic transformation of the continent.

In addition, the absence of an African regional monetary institution has meant that the only recourse which individual countries have, when confronted with both endogenously and exogenously induced monetary crisis, is the IMF. However, this institution does not, unfortunately, seem to understand fully the problems facing the continent nor was it originally set up to deal with more than short-term cyclical balance-of-payments problems. This is why the LPA called for effective mechanisms to ensure that a sound regional financial and monetary institution is established to protect the African economies from the adverse effect of world monetary crisis and to deal with the problems posed by a multiplicity of inconvertible national currencies, the lack of effective money markets, excruciating debt burden and severe shortage of foreign exchange reserves. Such an institution will also obviate or, at least, limit, the need to have recourse to the IMF as well as act as some kind of countervailing force to the rigid orthodoxy and conditionality of the IMF.

Indeed, efforts were made to establish the African Monetary Fund (AfMF). A series of feasibility studies was undertaken by the ECA, the OAU and the African Centre for Monetary Studies between 1981 and 1983. This was followed by a series of inter-governmental expert meetings which culminated in the preparation of a draft treaty establishing AfMF. Between 1984 and 1986, this draft treaty was the subject of intense negotiation by the member states and agreement was reached on all issues, except three – the subscribed capital, the membership in the Fund (i.e. whether Saharawi Republic should be a member) and the Headquarters of the Fund.

Unfortunately, at a meeting convened in 1986 at Libreville, to complete the negotiating process and fix the date for the signing of the treaty, unexpected opposition to the establishment of AfMF came from some member states which had, until that time, participated fully in the process and had been a party to the consensus that had evolved on all issues except those three. These countries expressed total opposition to the establishment of the Fund regardless of the fact that the LPA had unambiguously made this mandatory. Hence, a stalemate ensued. Up to now, as far as I know, that stalemate is still to be resolved. Unfortunately, the deepening economic crisis during the rest of the 1980s diverted attention away from this important project.

There is no doubt that AfMF is most urgently needed today. The IMF should play a positive role in its establishment as this will enable it to have a regional presence in Africa which would serve as a buffer between the African countries and itself.

CONCLUSIONS

The Bretton Woods institutions, which were not created with the interest of developing countries in mind, have become immensely important bodies for these countries since the 1970s – i.e. since the collapse of the Bretton Woods system. This is particularly true for Africa. The fact that the Bretton Woods institutions have mutated as regards their clientele has not led to the systematic restructuring and reorientation of their strategies, policies and management. They have thus not followed the trend of the United Nations which, beginning in the 1979s, embarked on a process of 'universalisation' – first in the General Assembly and then increasingly in the Secretariat, with discussions underway to also expand the Security Council beyond its post-Second World War constellation. If universality and global participation are indeed strategically important principles for a peaceful and sustainable life on this globe, the two Bretton Woods institutions can no longer be allowed to shelter themselves from reflecting major global forces, understanding that, in the medium-to-long term, force does not only derive from economic power. The distribution of power needs to be fundamentally rethought.

The rethinking should be informed by the fact that the Bretton Woods institutions in their current structure do not optimally allocate global financial resources and cause the misallocation of human resources, especially in developing countries. The combination of these factors result in devastating social, environmental and political costs in these countries.

These costs will, however, become increasingly 'transboundary' and become globally effective factors of destabilisation. The two Bretton Woods institutions have for much too long been allowed to conduct 'business as usual' and have, even though the negative impacts of their limited perspectives were amply analysed, not been held accountable in any significant sense. There is, therefore, a global and urgent interest to fundamentally restructure the Bretton Woods institutions so that they can fulfill the responsibility bestowed upon them.

At the organisational level this should take the form of 'federalisation'. In the case of the World Bank, a regional office for Africa, as well as for other regions, should be established to which true responsibilities – and not just rather inconsequential liaison functions – are transferred. A regional council should ensure that these offices are oriented towards Africa's fundamental problems, the need to restructure its economies so that its vulnerability to external and internal shocks can be reduced. The World Bank's support for regionally and nationally conceived development strategies, in particular for the basic principles of the New Agenda (NADAF), could be an important first indicator for the willingness to go beyond poverty-alleviation rhetoric and short-term crisis intervention.

As concerns the IMF, similar rethinking and opening up is necessary. Too often has the analysis which underpinned its policy prescriptions been flawed, marred by the obsession to apply standardised formulae ignoring empirical evidence. The principal instrument for African countries to gain a greater degree of control and flexibility in the management of their financial and monetary matters remains the establishment of a regional Fund of their own. The idea of an African Monetary Fund had been first ventilated in the Lagos Plan of Action. Its establishment was negotiated successfully for years but was unfortunately thwarted under mysterious circumstances just before the signing of the draft treaty. Yet an African Monetary Fund remains an inevitable prerequisite for rationalising Africa's external economic relations and domestic allocation of resources.

Apart from African governments, which do not have too good a track record in stubbornly pursuing their position *vis-à-vis* the Bank and the Fund and have often suffered from a lack of collective determination and solidarity, it is crucial to increasingly allow the many rumblings and amorphous protests in African countries – of youth, women, workers – to be given an audible voice internationally. Africa needs a continental watchdog in which economists and social scientists cooperate systematically with grassroots organisations to articulate African perspectives and concerns and insist on the reformulation of policies and on popular participation at all stages of implementation and evaluation. In linking up to citizens' groups in the North which have for years been calling for a fundamental restructuring of the Bretton Woods institutions, the political momentum for change needs to be created. Indeed, it would be desirable to convene a global people's assembly to establish an international watchdog to promote the rethinking and restructuring of the Bretton Woods institutions.

NOTES

1. Chakravarthi Raghavan, 'Will Clinton win herald less economic theology?', *Third World Economics – Trends and Analysis* (Issue No. 52/54, 16 November–15 December 1992), p. 22.
2. *Southern Africa Political and Economic Monthly* Vol. 2, no. 10, July 1989 (Harare, Zimbabwe), p 2.
3. Paratap Chatterjee, 'World Bank failures soar to 37.5 per cent of completed projects in 1991', *Third World Economics*, Issue No. 55, 16–31 December 1992, pp. 2–3.
4. *The Times* (London), 3 February 1993, p. 16.
5. Escott Reid, *The Future of the World Bank, An Essay* (Washington, DC: IBRD, 1965), pp. 20–1.
6. Alec Cairncross, *The International Bank for Reconstruction and Development, Essays in International Finance*, No. 33, March 1959, International Finance Section, Department of Economics and Sociology, Princeton University, p. 22.
7. The most seminal of these are the Monrovia Strategy (1979); the Lagos Plan of Action (LPA) and the Final Act of Lagos (1980); Africa's Priority Programme for Economic Recovery (APPER) (1985); the United Nations Programme of Action for African Economic Recovery and Development (UNPAAERD) (1986); the African Alternative Framework to Structural Adjustment Programmes for Socio-economic Recovery and Transformation (AAF–SAP) (1989); the African Charter for Popular Participation in Development and Transformation (1990); and the United Nations New Agenda for the Development of Africa in the 1990s (UN–NADAF). In fact, the last four blueprints – UNPAAERD, AAF–SAP, the African Charter for Popular Participation and UN-NADAF, were either the creation of Africa and the international community or have been endorsed by the community through the United Nations General Assembly.
8. R. F. Harrod, *The Life of John Maynard Keynes* (New York: Harcourt Brace), 1951, p. 580.
9. The North–South Roundtable from which the *Santiago Statement* emerged was held in that city in February 1984 and was co-sponsored by ECLAC, UNDP and UNU. At the time the Statement came out it was a landmark even if it failed to propose fundamental reforms of the Bretton Woods institutions.
10. The United Nations *New Agenda for the Development of Africa in the 1990s* (UN–NADAF) (New York: Office of the Special Coordinator for Africa and the Least Developed countries, DESD, 1992), pp. 6 and 7.

6 A West European Perspective On Bretton Woods

Andrea Boltho

INTRODUCTION

For most Western European observers, Bretton Woods is synonymous with the fixed exchange rate regime of the 1950s and 1960s. Little consideration has been given, outside Britain, to the negotiations of 1943–44, which were largely seen as an Anglo-American dispute that was bound to be won by the United States. And relatively little appears to have come for Europe from the institutions that were created at Bretton Woods. The World Bank, even if founded with European reconstruction in mind, was quickly marginalised by the Marshall Aid programme and by the activities of the OEEC. A similar fate befell GATT, whose efforts at trade liberalisation, however welcome, were, in the European context, overshadowed by those of the EEC and EFTA. Even the IMF, though clearly much more central to European preoccupations with the world monetary system, was usually seen as a relatively passive organisation, holding only limited funds and incapable of bold moves.

Yet, if the institutions did not seem to matter much, the international monetary system that was created turned out to be very important for Europe. Bretton Woods is to this day a name closely associated with what has often been called Europe's 'Golden Age' – the two decades or so that go from the end of postwar reconstruction to the outbreak of the first oil shock. During these years, Europe enjoyed its most rapid growth rate ever, was surprisingly free from sharp cyclical fluctuations, reached an unprecedented state of virtual full employment and was able to greatly extend the scope of its welfare systems. While the reasons that allowed such a favourable performance are, of course, numerous, many would argue that an indispensable element of this success story was the exchange rate fixity which the Bretton Woods agreements had ensured.

The first section of this chapter examines whether there is any truth behind such a claim. The second section considers Europe's more recent

83

attempts at recreating, on a much smaller scale, both the exchange rate stability and the international policy coordination that had existed in the 1950s and the 1960s. A concluding section summarises the main arguments and looks at some possible implications for the future.

BRETTON WOODS AND THE 'GOLDEN AGE'

As mentioned above, Europe enjoyed an exceptional economic perform-ance from the late 1940s onwards, and this despite the many fears expressed at the time, of endemic balance-of-payments problems and, consequently, low growth. Keynes had warned that the international monetary system that had been devised was likely to impart a deflationary bias to the world economy because of a fundamental asymmetry between the duties and obligations of deficit and surplus countries respectively. The former (which many associated with Europe) would be placed under strong pressure to rectify their external imbalances. Since exchange rate changes had virtually been ruled out except in ill-specified cases of 'fundamental disequilibrium', this could only come via restrictive policies. As for the surplus countries (or, better, country, since everyone expected this to be the United States) they (or it) were seen to operate under no such constraints.[1]

In the event, of course, almost the opposite happened. The United States, despite the dollar shortages of the reconstruction days, soon found itself in near-permanent balance-of-payments deficit, while the reverse was the case in most European countries (the major exception to the general rule being the United Kingdom, which was periodically beset by external difficulties).

Three major reasons probably lie behind this unexpected turn of events. First, the 1949 devaluations provided Europe with a fair measure of price competitiveness. Various indicators of purchasing power parity suggest that, on average, European prices were probably some 20 per cent below those of the United States in 1950 relative to the prewar period (Table 6.1). Second, the loss that Europe must have incurred in non-price competitive-ness *vis-à-vis* North America during the war and the reconstruction period, is likely to have diminished rapidly in subsequent years, thanks to the fast growth that was recorded. It has been plausibly argued that rapid growth, by enlarging the variety and quality of goods that are produced, improves a country's position on world markets (Krugman, 1989) . Third, the United States maintained a large transfer of funds (mainly in the form of militarily-linked aid and, especially, direct investment flows) which more than offset the country's continuing trade surpluses.

Table 6.1   Indicators of European competitiveness, 1950

	Absolute competitiveness	Relative competitiveness	
	Cost of tradeables basket[a] (US = 100)	GDP deflator	Wholesale prices
		relative to United States (1938 = 100)	
France	85	97	101
Germany	87	52	53
Italy	83	82	73
United Kingdom	81	62	72
Austria	–	67	72
Belgium	89	115	60
Denmark	83	78	85
Netherlands	76	66	75
Norway	82	63	58
Sweden	–	72	77
Switzerland	–	94	100

[a] Obtained by averaging the United States and own country basket figures shown in the original source.

Sources: Author's estimates using data from: Gilbert (1958); IMF, *International Financial Statistics Yearbook*, 1980; Triffin (1957); United Nations, *Statistical Yearbook*, 1954; United Nations Economic Commission for Europe, *Economic Survey of Europe in 1951*, Geneva 1952.

For Europe, high and rising competitiveness meant that external demand was growing relatively rapidly, while rising inflows of capital further facilitated the achievement of healthy balance-of-payments surpluses. European governments could thus add to their reserves whose level quadrupled through the two decades (Table 6.2). Even more importantly, freed from an external constraint, European governments were able to fully exploit their growth potential by following macro-economic policies that were probably more expansionary than they would otherwise have been (Lamfalussy, 1964; Maddison, 1964). In some ways, Europe benefited from a form of export-led growth, a mechanism in which initial high external demand and, in this case, also capital inflows raise investment and productivity, strengthen competitiveness and reinforce business confidence (Beckerman, 1962).

Table 6.2   Western Europe's foreign reserves
(US $ billion; end-years)

	1950	1955	1960	1965	1970
Gold	6.8	8.8	16.0	22.9	20.4
Foreign exchange	3.2	6.7	8.6	10.0	22.5
Total	10.0	15.5	24.6	32.9	42.9

Source: IMF, *International Financial Statistics Yearbook*, 1980.

For the United States, on the other hand, continuing deficits were not seen as a major problem that needed deflationary action. Rather than financing them by drawing down its gold reserves, the United States was able to balance its external accounts by short-term borrowing, i.e. *de facto* by supplying dollars to Europe. Europeans willingly held these dollars on the New York financial markets. Americans, in exchange, obtained goods or assets abroad. While the Macchiavellian idea that the United States followed such policies purposively, so as to maximise its collective utility, seems far-fetched, the country clearly derived some gains from its seignorage position (Yeager, 1976).

The unexpected outcome of the monetary arrangements of Bretton Woods was thus 'that neither Western Europe nor North America had to worry about their external balance' (Lamfalussy, 1964, p. 268). Unfortunately, however, this happy state of affairs was bound to come to an end. While the fear that Bretton Woods would succumb to an insufficiency of American gold reserves (Triffin, 1960) could be, and was, tackled by the creation of the SDR, two other well-known problems undermined the system. On the one hand, fixed exchange rates, in the face of diverging productivity trends, created growing currency misalignments that proved to be unsustainable over the longer run. On the other hand, the system was always vulnerable because of the asymmetric position of the United States – the sole country that could conduct an independent monetary policy.

As it so happened, American governments pursued relatively prudent policies until the mid-1960s. Thereafter, however, the United States embarked on two major spending sprees (the 'Great Society' project and the Vietnam war) which it was unwilling to finance through tax increases. The breakdown of the early 1970s then followed when Germany in particular (already beset by domestic inflationary pressures) refused to countenance further imported inflation. Ironically, rather than the system exhibiting a deflationary bias, it was an inflationary one that progressively undermined it.

Overall, however, and while it lasted, the Bretton Woods system served Western Europe extremely well. Fixed exchange rates almost certainly facilitated the trade liberalisation that took place. They also provided the rapidly growing Europe with a rising non-price competitive advantage *vis-à-vis* the United States that was not offset by appreciation. Finally, they contributed to the putting in place of various forms of international economic cooperation, such as the Central Banks' swap network, the General Agreements to Borrow, or the monitoring carried out by the OECD Working Party No. 3 (Boltho, 1988). Yet, a lot of this was both unexpected and bound to be temporary. It was unexpected because of the way the gold-exchange standard had evolved, with dollar liabilities taking the place of gold as the major reserve asset of most economies. And it was temporary because it was dependent on the anchor country (the United States) following policies that were in the interests of the international community. In the absence of this latter condition, breakdown was inevitable.

While for most countries, the assessment is favourable, mention must be made of some dissenting voices. Two, in particular, stand out, if for opposite reasons. Both Britain and France expressed some disquiet about the monetary arangements of the 'Golden Age' – the former because its relatively low competitiveness generated a balance-of-payments constraint which, in turn, imposed the need for stop–go policies; the latter because it resented the hegemonic role of the United States and of the dollar. Some division also appeared in Germany, with the Bundesbank gradually moving in favour of a floating system, but the government content with an export-led strategy which relied on a relatively low exchange rate. Interestingly, these various national strands continued to operate in the world of the 1970s and 1980s.

THE QUEST FOR EXCHANGE RATE STABILITY

The slowdown that began in the early 1970s has been much more traumatic in Western Europe than in either the United States or Japan. Growth since 1973 has been less than half that of the 1950s and 1960s, international competitiveness seems to have slipped, public-sector deficits have increased almost everywhere and, most serious of all, unemployment has risen inexorably to levels which, in the early to mid-1990s, may well be *above* those recorded during the Great Depression. Gone is the stability of the Golden Age, its place taken by Eurosclerosis, a thesis according to which the European economy is hopelessly ossified by, *inter alia*, overblown welfare states and powerful trade unions.

Clearly, the breakdown of the Bretton Woods arrangements has little to do with these highly Euro-specific problems. Yet a recurrent element of dissatisfaction with the events of the last 20 years has been the performance of the international monetary system. The absence of established rules of the game, the sharp gyrations in exchange rates, the appearance of currency misalignments probably greater than those that contributed to the downfall of Bretton Woods (Thygesen, 1986) have convinced most European governments that some form of international monetary stability is an essential ingredient in a return to a more satisfactory economic performance.

Even before generalised floating began, efforts were made by some countries to prevent undue intra-European fluctuations in the framework of the so-called 'snake' agreements, by which several European currencies linked themselves to the Deutschmark. The late 1970s then saw the launching of a more ambitious scheme, the European Monetary System (EMS). This involved not only greater exchange-rate stability but also attempts at policy coordination. If on a smaller scale, the EMS clearly had some ambitions of emulating the Bretton Woods arrangements.

Despite the difficulties which have plagued, and, indeed, virtually destroyed the EMS in 1992–93, most observers would concur in the view that the system benefited Europe through most of its existence. Exchange rate volatility was dampened, be this relative to what was occurring elsewehere, or in comparison with the participating countries' previous experience. More interestingly, and contrary perhaps to expectations, the same was also broadly true for interest-rate volatility (Artis and Taylor, 1989). Partly this reflected the maintenance of controls on capital movements in several countries until the late 1980s, yet it was also proof that through much of its existence, the EMS arrangements had looked reasonably credible to financial markets. Nor did the fixed exchange rates of the 1980s create the same misalignments that Bretton Woods suffered from, in part thanks to governments' greater willingness to realign their currencies (at least until 1987), in part also to the greater economic similarities of the participating EEC member countries.

Yet the EMS has been subject to a very similar type of pressure as that which ultimately brought down Bretton Woods – the asymmetric position of the hegemonic country, in this instance Germany. As long as Germany pursued policies that were seen to be in the interest of the other EMS countries, all was well. Since inflation-control was the major policy priority in Europe through most of the 1980s, following the orthodox stance of the Bundesbank, however painful in terms of unemployment, seemed broadly acceptable to public opinion.

The situation changed, however, in the early 1990s, after the fall of the Berlin Wall. Germany now entered into a period of relatively high inflation and large budget deficits which prompted an even more restrictive Bundesbank stance – a stance totally inappropriate for most other EMS member countries, whose inflation rates had come down to, or were even below, German levels, and whose economies were moving into recession. The ensuing near-collapse of the system in summer 1993 was probably inevitable despite the tenacity with which most participating countries tried to preserve it.

In many ways, the Bretton Woods breakdown of the early 1970s and the EMS breakdown of the early 1990s have a similar cause – a divergence between the interests of the anchor country (the United States or Germany) and those of everyone else. In both instances, an exogenous shock (war in one case, unification in the other) generated sizeable demands on public finances. An unwillingness to raise taxes sufficiently to pay for these demands led, in turn, to massive budget deficits. In the United States, these were largely accommodated by an overexpansion of the money supply (De Grauwe, 1989) which added to worldwide inflation. In Germany, by contrast, they prompted a sharp rise in interest rates that was transmitted to the rest of Western Europe where it strengthened incipient deflationary forces.

It is the growing realisation that fixed exchange rate systems that rely on an anchor country are prone to virtually inevitable instability that has prompted Western Europe to resurrect the search for an even more binding mechanism in the form of a fully-fledged monetary union. In this, control of money would be vested in a central bank that would, in some ways at least, resemble, at the European level, the world institution that Keynes had in mind in his blueprint for the postwar world. It remains to be seen, however, whether the European Community will succeed. Prospects for a European Monetary Union (EMU) by the end of this century, as laid out in the Maastrich Treaty, hardly look promising – quite apart from the setback suffered by the EMS, there is a growing realisation among economists and policy-makers that the EEC is far from fulfilling the criteria of an optimum currency area (Eichengreen, 1991), and there is mounting scepticism in public opinion with the prospect of relinquishing one's own currency for an untested pan-European equivalent.

The earlier divisions among the major European countries that had surfaced under Bretton Woods have reappeared in the latest debates and events. France, always at the forefront in the battle for fixed exchange rates, sees a further advantage in EMU stemming from an enhanced role for the Ecu relative to the dollar. Britain, by contrast, remains profoundly averse to the freezing of exchange rate parities. And within Germany, Bundesbank scepticism about the virtues of monetary unification is countered, at the governmental level, by the politicians' enthusiasm for a more federal Europe

CONCLUSIONS

Bretton Woods remains firmly associated in Western European views with the area's most successful period of economic expansion. While the causes of that expansion were many, the fixed exchange rate system of the period is usually seen as having been one important ingredient. More generally, Western Europe has clearly revealed through time a strong preference for fixed (or, at least, relatively stable) exchange rates. The United Kingdom may be a partial exception to this general rule, as is, on the whole, the Bundesbank, but most other governments have preferred, through time, the certainty provided to the tradeable sector by stable exchange rates to the monetary policy 'freedom' that, in theory at least, accompanies floating.

The reasons for this are numerous and often rooted in history. The years of the Gold Standard, at the turn of the century, are remembered as a period of great political stability and prosperity. Growth rates at the time may have been low by the benchmark of the 1950s and 1960s, but they were, nonetheless, rapid by comparison with what had preceded them. By contrast, the performance of the interwar years is obviously viewed with dismay. Though many European countries were forced into floating arrangements of some sort, most at the time desired a return to fixed exchange rates (Nurkse, 1944).

Clearly, stable exchange rates are seen as desirable for relatively small, very open and closely linked economies (incidentally, they also greatly facilitate the workings of the EEC's Common Agricultural Policy). Hence Europe's more or less permanent quest for them – a quest that has only been partially successful. At the turn of this century, completely fixed exchange rates embraced virtually all the industrialised and many of the industrialising countries of the time. Fifty years later, though widespread, they were no longer quite as fixed and, for Western Europe in particular, their scope had shrunk since the whole of Eastern Europe and Russia were now out of bounds. By the 1980s, they were even less fixed and covered only the EEC area (with some exceptions). By the beginning of the next century, a greater degree of stability may be possible, within the context of some form of EMU, but the geographic scope of the latter is bound to be limited to a Deutschmark (or French Franc-DM) area.

From broad world-wide schemes, as that of Bretton Woods, Europe has retreated to the more parochial interests of strengthening and, possibly, widening the Community. It is unlikely that these priorities will change in the foreseeable future. Europe seems far too preoccupied with its own divisions and problems, in both West and East, for it to wish to play a greater international role. The United States, whether under Republican or Democrat leadership, seems similarly uninterested in most forms of international economic cooperation, particularly in the domain which is most crucial to Europe – exchange rate control. In addition, the growing trend of regionalisation in world trade (to which the EEC, of course, contributes) is making for a world economy in which global cooperation may be less practised. Finally, that all-important glue that kept the OECD countries together for so long – the presence of a Soviet threat – has dissolved. Trying to reconstitute a world order in such a fragmented situation hardly looks a promising proposition.

NOTE

1. It should be noted, however, that (as Paul Streeten pointed out to the present author), Keynes himself did not share the widespread fears of a persistent United States surplus: 'the chances of the dollar becoming dangerously scarce in the course of the next five to ten years are not very high' (Keynes, 1946, p. 185). And he added: 'The United States is becoming a high-living, high-cost country beyond any previous experience ... they will discover ways of life which ... must tend towards, and not away from, external equilibrium' (ibid.).

REFERENCES

Artis, M. J. and M. P. Taylor (1989), 'The Achievements of the European Monetary System', *Economic and Social Review*, Vol. 20, no. 2, January, 121–45.

Beckerman, W. (1962), 'Projecting Europe's Growth', *Economic Journal*, Vol. 72, no. 288, December, 912–25.

Boltho, A. (1988), 'International Economic Cooperation: Some Lessons from History', *Rivista di storia economica*, Vol. 5, no. 2, June, 173–92.

De Grauwe, P. (1989), *International Money*, (Oxford: The Clarendon Press).

Eichengreen, B. (1991), 'Is Europe an Optimum Currency Area?', NBER Working Paper, No. 3579, January.

Gilbert, M. and Associates (1958), *Comparative National Products and Price Levels* (Paris: OEEC).

Keynes, J. M. (1946), 'The Balance of Payments of the United States', *Economic Journal*, Vol. 56, no. 2, June, 172–87.

Krugman, P. (1989), 'Differences in Income Elasticities and Trends in Real Exchange Rates', *European Economic Review*, Vol. 33, no. 5, June, 1031–54.

Lamfalussy, A. (1964), 'International Trade and Trade Cycles, 1950–60', in R. Harrod and D. Hague (eds.), *International Trade Theory in a Developing World* (London: Macmillan).

Maddison, A. (1964), *Economic Growth in the West* (London: George Allen & Unwin).

Nurkse, R. (1944), *International Currency Experience* (Geneva: League of Nations).

Triffin, R. (1957), *Europe and the Money Muddle* (New Haven, CT: Yale University Press).

Triffin, R. (1960), *Gold and the Dollar Crisis* (New Haven, CT: Yale University Press).

Thygesen, N. (1986), 'Flexible Exchange Rates and National Monetary Policies', in L. Tsoukalis (ed.), *Europe, America and the World Economy* (Oxford: Basil Blackwell).

Yeager, L. B. (1976), *International Monetary Relations: Theory, History and Policy*, (2nd edn) (New York: Harper & Row).

Part III

Reforms in the UN and the Bretton Woods Institutions

7 A Comparative Assessment
Catherine Gwin

INTRODUCTION

Changed international circumstances have created both the opportunity and
the need to look afresh at the performance and potential of multilateral
institutions. Key changes include:

(1) The end of the cold war and the opportunities and challenges posed by
    transformations taking place both within former communist countries
    and across the former East–West divide.
(2) The setbacks in growth and development that occurred in the 1980s
    and the new thinking on development that emerged in the course of the
    'lost decade' – notably the turn to democracy, markets and social
    development needs.
(3) Irreversible developments in technology and global economic inter-
    dependence, heightened attention to emergent global problems – such
    as environmental degradation, narcotic trafficking and use, the spread
    of AIDS, and the proliferation of weapons of mass destruction – and
    the growing recognition of the need to forge new cooperative,
    public–private arrangements to deal with transborder problems.
(4) The tightening of aid resources, because of competing demands (both
    domestic and foreign), and the corresponding new emphasis on aid
    effectiveness.

Together, these circumstances are creating radically new demands on the
existing international institutions. And they are contributing to a growing
consensus that neither the Bretton Woods nor the UN development
institutions are working adequately.

This chapter seeks to contribute to ongoing discussions of needed reform
by looking comparatively at the two Bretton Woods institutions – the
International Monetary Fund (IMF) and the World Bank – and two UN
development agencies – the United Nations Development Program
(UNDP) and the United Nations Children's Fund (UNICEF). In so doing,
the chapter will (a) review the major changes that have occurred in Bretton
Woods and UN development institutions since their foundings in the
forties; (b) provide an assessment of the comparative strengths and

weaknesses of both groups of agencies, and (c) highlight key issues that will need to be addressed, over the medium-term future, if the multilateral system is to be rationalised, improved and set on the right course for increased international cooperation in the twenty-first century.

One of the main themes of this assessment is that, in any effort to strengthen the multilateral system, the existing institutions need to be reviewed not individually but as parts of a whole. In other words, serious attention needs to be given to each institution's 'comparative advantage' as well as its current performance. A second, related theme is that improvements in the performance of existing institutions, consistent with a sharpened notion of their respective 'divisions of responsibilities', is a prerequisite to the elusive aim of improved coordination among them.

A MUCH-ALTERED SYSTEM

The multilateral development system in place today is markedly different from the one envisaged half a century ago at the Bretton Woods and San Francisco conferences.

● For both the UN and the Bretton Woods organisations, development was a secondary concern.
● In the original descriptions of their respective mandates, there was a clear division of responsibility between the IMF and the World Bank, and between the World Bank and the central UN system.
● Formally, as designated in the UN Charter, the Bretton Woods institutions were specialised agencies of the UN and their activities, along with those of the other specialised agencies, were to be coordinated by ECOSOC.

The current situation bears little resemblance to this original conception.

● Development has become a core concern of both the Bretton Woods and UN institutions. The last IMF loan to a developed country was in 1977. Since then all IMF balance of payments assistance has been to developing countries and, recently, the transforming economies of Eastern Europe and the former Soviet Union. The World Bank has become the dominant international development institution, having surpassed the largest bilateral programme in scale, in programme scope and in policy influence in the 1970s. Similarly, development has become as central a function of the UN as humanitarian relief and peaceful settlement of disputes. In the process, the UN has added numerous agencies and programmes and some agencies, whose mandates were originally 'emergency assistance', have taken on development roles.

- These institutional changes have been evolutionary and, to a large extent, *ad hoc*. As a result, there has been some overlap of activities, some blurring of lines of responsibility – between the IMF and World Bank and between the World Bank and UN, and some gaps as well as failures in the delivery of development assistance.
- The result is a much larger but also less coherent system than earlier envisaged, marked by strengths and weaknesses in each of the institutions, inadequate coordination among them, and no unified or central steering.

This last aspect, of central steering, is far from imaginable if it is taken to mean that any one international entity would set the policy directions for all the others. Nonetheless, the global development agenda has substantially broadened in recent years. The agenda now embraces some new goals, and integrates elements that earlier were largely perceived as independent of each other. Indeed, 'the basic insight' of the broadened concept of 'sustainable human development' is that its elements are intrinsically interrelated.[1] With these changes has come the obvious need to step back and look systematically at (a) what functions must be performed collectively in the decades ahead; (b) where the institutional capacity resides, or could be created, to perform those essential functions; and (c) how coordination among core functions can be assured. A clear picture of the comparative advantages of existing institutions is necessary background for that assessment.

DISTINGUISHING FEATURES

To a large extent, the comparative strengths and weaknesses of the Bretton Woods and UN development institutions are a reflection of certain core characteristics or 'distinguishing features' of the two sets of agencies. Those distinctions, which have significantly shaped and constrained the performance of each of the institutions, include the following:

Membership

Although the Bretton Woods institutions were to have been open to all interested parties, the decision of the Soviet Union not to join and the later withdrawal of several communist-bloc countries left Bretton Woods as a less-than-universal system, in sharp contrast to the United Nations. As a result, the Bretton Woods institutions became something of an instrument of the cold war and they received far more financial support than did the 'more unruly' UN system. With the end of the cold war, the disintegration of the Soviet Union, and the entry or re-entry of the former communist-bloc states into the IMF and World Bank, this distinction disappears; but the legacy of the difference in donor commitment to the two sets of institutions is marked and not likely to wear off quickly.

Mandate and Scope

The IMF, the World Bank and the UN agencies were designed with distinctly different mandates. Although all have grown in size and scope, the basic distinctions still hold.

● The IMF, created to foster stable trade and payments relations among countries conducive to growth and employment, was designed to provide central steering to the international monetary system and short-term assistance to countries in balance-of-payments difficulties. In the last twenty years, it has seen its central steering and surveillance function eroded. At the same time, its involvement with developing countries has increased – through extended and, for some countries, subsidized credit; the conditionality attached to its credit has become more extensive; it has become more actively involved in the provision of technical as well as financial assistance in areas of monetary and fiscal reform; and, most recently, involved with the content of public sector expenditures (much belatedly, some would argue).

● When the World Bank was created, the provision of capital was seen as the key ingredient needed to stimulate growth and development in the 'less developed' parts of the world. Although its activities have grown enormously in size and scope, the transfer of capital has remained the World Bank's core function. Focused first on the financing of infra-structure projects, the World Bank in the late 1960s and 1970s increased its lending for agriculture and social sectors projects; and then in the 1980s became heavily involved in policy-based, structural adjustment and sector lending. In this latter phase, World Bank and IMF activities in support of macroeconomic policy reform have become overlapping; and the World Bank has become a larger funder of technical assistance than the UN's central technical cooperation agency, the UNDP. But, the World Bank remains, in the main, a provider of capital for long-term investments in economic and social development and, now, the major provider of economic policy advice.

● It was largely at the insistence of the United States that the division was made initially between UN humanitarian and technical assistance activities and the capital investment functions of the World Bank. Also, an institutional separation between funding and project execution was built into the UN system. Those divisions have begun to break down. Not only is the World Bank now a major funder of technical cooperation, but many UN programmes go beyond narrow definitions of both humanitarian and technical assistance. Moreover, both UNDP and UNICEF, in particular, have shown an unwillingness to leave development policy reform to the Bretton Woods institutions and a determination to move beyond project-based technical assistance to social sector and social policy reform.

Governance

Two aspects of governance have sharply distinguished the Bretton Woods and UN institutions – voting rules and the roles of governing boards.

● The contrasting systems of voting – with weighted voting the rule in the World Bank and IMF and one-country-one-vote the rule in the UN agencies – gained importance as the number of developing-country members increased in both sets of institutions. This difference has reinforced donor country preference for the IMF and World Bank and, conversely, contributed to the relatively greater developing-country enthusiasm for UN agencies where they have more influence and voice.

● Moreover, the Bretton Woods institutions are governed by executive boards organised on the basis of constituency representation which meet continuously to oversee activities. In contrast, the UN agencies' governing councils have in the past comprised all members, met annually and, consequently, been a more unwieldy and less influential structure. This has, among other things, left more discretion in the hands of the agency and the recipient country. It has also meant that the quality of leadership of the head of the UN agencies has had an even more significant bearing on the quality of performance of those agencies than is the case for the IMF and World Bank.

Dissatisfaction with governance features in both sets of institutions is evident in current international debates. For example, discussions about the governance of the new Global Environment Facility may point to some new notions about constituency representation with different patterns of voting for different types of decisions; and recent proposals for UN reform have emphasised the need for more active governing bodies based on some form of constituency representation. But the initial distinctions still prevail.

Funding

The distinctions in regard to funding are twofold.

- While the UN system offers assistance in the form of grants, the Bretton Woods institutions lend, with interest. The creation of IDA in 1960 added a 'soft loan window' to the Bank (rather than a development fund to the UN) and, beginning in the 1970s, special arrangements allowed for the subsidisation of some Fund drawings – but the basic distinction still holds. Bretton Woods financing is in the form of repayable credits and loans, the bulk on near-commercial terms. This can lead, as is now the case for a number of countries, to a negative flow of resources from borrowers to the Bretton Woods institutions. Indeed, World Bank funding net of repayments is likely to be positive later in the 1990s only to sub-Saharan Africa, South Asia, and perhaps a number of transforming economies.
- The sources of funds also differ. Neither the IMF nor the World Bank depend on voluntary contributions. Rather, IMF 'quotas' and World Bank 'shares' (which provide the basis for Bank borrowing on the private capital markets) are allocated by formula and IDA replenishments are negotiated on a 'burden-sharing' basis.

As a result, the Bretton Woods institutions have substantially more resources than the UN system; but the use of those funds is constrained by provisions designed to keep the institutions 'solvent' and by the cost of the credit to borrowers.

Organisation and Staffing

As a reflection of their different mandates and funding bases, the UN and Bretton Woods institutions have evolved markedly different organisational features.

- Both the IMF and World Bank are headquarter-based institutions with large professional staff that are relatively highly paid and high quality. While this may have suited the original tasks of the World Bank (i.e. large-scale infrastructure investment), as the business of development has changed over the course of the past decade, the Bank has begun to increase its number of field offices and questions have begun to be asked about whether the Bank has the appropriate staff composition for the tasks at hand.

● In contrast, both the UNDP and UNICEF are field-based organizations with representatives resident in recipient countries. This decentralisation to the field gives the UN agencies certain operational strengths but, because of central UN personnel procedures, the quality of UN staff is highly uneven.

COMPARATIVE STRENGTHS AND WEAKNESSES

The strengths and weaknesses of each of the institutions, which derive for the most part from the core distinguishing features, can be summarised as follows.

The International Monetary Fund

The principal strength of the IMF lies in its focused mandate as the world's central monetary institution. Its Articles of Agreement give the IMF responsibilities to regulate the volume of international liquidity, ensure the stability of exchange rates, promote trade and employment, coordinate the macroeconomic policies of member states, and assist members with balance-of-payments difficulties. And, over time, it has become an important source of data and analysis on the international monetary system.

Since the breakdown of the fixed exchange rate system in the early 1970s, however, the IMF has not played a central role in the functioning of the international monetary system. In the context of an explosive growth of international capital markets, the system has evolved in many directions – floating rates under various regimes of management, the European Monetary System, 'monetary anchors', 'crawling pegs,' and so on – without major Fund involvement at most critical junctures. Special drawing rights (SDRs), created to supplement countries' reserves, have not been issued for over a decade and are little used as other than a unit of account. More generally, the IMF has no effective pressure on surplus countries or on the largest deficit country, the United States. Many proposals have been made to strengthen the central monetary function of the IMF. Those issues are left to treatment elsewhere.

More directly related to this chapter's comparative assessment is the IMF's principal task of over a decade – providing balance-of-payments assistance to developing and, now, transforming countries. In that role, it gets mixed, though improving, grades.[2] Two main problems – conditionality and the cost of IMF financing – were discussed extensively through the 1980s. While there has been important 'learning by doing' on the part of both the IMF and developing countries in the design of stabilization programmes, several problems remain.

● Limited impact. While the specifics of IMF financial programmes continue to be disputed, there is less controversy than formerly about the main thrust of the IMF's advice, about the importance of macro-economic stability, and about the need for fiscal and monetary discipline to that end. At the same time, empirical research suggests that IMF effects – positive and negative – have been overrated. IMF programmes usually strengthen the balance of payments and strongly affect the exchange rate; but they have limited impact on the inflation rate, economic growth and fiscal policy. There is also little evidence that programmes typically impose large social costs. This record suggests, among other things, that there is need for continuing improvements in the interface between IMF programmes and longer-term World Bank adjustment lending.

● Breakdown. About half the IMF programmes break down before completion – many because of adverse external conditions. In the absence of adequate contingency financing, countries get into difficulties because world prices turn against them and, quite often, because of natural disasters, such as hurricanes or droughts. The record provides a strong case for returning the Contingency and Compensatory Financing Facility (CCFF) to a streamlined, low-conditionality mechanism.

● Inadequate financing. Not only do IMF programmes provide inadequate contingency financing, they also fail to trigger additional inflows of capital from the rest of the world, despite claims that the IMF's 'seal of approval' has a catalytic effect on capital flows. In the case of low-income countries, moreover, IMF credits other than from certain special facilities, carry rates of interest too costly to bear. For these countries, there is need for a degree of concessionality to be built into all of their Fund drawings.

● Ownership. There is a general sense, though not much supporting empirical research, that programme effectiveness is undermined by the limited extent to which borrowing governments regard an IMF programme as their own. This is due, only in part, to the modalities of IMF relations with governments; in part, to the crisis conditions under which governments turn to the IMF; and, in part, to the tendency of governments to use the IMF as a scapegoat, blaming it for unpopular policies which the government knows must be undertaken. Increased attention to, and coordination with other international agencies involved in building government capacities has been, and should continue to be, an important response to this problem.

The World Bank

The World Bank is, today, the 'heavyweight' in the international development system – approving about $25 billion per year in commitments. Given its broad substantive scope, the size of its staff and the size of its loans (which now exceed $100 million on average), the Bank is better equipped than other agencies to take a broad overview of national economic and sectoral issues and to influence policy at the national and sectoral level. It has, in other words, the unique capacity to combine analytic rigour, policy influence and financial support. It is highly professional and technically strong, has demonstrated a capacity for institutional innovation and change, and has a record of intellectual leadership in certain regards.

To a large extent, the sources of the World Bank's strengths are, also, the sources of its weaknesses. The World Bank is a donor-dominated, headquarter-based institution, whose role has been to transfer capital in the form, until the 1980s, of project financing and whose staff incentives have been structured, accordingly, in terms of getting loans out.

Donor domination, especially US, has at times (though less often than generally assumed) influenced to whom and for what the World Bank can lend. Also, many would argue, it is a principal reason why the World Bank was not more active, earlier on, in the debt crisis.

The substantive rationale for the project-driven orientation of World Bank lending stems from the emphasis given in the economic development literature of the 1940s, 1950s, and 1960s to capital investment. But project lending proved ineffective as a vehicle for fostering and monitoring needed policy and broad institutional reforms.

Structural adjustment lending was introduced in the 1980s as a response to both the slow disbursement and policy reform limitations of project financing. But as the World Bank has moved into policy-based lending, other weaknesses inherent in the structure and ethos of the institution have become increasingly evident.

- Limited institutional development function. The strong (some would say single-minded) economics perspective and dominant (almost exclusive) role of economists on the staff have made the World Bank slow to recognise and ill-equipped to deal with important human and institutional dimensions of development. The World Bank is further impeded in these matters by its headquarter-based structure and by the fact that needed technical cooperation does not fit easily into its large-loan operations. There is, therefore, a clear need for closer cooperation with other agencies whose mandate and organisational structure better suit these particular development requirements.

- Constrained private sector development role. With the shift in its client countries toward more market-oriented, private-sector-led development strategies, the World Bank's concentration on the roles and responsibilities of the public sector becomes a significant limitation. The Bank, in accordance with its charter's joint and sovereign guarantee provisions, has not made support for the private (profit or not-for-profit) sector central to its efforts and has not developed adequate techniques for encouraging its development. This is an area ripe for major institutional reform and development.

- Portfolio performance. Recently, the World Bank, its member governments, and outside observers have focused on matters of operational effectiveness. Two major Bank-initiated evaluations which address this issue make clear the need for improvements in the World Bank's performance. They emphasise the need for greater attention to loan implementation, transparency in policy and decision-making, more public access to information about World Bank activities, greater participation of local groups and strengthened borrower commitment to programmes. A logical extension of these recommendations, in the view of many World Bank observers, is the need for substantial decentralisation of staff to the field.

- The goal of sustainable development. Most challenging of all is the task that lies ahead for the World Bank to work with countries to give concrete meaning to the goal of sustainable development. This will require integration (both analytic and programmatic) of the objectives of growth, poverty reduction and environmental protection. This is, clearly, the central role of the World Bank in the decade or so ahead and given its comparative analytic and financial capacities, it can and should have 'lead responsibility'. But not all of the tasks of standard-setting, provision of assistance, and monitoring can or should be handled by the World Bank and it will, therefore, have to learn to function in closer cooperation both with other MDBs and with relevant parts of the UN system.[3]

United Nations Development Programme

The UNDP is the UN's central funding agency for technical cooperation. It is the UN system's 'impresario' of international technical assistance and principal in-country representative. But the UNDP has, in a sense, always been in search of a role and its lack of clarity of purpose has been one of its major weaknesses.[4]

Started in 1949 as the Expanded Programme for Technical Assistance, its mandate was to finance technical assistance and expertise from the UN system to developing countries. With the merger of EPTA and the UN Special Fund in 1965, UNDP was created and, in 1970, was given responsibility for the central funding and coordination of UN technical assistance activities which the specialised agencies were to execute. However, neither the specialised agencies nor the donors have ever been willing to allow UNDP that degree of influence over the UN's technical cooperation activities. Today, only about half of the technical assistance of the UN system is funded through UNDP; the other half is provided by donors directly to the budget or trust funds of the various specialised agencies for specific purposes.

Compared to the Bretton Woods institutions, the UNDP has been more a recipient-driven than donor-driven agency and this has been both a strength and weakness of the organisation. UNDP now operates on the basis of a five-year country programming cycle (which entails resource 'indicative planning figures' for each recipient country). This programming cycle forms the basis of a 'tripartite system' in which recipient governments are responsible for the programming of UNDP technical assistance funds, UNDP is responsible for approval, financing and monitoring of the country programmes, and the UN specialised agencies and, increasingly, national organisations, are responsible for project execution.

The strengths of this unique assistance programme are threefold:

(1) UNDP has close working relations with central government institutions and focuses on capacity-building within those institutions. This is said to account for:

- A sense of 'national ownership' of UNDP assistance and of a greater responsiveness to country objectives and priorities than in the case of World Bank assistance;
- A relative 'neutrality' of approach or diversity, openness and broad view of development strategies.
- A relative absence of 'political strings' in the allocation of UNDP funds.

(2) UNDP has a substantial field presence and decentralised decision-making structure that gives the programme:

- flexibility in the financing of a diversity of both large and small technical transfer and institution-building projects, whose design and adaptation can be decided on the spot;
- Country-specific knowledge and working relations not only with governments but also a wide range of non-governmental organisations;
- A major role in advising both donors and recipients on technical cooperation operations; and
- Though to a lesser extent than its original mandate envisaged, its country presence enables UNDP to play a useful aid coordination role (particularly where it has dynamic residential representatives).

(3) UNDP provides technical assistance on a grant basis; it works on a much smaller scale than the MDBs; much less of its technical assistance is tied directly to capital investment projects; and more than the MDBs, UNDP has given some emphasis to developing South–South cooperation.

Despite these strengths, UNDP's role in the funding and coordination of technical cooperation has been a declining one – due to several major weaknesses. Some of the shortcomings are internal to the agency and the way it has organized and operated its programmes; some external, i.e. a function of shortcomings of the wider UN system within which UNDP operates; still others a function of the way technical assistance has been conceived and delivered not only by UNDP but all assistance agencies. The major agency weaknesses include the following:

(1) Narrow and weak funding base. UNDP's funding, based on annually pledged voluntary contributions in national currencies, has never allowed it to live up to its role as the UN's central funding organisation for technical assistance. Its recent decline has further limited UNDP effectiveness.

- Even the major recipient of UNDP funds, FAO, now receives considerably more funding for technical assistance from sources other than the UNDP. And as already noted, the World Bank has become a larger funder of technical assistance than the UNDP.
- UNDP's declining resource base reflects a lack of confidence in the agency on the part of some major donors, a desire on the part of a growing number of donors to exercise greater influence over project targets and purposes, and fierce competition with and among the UN specialised agencies.

● The central funding concept which stands as the cornerstone of the country programming approach of UNDP has, as a result, broken down.

(2) Lack of focus. UNDP has been criticised over the years both for spreading itself too thin and for not targeting its grant resources on countries most in need. This shortcoming is, in part, an outcome of the country programming process (which needs to be reformed) and, in part, a result of the failure of member states to agree on the strategic purpose of UNDP. In a recent internal assessment of the agency's future, its 'functional' comparative advantages were identified as: the mechanism for designing and delivering technical cooperation; the relationship of the agency with governments, NGOs, the UN system and other development agencies; and its catalytic role in promoting regional and South–South interaction. But as that same document stated, UNDP's 'substantive' comparative advantages 'are at present potential rather than actual'. [5]

(3) The division between funding and execution. UNDP was established as a funding, not an operating agency. However, in recent years it has reduced its reliance on UN agencies for design and execution – as the technical expertise of UN specialised agencies has declined relative to that of other organisations and as UNDP has increased its reliance on national entities for project execution. As a result, UNDP is no longer a central funding mechanism for the UN system, and not yet an autonomous development agency.

(4) The quality of UNDP personnel. UNDP faces at least two personnel problems.

● It is largely staffed by technical assistance generalists expert in the management of technical cooperation financing but dependent on the specialised agencies and outside consultants for programme design and execution.
● Due mainly to current UN personnel procedures, it lacks uniformly high-quality reps, and this, in turn, hinders its ability to retain talented and energetic staff in its field offices. It also lacks a strong analytic capacity in its central office.

UNDP has taken some important steps in recent years to build on its strengths and overcome some of its weaknesses. Three seem particularly significant for the future direction of the organisation.

(1) With the publication of its first annual *Human Development Report*, 1990, UNDP began to define and stake out for itself a more purposeful and strategic focus.

(2) Two years ago, UNDP's governing council directed the organisation to focus on six themes or areas within an overall human development focus: environment and natural resources management, poverty alleviation, women in development, public sector management, and technical cooperation among developing countries. More recently, UNCED designated UNDP as lead agency for capacity-building assistance in pursuit of the goals of *Agenda 21.*

It is not yet clear that this offers much clarity of focus or represents a substantive agenda which UNDP can effectively meet. At the same time, it would seem that there are missing from that substantive orientation some critical 'niches' which UNDP uniquely could/should fill in the politically sensitive areas of peacebuilding (as it is already doing in Nicaragua), promotion of human rights through the establishment of the rule of law, and good governance. These are tasks which do not now fall squarely within the gambit of any international institution, which entail human and institutional development more than capital-intensive investment, and require close working relations with both governments and NGOs – all strong suits of UNDP. It is not, however, the task of this chapter to define UNDP's substantive focus – but rather to assess its role and function in comparison to other international organisations and, for UNDP, that would seem to entail identifying potential as well as existing roles.

(3) UNDP has also begun to shift its emphasis from funding foreign experts to relying more on local expertise in its effort to build national capacity. This change is reflected in both an increased use of national entities for project execution and the funding of National Technical Assessments and Programmes (NaTCAPS) as a means for countries to look systematically at the way technical cooperation is used for national development and to build their own capabilities for better managing those resources.

This third step is consistent with the conclusions drawn by recent evaluations of technical assistance – whether provided by the UN, the MDBs, or bilateral agencies.[6] The key conclusions are that

- Technical assistance has proved a more demanding instrument than originally anticipated;
- The persistent use of outside experts is, increasingly, out of sync with the availability of trained personnel in recipient countries;
- Overall, it has had limited positive impact on national capacity-building or institutional development; and
- Of all the types of technical assistance, that aimed at institution-building has been the least effective.

These conclusions suggest that technical assistance is not an area in which any development assistance agency has done particularly well; that a sharper emphasis needs to be put on national capacity building; and that, so defined, it is an area in which there is both opportunity and need for a reformed UNDP to play a leading role – in closer cooperation with other parts of the international development cooperation system, especially the MDBs. But this outcome would require significant agency reform, and, subsequently, adequate budgetary support for a strategically revitalised UNDP role. In fact, in his maiden speech to the UNDP staff in July 1993, the newly-appointed UNDP Administrator, James Gustave Speth, stated his commitment to just this kind of change. There are, he said, three broad areas where changes must be made: (1) UNDP needs to strengthen its 'ability to be of service to the UN system'; (2) it needs to improve its own programmes in countries by becoming more focused and more engaged in policy, moving away from small, isolated projects upstream, to greater involvement on policy issues and programme planning; and (3) it must seek to mobilise increased resources, both financial and technological, in support of sustainable human development.

United Nations Children's Fund

UNICEF, unlike UNDP, is both a funding and an executing agency. It is focused on a designated segment of the world's population, and mandated to 'advocate' as well as fund and operate programmes on its 'clients' behalf.

Started as an emergency fund for children, UNICEF has evolved significantly since the 1940s and 1950s. In the 1960s, it moved beyond emergency relief to development, and became involved in education at all levels. In the 1970s, it withdrew from a number of activities and focused its programme on the least-privileged children and women and their most pressing human problems.

In the 1980s, UNICEF evolved this basic needs focus into a unique approach targeted on selected, quantifiable problems. As a part of its new approach, UNICEF shifted from an emphasis on the demonstration of effective field operations to the achievement of specific goals through a multi-pronged, social mobilisation process. This approach, together with an aggressive fund-raising effort, enabled the agency to more than double its expenditure over the last decade.

In a recent evaluation, UNICEF was described as an active, innovative, agency capable of working fast and efficiently.[7] Its several strengths include the following:

(1) Sense of mission. UNICEF not only has a mandate, it has a sense of mission – one which has universal relevance and appeal. This creates a 'culture' within the agency – or commitment to both the organisation and its purpose on the part of both its staff and governing board.

(2) Focus. Its programmes are focused not only on the neediest children and women, but within that framework on selected issues and, in part, on measurable goals which can be achieved in 'politically relevant' time-frames. This focus has proved significant in building support for its efforts both among donors and recipient governments and communities.

(3) Decentralisation. UNICEF is the most highly decentralised international development programme.

- Nearly 85 per cent of its staff are stationed in the field and the field offices are vested with substantial programme authority. While resources are allocated among recipient countries at headquarters, their distribution among programme priorities is largely in the hands of in-country staff.
- It was from its 'position on the ground' that UNICEF detected and, subsequently, called attention to the 'human costs' of early structural adjustment programmes promoted by the Fund and the Bank.

(4) Effective advocacy. More than any other international development agency, UNICEF has effectively mobilised global concern and action. Its targeted drives (e.g., for children's immunisation and oral rehydration), its publication of *The State of the World's Children*, and its Summit and Convention on the Rights of Children have all been powerful techniques in this regard.

UNICEF faces the challenge, however, of not becoming the victim of its own success. Among the principal pitfalls and potential weaknesses that it needs to avoid are the following:

(1) Pressure to expand. In light of the success of its immunisation and oral rehydration drives, there is a danger that UNICEF will be pressed to expand beyond its capacity by donors in search of enhanced 'aid effectiveness'.

(2) Sustainability. There is an even greater danger that UNICEF-led efforts will not translate into sustainable national programmes. This problem was strongly emphasised in an otherwise highly positive assessment of UNICEF undertaken by DANIDA. As stated in that report:

- 'There is a significant **trade-off** between UNICEF's choice of establishing an often **effective project implementation** structure in parallel to existing government execution structures, and the **likely sustainability** of activities. UNICEF has not yet fully realized the extent of this trade-off....'

● 'Besides the parallel project implementation approach..., UNICEF in a number of cases chooses a "semi-parallel" implementation structure, where it cooperates with a well known and responsive government partner only marginally involved in that particular field.... While this implementation approach often proves effective in terms of project delivery, it is basically in conflict with concerns for capacity-building in governments.'

(3) The link between child survival and human development. While UNICEF's social mobilisation approach and high energy advocacy seem well suited to the programme's current emphasis on child survival, it is not equally clear that UNICEF's efforts are as effective in supporting longer-term development activities. The Summit commitment to the establishment of 'national plans of action', with defined government priorities and benchmarks, is intended to make the link. But much is likely to depend on UNICEF's policy influence at the national level and that, in turn, will depend on its ability to leverage other resources through greater interaction/coordination with other parts of the international development assistance system. UNICEF's high degree of decentralised authority compared to that of other agencies is said, however, to make for difficulties in coordination.

(4) UNICEF's strategic choices for the future. As outlined in an independent evaluation of UNICEF completed earlier this year, the agency 'faces a series of strategic choices if it is to sustain the achievements of the past decade and enhance its effectiveness as a multilateral agency with a specific mandate for children and women.'[8]

Specifically, the evaluation noted that the bulk of UNICEF's activities had followed three basic intervention strategies: (a) support to the delivery of social services; (b) capacity building for sustained programme delivery; and (c) empowerment of target group members. Over the past decade, UNICEF has placed greatest emphasis on support to public service delivery, aimed at rapid achievement of global goals, in particular, Universal Child Immunisation by 1990. UNICEF's use of the second and third strategies, capacity building and empowerment, has been more limited and aimed mainly at securing effective management of UNICEF-supported programme operations. As the evaluation stresses, these strategies are not mutually exclusive, but they call for somewhat different modes of operation. Therefore, the evaluation urges a more transparent and self-conscious choice of overall strategy. It also calls for more attention to, and more transparency in accounting for, the impact of agency-supported programmes. And, as said elsewhere in this chapter about other agencies, it calls for greater policy coordination and increased technical dialogue between UNICEF and parts of the UN system as well as with the MDBs.

THE ISSUE OF COORDINATION

Coordination among development institutions (bilateral and multilateral) has become increasingly important as development agencies have proliferated and the list of development 'objectives' have broadened. One of the clear indications of significant international cooperation over the past fifty years has been the thickening of the web of institutions – at the global, regional and sub-regional levels. This development has created much increased capacity for the collective management of shared problems. But this institution-building has occurred in such a way as to produce much incoherence and leave major gaps. At the same time, there has been a broadening of the process of development cooperation. From a focus on the provision of capital and technical assistance for physical infrastructure development, the development cooperation effort has extended across sectors, processes and problems. The broadening of the process has greatly added to the problems of coordination among agencies. Never an easy matter, inter-agency coordination has become both more of a necessity and more of a challenge as development cooperation has moved up the ladder from project finance to policy reform, across a wide range of economic, social and, increasingly, political development concerns, and into interaction not only with governments but also with an array of NGOs.

Formally, relations between the UN and the Bretton Woods institutions are governed by certain provisions of the UN Charter and the Articles of Agreement of the IMF and World Bank. Specifically, the UN Charter provides for the UN bodies to make recommendations to and obtain reports from the Bretton Woods institutions, and for ECOSOC to coordinate the activities of the UN specialised agencies (which, under the Charter, include the IMF and World Bank).

The record, of course, has been quite different. Efforts at coordination by ECOSOC of the activities of the specialised agencies have never been successful. The agencies have insisted on autonomy as independent institutions responsible only to their governing boards. In addition, early agreements between the Bretton Woods institutions and the UN were designed to put a distance between them, despite the Charter provisions. This was pressed by the major industrial countries, notably the United States, in accordance with their greater voting power in the Bretton Woods institutions. Agreements also established arrangements whereby the IMF and World Bank rights of representation before UN bodies were far more extensive than reciprocal rights of UN institutions.[9]

There are important examples of UN analysis and debate having impact on the IMF or World Bank. For example,

- The creation of IDA as a soft-loan window of the World Bank derived from debates begun in the UN;
- The creation of the compensatory financing facility in the IMF emerged out of LDC pressure within UN bodies; and
- More recently, analysis and pressure by UNICEF contributed importantly to increased IMF attention to the social costs of adjustment.

There is also a variety of coordination mechanisms devised over the years to try to build coherence at a policy level and increase interaction, in recipient countries, at a programme or project level. For example, bilateral donors sometimes co-finance efforts with multilateral agencies. There is considerable coordination of capital and technical assistance among multilateral institutions and between them and bilateral agencies. World Bank-chaired Consultative Groups and UNDP-led Round Tables bring multiple donors together with a recipient to discuss needs and performance. The Development Assistance Committee (DAC) of the OECD, with a membership of 20 industrialised nations, is a main channel for the development of common policies among bilateral donors. The new Global Environment Facility (GEF) has been established as a joint undertaking of UNDP, UNEP and the World Bank. Many other examples could be cited. Still, the lack of adequate inter-agency coordination remains a common refrain of virtually all evaluations of the UN and Bretton Woods institutions.

Much of the explanation for this inadequacy lies in the fact that the institutions' member countries have simply not made coordination a priority. To the contrary, both donor and recipient countries have often acted, for different reasons, to undermine coordination. The institutions have competed for autonomy, resources and turf.

As indicated in this chapter, however, agencies operate under different constraints and have different areas of comparative advantage. This, plus the danger that an explosion of international goals is threatening to overload individual agencies, suggests that different agencies should take leading responsibility for different tasks or sets of objectives. The division of leading responsibility should reflect agencies' varying *mandates*, including the strength of consensus among member countries on core institutional roles; *capacities*, including their technical and financial resources; and their *credibility* with regard to specific goals or in specific geographic regions. And better coordination should follow and be built on a strengthening of their complementarities.

Under the present tight resource conditions, both member governments and international bureaucracies may be recognising that they can no longer afford weak coordination. It is member governments rather than agency staff that must take the initiative to look at the total system of international development cooperation, to find the complementarities among institutions, or to develop the complementarities along lines of current and potential comparative advantage, if significant improvements in development cooperation are to occur.

TOWARD AN IMPROVED SYSTEM

To paraphrase, it's time to 'reinvent international governance'.

One alternative is merger. This has been proposed by some in regard to: (a) the IMF and the World Bank, (b) the UN development agencies, and (c) the capital assistance and technical assistance functions. Such steps might bring about a reduction of bureaucracy and lessen confusion and the waste of scarce resources (including the time and energy of both donors and recipients) in the delivery of assistance.

However, it is the view of this assessment that the several organisations described have importantly different features and that there are strong reasons for a 'pluralistic' as well as functionally distinct system. Other conclusions that emerge from this brief comparative assessment include the following:

(1) There is need for change throughout the international development cooperation system. Each component of the system is differently constrained. And each faces important strategic choices over the medium term which ought to be approached with a view to comparative strengths and weaknesses in the system as a whole.

(2) At present, there is a danger of the World Bank being overloaded with tasks – some of which it is ill-suited to perform – largely because donor countries lack confidence in other international development institutions. For any number of tasks, there is need for institutional strengthening elsewhere.

(3) Of the institutions reviewed, UNDP seems the one needing the most substantial reform and revitalisation. Not only does it stand as the centrepiece of international technological cooperation – an area widely recognised as requiring improvement; but also, UNDP's institutional features would seem to make it potentially well-suited to take on some of the new tasks, especially in politically sensitive areas of cooperation. But if it is to play an enhanced role, its strategic purpose will need to be more sharply defined and other aspects of governance, programming, staffing and financing revised.

(4) There is need for greater transparency, accountability and evaluation throughout the entire system.

(5) Better coordination should be sought, not merely to avoid duplication and overlap, but, more importantly, to attend to the interrelatedness among issues and build on the actual and potential complementarities among the UN and Bretton Woods institutions.

NOTES

1. For a discussion of the broadened development agenda and the interrelatedness among goals, see Joan Nelson, 'Global Goals, Contentious Means: Issues of Multiple Conditionality', (Washington, DC: Overseas Development Council, 1993).

2. This condensed assessment of the IMF's role in developing countries draws on much previous analysis, especially the research work of Tony Killick and Graham Bird summarised in the Overseas Development Institute Briefing Paper, 'Does the IMF Really Help Developing Countries?' (April 1993).

3. For a fuller discussion of the division of responsibility among international institutions in the pursuit of sustainable development, see Maurice J. Williams and Patti L. Petesch, 'Sustaining the Earth: Role of Multilateral Development Institutions' (Washington, DC: Overseas Development Council, 1993).

4. This discussion of the UNDP draws particularly on three recent studies: DANIDA, 'Effectiveness of Multilateral Agencies at Country Level: UNDP in Kenya, Nepal, Sudan, and Thailand', 1991; the Nordic UN Project, 'The United Nations in Development' and 'The United Nations: Issues and Options', 1991; and UNDP, 'UNDP and the World Bank: Roles and Relationships', 28 May 1992.

5. UNDP, Report of the Administrator, 'Efficiency of programming and the comparative advantage of UNDP', DP/1993/28, 2 March 1993.

6. See, for example, Elliot J. Berg, *Rethinking Technical Cooperation* (New York: UNDP, 1993) and Beatrice Buyck, 'Technical Assistance as a Delivery Mechanism for Institutional Development: A Review of Issue and Lessons of Bank Experience', paper prepared for the World Bank's Conference on Institutional Development, 14–15 December 1989.

7.   DANIDA, 'Effectiveness of Multilateral Agencies at Country Level: UNICEF in Kenya, Nepal, Sudan and Thailand', 1991.
8.   'Strategic Choices for UNICEF: Service Delivery, Capacity Building, Empowerment', a joint evaluation sponsored by AIDAB, CIDA, DANIDA, and SDC, 1992.
9.   For a more extensive discussion of this issue, see Sidney Dell, 'Relations between the United Nations and the Bretton Woods Institutions', paper presented to the North–South Roundtable on the Future Role of the UN, Uppsala, 6–8 September 1989.

8 A Blueprint for Reform

Paul Streeten

INTRODUCTION

With the end of the cold war, the role of the United Nations in peace-making and peace-keeping has increased, but in the social and economic sphere it has been reduced. No longer is an arbiter above the cold-war battleground needed, and many of its functions have been handed over to the World Bank, to NGOs and to bilateral donors.

There are, however, areas in which the UN is particularly well-equipped to act: responding to the needs of refugees, emergencies, famines, health hazards. The UN will presumably continue to be active in these fields. If one were to look for gaps in the generation of ideas and their application to policy, the links between economic development, democracy, freedom and human rights are particularly suited for the UN family. They can provide a bridge between the political and the social and economic functions. The UNDP's Human Development Reports, and the policies resulting from them, by putting people at the centre of our concern, have made a beginning. If human development is defined as incomes plus social services plus participation, or as development of the people, for the people, by the people, it is the third term, participation or development by the people, that can become the special concern of the UN. The large UN conferences on human rights in Vienna in 1993, on population in Cairo in 1994, on women in Beijing and the social summit in Copenhagen in 1995 all concentrate on people. If the specialised agencies could be reorientated towards this aim, the effectiveness of the UN could be greatly improved.

Thus far the attempt has been made to avoid duplication (or competition), by limiting an area of 'soft' concerns for the UN, while the 'hard' matters of money and capital flows are reserved for the Bretton Woods institutions. But there are activities which the Bank or the Fund might be thought to be well suited to conduct, but where a case can be made for the UN to step in. Since one man's coordination is another's ganging up, there is a lot to be said for a diversity of approaches and some competition.

FINANCIAL INNOVATION UNDER THE UN

Most of our current economic troubles are the result of chronic global macro-economic imbalances. Conventional (progressive) wisdom has it that these should be cured by symmetrical action, on the side of both surplus and deficit countries, and not just by one-sided pressure on deficit countries. Japan,[1] with an estimated current account surplus of $130 billion this year, should expand its consumption and investment, while the USA should contract. Thus C. Fred Bergsten is recently reported to have said: 'Recycling is really a smokescreen. It looks too much like an excuse not to make the adjustments in the trade surplus that are necessary. The real point is that we have to get the surpluses down, not recycle them.'[2]

This would, of course, be better than one-sided deflation in the USA, with its contractionist implications for other OECD countries, reduced aid flows to the developing countries, lower commodity prices, rising protectionist barriers, rising interest rates, growing difficulties in debt service, threats of global fragmentation, etc.

But there is a better solution. A country that exports more than it imports is saving more than it invests domestically (and produces more than it consumes and invests at home). In a world starved of capital, far from wishing to discourage such excess saving, we should go down on our knees and be grateful for such behaviour. Of course, the export surpluses should not be permitted to put deflationary pressures on the deficit countries, but should be lent or invested on acceptable terms in areas in need of capital.

The free market has looked after this up to a point, but, as we have seen, not very well. The growth of the Eurocurrency market in the 1970s is witness to the possibility of private recycling, but at excessively high interest rates and for projects and to countries that should not always have been financed. Many loans were spent on armies, loss-making public enterprises, and swollen bureaucracies, if they did not disappear as capital flight to American or European private bank accounts.

What is needed, therefore, is financial innovation. As things are, the Japanese try to invest part of their surpluses in the capital-richest countries of the world: the USA (although investment there has recently declined) and Europe. And they do this, facing the risk of devaluation and inflation. The assets issued by an International Investment Trust, multilaterally guaranteed by governments, would provide a safer return to private investors. The Trust would then on-lend the funds on commercial terms to developing countries. If such a Fund had existed in the 1970s during the oil shocks, we should not have had a debt crisis. If an interest rate subsidy for the low-income countries could be grafted on to such a scheme, financed by government contributions, all the better. But it is not an essential part of this particular proposal.

Part of the current account surpluses[3] would be lent to the Trust on terms preferable to the present dollar investments, which are subject to devaluation and inflation. They would be lent to developing countries at reasonable interest rates, and invested in carefully examined projects, sectors and programmes. And the loans or investments would be spent on the exports of other OECD countries, which would earn foreign exchange, and be freed from the fear of balance-of-payments difficulties and contraction.[4]

Such an inter-governmental International Investment Trust would bring together in a fruitful union three surpluses in search of coordination, and at present wasted: the current account surplus of Japan (and any country likely to generate one in the future), the surpluses of unemployed skilled labour and industrial capacity in the OECD countries, and the vast surpluses of unskilled and semi-skilled manpower in the developing countries; and all this in the context of a growing, prosperous world economy. Here is a positive-sum game that players have avoided so far for want of coordination: a typical prisoner's dilemma outcome, for no country could by itself move in this direction.

Which institution should initiate and implement such an International Investment Trust? The World Bank would be an obvious candidate. And those fearful of the proliferation of international bureaucracies would advocate this. But those who believe in the value of competitive markets should not wish to increase the threatening monopoly power of the Bank. The proliferation of international lending institutions has considerable merits. Not only does competition keep each alert, but each can do things in different ways and all can learn from one another, as IFAD and the regional development banks have shown. So I would suggest that the International Investment Trust might come under the UN umbrella, as a new agency. If the graft of an interest subsidy is accepted, contributions would be according to income per head, not according to the current account surplus. A surplus constitutes a case for commercial lending and investing; higher incomes for giving more aid.[5]

A GLOBAL ENVIRONMENTAL PROTECTION AGENCY

Just as in an uncoordinated world each country has an incentive to pour its problem of unemployment, metaphorically, into the yards of others, so does it, literally, cast its muck into the neighbouring fields or into the oceans, the atmosphere or the land which are the global commons. Acid rain that kills forests, the emission of chlorofluorocarbons that destroy the ozone layer, the global warming resulting from the burning of fossil fuels, overfishing in common waters, are examples of global abuse that can be stopped only by global agreements that limit national sovereignty.

The domestic environmental problems of rich countries are often in conflict with poverty reduction in developing countries, while the domestic environmental problems of poor countries both arise from, and contribute to, poverty. The poor are both the cause and the victims of their local environmental degradation (soil erosion, deforestation, desertification). But the global environmental problems are shared by the whole of humanity and call for global solutions.

Add to the prisoners' dilemma the free-rider problem, according to which each country relies on others to bear the costs of arrangements that benefit everybody. As a result, public goods, such as peace, an open trading system, including freedom of the seas, well-defined property rights, standards of weights and measures, international stability, a working monetary system, and conservation of the global environment, are undersupplied, while public bads, such as wars, pollution, unemployment and poverty are oversupplied. The situation has been described in parables and similes such as the tragedy of the commons, social traps, the isolation paradox, etc. Everybody free-rides, and thereby ensures that there is no horse.

The ranking of preferences by each country is the following:

(1) My country does not contribute (financially or by refraining from damaging action) while others do. (Free rider, defection of one.)
(2) My country contributes together with others. (Cooperation.)
(3) No country contributes. (Prisoners' dilemma outcome.)
(4) My country contributes while no other country does. (Sucker.)

Behaviour by each according to (1), or the fear of (4), leads to outcome (3). Although (2) is preferred to (3), we end up with (3), unless either rewards and penalties, or autonomous cooperative motivations lead to (2). Incentives and expectations must be such as to rule out outcomes (4) and (1), so that if I (or you) contribute, I (or you) will not end up a sucker. In the absence of such motivations and coordination, the result is that peace, monetary stability, absence of inflation, an open world economy, debt relief, raw material conservation, poverty reduction, world development and environmental protection will be undersupplied.

It has been shown that iterative games of the prisoners' dilemma type lead to non-destructive outcomes. The partners learn and adopt mutually beneficial strategies. For several reasons it is harder to reach cooperative agreements in international transactions than in others, in which mutual trust and a sense of duty play stronger parts. There are now many states, and large numbers make agreements more difficult. We do not have a world government that could enforce agreements. Change is rapid, which undermines the basis of stability on which agreements are based. The absence of a dominant world power also removes the sanctions against breaking the agreement. And all these factors prevent trust from being built up, which is an essential prerequisite for international agreements.

The United Nations and its agencies could provide the forum in which this trust is built up, in which actions can be coordinated, and benefits for all can be achieved. The environment, following the Rio meeting, has been a concern of the UN.

The solution to mutually destructive actions pursued by each country separately is the establishment of a global environmental protection agency, with powers of enforcement. Each country, by sacrificing some of its national sovereignty, gains more in the pursuit of its national interests than it would have done had it continued to act independently.

Such an agency would require substantial finance and powers. A tiny step in this direction was taken in November 1990. Twenty-five industrial and developing countries agreed to establish a Global Environmental Facility (GEF), which is run jointly by the World Bank, the United Nations Development Programme (UNDP), and the United Nations Environment Programme (UNEP). It started off with a fund of about $1.3 billion. A little progress was made at the Rio United Nations Conference on the Environment and Development, which gave strong verbal support to the Facility. Pledges of about $2.5 billion a year were made in Rio. This compares with $70 billion which the UN said was needed for environmental purposes, and about $5 billion which had been predicted.

Initially modest resources are to be devoted to providing help in financing programmes and projects that affect the global environment. Four areas have been selected for the operations of the Facility.

(1) Protecting the ozone layer. The GEF's work will be coordinated with the implementation of the Montreal Protocol to phase out the use of CFCs, halons, and other harmful gases.
(2) Limiting greenhouse gas emissions. The emission of carbon dioxide, CFCs, and methane will be limited, the adoption of cleaner technologies and fuels will be encouraged, as well as reforestation and forestry conservation.
(3) Protecting biodiversity. The diversity of species contributes to materials for medicines and industrial products, genetic resources for food production, and the regulation of climatic and rainfall patterns.

(4) Protecting global water resources. The Facility will support programmes that encourage planning against oil spills; to abate water
pollution, to prevent and clean up toxic waste pollution along major
rivers and to conserve water bodies.

Developing countries with GNP per head of less than $4000 will be
eligible for GEF funding for investment projects and supporting services.

The initial steps towards a Global Environmental Protection Agency
should be on very specific issues, such as the Montreal Protocol or the
International Whaling Commission. A sharp and narrow focus in the early
stages will prevent endless discussion, frustration and acrimony. But the
problems of primary concern to the poor people in the developing countries
– clean air in the towns, access to safe water and sanitation, the prevention
of soil erosion, and population control – are not touched by the Facility.
From the point of view of these concerns, the Rio conference was a failure.

Programme versus Project Aid

In the golden age of development aid, men and women of good will tended
to favour programme aid, while the hard-nosed, hard-boiled conservatives
favoured project aid. The latter was supposed to be subject to the discipline
of project appraisal and could be controlled by a knowledgeable donor,
whereas the former permitted the recipient to spend the money freely.
Anyone who has had to collect money for a university or research institute
knows the dilemma, and knows how to get out of it. You collect the money
for a building or a chair named after the donor that you would have wanted
to have anyway (the project), and you use the money for what you consider
priority causes: improving the kitchen, or the garden, or the salaries. This is
called fungibility. Hans Singer's seminal article put the case admirably.[6]

The advocates of programme aid were not against conditionality attached
to the aid. They thought that macroeconomic policies are more important
than project design. Even the best project can be ruined by the wrong
exchange rate, or the wrong demand management, or the wrong prices for its
products. Indeed, many thought that it is the virtue of concessionary loans
that you could buy the right policies with the concessionary component.
Those who argued that efficient project execution required the discipline of
full commercial interest rates were wrong (it was thought). Concessionary
loans or grants were more efficient, because they could be accompanied by
conditions of good management that went beyond those necessary for the
repayment of the loan and covered good policies for the whole economy. It
was these that were important for the success of the projects.

In the present dross age, the roles seem to have been reversed. Conservatives (and one began to be suspicious when US ex-Treasury Secretary James Baker advocated it) are for programme aid, while the people on the left are for project aid. Why this role reversal? I can think of four reasons.

First, in the current debt crisis programme aid is often aid to the banks in the USA and other creditor countries, not aid for the poor or for development. The alternative may be default or debt-forgiveness. It is then understandable that people with sympathy for bank managers and bank shareholders (and perhaps depositors) are happy to see money intended for development aid spent on repaying bank loans. A drawback of conditionality attached to loans that are used for the repayment of debt is that the reward for obedient economic performance goes to the creditors, and this reduces the incentive of the debtor to conform to the conditions.

Second, it may not have been immediately obvious that not only projects, but also policies are fungible, or rather substitutable. Complete fungibility would mean that the policy that is imposed as a condition would have been carried out anyway, whereas in this case ways are found to get round it. The donor makes devaluation a condition, but the recipient, while following the advice, inflates to restore the initial real exchange rate.[7] Or open and concealed taxes and subsidies can undo policies with respect to tariffs or credit. A conditionality that embraces all possible measures would be impossible to implement or monitor. Awareness that not only 'top priority' pet projects, but also 'top priority' pet policies can permit escape mechanisms has come only slowly.

Third, the conditions imposed by lenders reflect often prematurely crystallised, but flawed orthodoxies. The current fashion of state minimalism and pricism, with its prime emphasis on getting prices right in the free play of market forces, cannot be said to be based on sound scientific principles. Doctrines have hardened into ideological stances, and the plurality of donors' views and conditions has been greatly weakened.

In the golden age, borrowers, if they did not like the conditions, could turn to other lenders, or do with less aid. With high growth rates, booming world trade and a working financial system, this was not a great loss. Today, by contrast, recipients are in such a desperate situation that they must bow to the donors' views against their own judgement, and a single donor, the Bank and Fund, controls all other donors so that aid from *all* sources is cut off if conditions are not accepted.

Fourth, confidence in the ability of recipient countries to carry out the policies incorporated in the conditions has declined. This is partly because, with the breakdown of the Keynesian consensus, the political obstacles and psychological inhibitions to the new prescriptions (e.g. dismantling the state) are greater, and partly because the training and skills are seen to be absent in many developing countries. To be critical of the narrow ideology reflected in some donor conditionality does not imply approval of the policies carried out in the recipient countries. Some of the early faith in programme aid was based on excessive confidence in the capability of these countries to carry out good policies.

If these arguments are accepted, there is a role for the UN and its specialised agencies to move into giving project aid. First, technical assistance is often most effective when combined with project lending. And the UN and its agencies have unrivalled experience in providing technical assistance. Second, a variety of experiences, approaches and lending practices is useful as a learning process. Third, the competition introduced by different agencies providing loans and grants keeps each alert and efficient.

DECENTRALISATION AND MANAGEMENT

Criticisms of the Bank and the Fund are legion, from both right and left. Here I wish to concentrate on two, not usually high on the list of commonly voiced complaints.

First, the Bank is too centralised. When it talks of decentralisation, it means decentralisation of the organisation in Washington. The Commonwealth Development Corporation only began to be an effective development agency when, under Lord Reith, it decentralised its activities to regional (not national) offices, which produced proposals for projects to headquarters in London. Living in the country, the daily contact with local people, and the dialogues with policy-makers, make the decisions sensitive to social and political, as well as to economic and engineering factors. It also reduces the acrimony so often found in conditionality attached to loans. Technocracy can be desirable professionalism, but it has to be embedded in awareness of the human setting. This is impossible for short-term missions who fly in and out of the country. Only residents can achieve the feel for the opportunities for, and constraints within which the economic and technical variables operate. Here again, there is scope for experimentation and different ways of doing things. Some of the UN Resident Representatives and their staff could be charged with introducing into the aid dialogue such sensitivity.

The other proposal is more controversial. It applies mainly to Africa. We all know that there are now more foreign experts in Africa than under colonialism. Yet their impact on self-reliant development is small, if not negative. Here again, I should like to propose a lesson learned from the

Commonwealth Development Corporation. It is unique (I believe) in not only lending, and withdrawing when the project has been built, and when involvement becomes most important, but also managing the project, with the mandate to train and hand over to local people when they are ready. This is particularly important in the low-income countries of Africa. The commitment of a manager is of a different kind from that of a detached adviser. The charge of neo-colonialism may be raised against such foreign managers. But a genuinely multilateral institution, with a staff that is trusted to have the interests of the host country at heart, can escape such suspicions. The UN should be particularly suited to recruit, train, and send out such a corps of managers.

It is true that the ability to manage does not necessarily go with the ability to train counterparts to take over. Indeed, they may be in inevitable conflict. But institutions such as the Commonwealth Developmnent Corporation have done well on both fronts, and it would be quite possible to divide the two tasks between different people.

CONCLUSION

This chapter approached the division of labour between the Bretton Woods institutions and the UN by proposing new institutions, functions or responsibilities, and allocating them to the UN. Where precisely they should fit into the structure of the organisation remains to be settled. I have no special expertise in this.

Mahbub ul Haq, as quoted by Carlos Fortin, wrote: 'In discussing the substantive role of the UN in the 90s, a good starting-point may be to analyse the comparative advantage of the UN in various socio-economic fields.'[8] I agree that it is a good starting point. But we know that comparative advantage is no longer God-given, once-for-all, but can be created. Like the South Korean shipbuilding and steel industries, which gained world preeminence without the required initial skills or raw materials, the comparative advantage of the UN, in some of the areas I have sketched out above, may be capable of being created. And variety, diversity and competition are to be welcomed.

NOTES

1. Different countries have in the past generated large surpluses: first the USA, then the capital-surplus oil-exporting countries, and, before unification,

Germany. Even if the Japanese surpluses should, against all expectations, disappear, another country or group of countries will take their place.

2.   'Japan's "Recycling" of Trade Surplus Declines', *New York Times*, 22 February 1993, p. D3.

3.   Some stimulus to the Japanese economy is justified, and investment in housing and infrastructure is necessary.

4.   It may be said that a tax on surpluses, as proposed by Keynes, would also encourage foreign lending. But it would at the same time encourage more consumption and domestic investment, so that the lending or investing would be only one of several options to reduce the surplus.

5.   Japan is often urged to increase aid because of its large current account surplus, and has in fact done so. Several billion dollars, for instance, were used to support the Brady Plan, helping to resolve the debt crisis. But it would then be too easy for deficit countries to plead justification for reducing their aid. Surpluses and deficits are grounds for lending and borrowing, not for aid-giving.

6.   H.W. Singer, 'External Aid: for Plans or Projects?', *Economic Journal*, Vol. 75, September 1965.

7.   Of course, donors will wish to attach additional conditions, relating to monetary and fiscal policies to avoid inflation. But implementation may not always be possible.

8.   Carlos Fortin, 'The United Nations and Development in the 1990s', in Paul Streeten, Louis Emerij, Carlos Fortin, *International Governance*, Silver Jubilee Papers, Institute of Development Studies, 1992, p. 74. The quotation is from Mahbub ul Haq, 'Issues before the Uppsala roundtable on the future role of the United Nations', *Development*, No. 4, 1989, p. 2.

9 A New International Monetary System for the Future[1]

Carlos Massad

INTRODUCTION

The discussions about the reform of the international monetary system dominated internal debates at the IMF during the first part of the seventies. They also consumed great analytical and political efforts at the time, leading nowhere. By 1975, interest in reform was fading and attention was being directed to surviving with the existing state of affairs. Now, close to commemorating 50 years since the creation of the postwar monetary arrangements, interest in reform is coming back, as the IMF is now really becoming a global institution and as experience gained in the last 15 years shows that even imperfect cooperation in the monetary and adjustment fields is clearly more productive than open confrontation.

This chapter contains six sections. The first summarises the analytical basis of the International Monetary System prevailing since the end of the Second World War up to the formal declaration of inconvertibility of the US dollar on 15 August 1971, and shortly thereafter. The second section contrasts the theory with the facts, and points out the main deficiencies of the system. The third describes international monetary arrangements prevailing at present. The fourth points out differential effects of the international monetary system, or non-system, on developing and developed countries. The fifth section presents an outline of a new international monetary system. Finally, the sixth section discusses some of the problems involved in the transition from the present situation to the new system envisaged, and suggests lines of approach to face them.

BRIEF HISTORY

It took only two years to go from the drawing board to the most ambitious international agreement on economic matters of all time. The facts that the

Second World War was going on and that the most brilliant minds of the Allies were addressing the subject certainly helped: the Articles of Agreement of the International Monetary Fund were adopted at Bretton Woods, New Hampshire, on 22 July 1944. They came into force on 27 December 1945, and ruled international monetary affairs, unchanged, for almost 25 years.[2]

The Agreement covered two main problems: the correction of balance-of-payments imbalances and the creation of international liquidity. Imbalances were supposed to be corrected essentially through monetary and fiscal policies, while exchange rate changes were considered a tool of last resort. A system of medium-term lending by the Fund was established for countries in deficit to bridge the gap between monetary and fiscal policy decisions and the materialisation of policy effects. For surplus countries, moral suasion and the risk of their currencies being declared 'scarce' were the stimulus to adjust: such declaration would trigger actions by other countries limiting the use of the 'scarce' currency. 'Parities', the inverse of the price of gold in terms of each of the currencies, were supposed to be fixed; through gold parities, a constellation of fixed exchange rates, the prices of currencies in terms of each other, was established.

Liquidity was to be created, or destroyed, essentially through transfers between monetary and non-monetary uses of gold as well as through new production of the metal. Under special circumstances, uniform changes in par values could be made to change liquidity measured in terms of currencies, in what amounted to a generalized, 'uniform', change in the price of gold.

Countries undertook to defend the exchange rate of their currencies by buying and selling unlimited amounts of it in the market, at prices within a band of 1 per cent above and below parity, against the currencies of other members. The US, the only industrial country essentially undamaged by the war, in order to avoid inconsistencies in the exchange rate system, committed itself not to intervene in the markets but to guarantee free conversion of dollars into gold at the established parity (plus or minus 1 per cent). Thus, the relation between the US dollar and gold, at $35 per ounce, became the anchor of the whole system of exchange rates.

FROM THEORY TO PRACTICE: THE FIRST 25 YEARS

The world economy used dollars for transaction and reserve purposes, as the direct use of gold was more expensive and inconvenient. After all, the dollar was supposed to be a 'gold certificate', convertible on demand. So, official reserves in dollars grew the world over, allowing the US to run sustained deficits in its balance of payments financed with her own currency: no adjustment measures were triggered by the external deficit of the US as it was, in a very real sense, demand-determined. The US dollar became the reserve currency in the world.

The other side of the coin were surpluses in Europe and Japan, which allowed them to accumulate the reserves they needed. Developing countries did not show a systematic pattern in their external accounts, which moved back and forth between surpluses and deficits in tune with world commodity prices and domestic policies.

Developing countries, mostly in Latin America, as well as developed non-reserve currency countries, when in deficit, had no other alternative but to adjust once their reserves reached critical levels; they could rely on IMF credit (and also other support from official sources subject to agreement with the IMF) while adjustment measures took hold. The Fund developed its lending policies mostly in its Western Hemisphere Department, on the basis of theoretical work done at its Research Department and elsewhere.[3] Conditionality was experimented in Latin America, and increasingly incorporated into the lending policies of the Fund.

In practice, the system agreed upon in Bretton Woods proved to contain three types of asymmetries: an asymmetry of intervention, as the US could not intervene in the exchange markets, in order to avoid inconsistencies; an asymmetry of adjustment, as there was no incentive for surplus and for reserve currency (surplus or deficit) countries to adjust; and an asymmetry of liquidity creation, as liquidity was created by the reserve currency country of the time: the US.[4]

The events leading to the demise of the Bretton Woods system are well-known: dollar reserves were accumulated abroad in amounts that largely exceeded US gold reserves; attempts by countries to convert them into gold led to gold price and market regulations resulting in a black market for gold and wide differences between the black market and the official prices. Finally, on 15 August 1971, the US made a formal declaration of inconvertibility of the dollar into gold.

A period of futile attempts to rebuild the system followed. Three years later, such attempts were abandoned.

INTERNATIONAL MONETARY AFFAIRS AT PRESENT

The dangers of the large accumulation of dollar reserves had been foreseen, particularly by Triffin.[5] The analysts had concluded that the US would be forced to adjust by peer pressure, and that the source of world liquidity would then disappear. It was this conclusion, widely shared, that led, on

31 May 1968 to the creation of a new, collectively managed source of liquidity: Special Drawing Rights.

But the conclusion of the analysts had been wrong. In fact, the external deficit of the US widened, and the markets developed new financial 'products' around dollar deposits outside the US which enlarged dollar-holdings by both the private and the official sectors. Exchange markets became erratic and short-term capital movements overshadowed the influence of trade on external balances. Attempts to manage exchange rates world-wide failed, and main currencies entered a period of different forms of floating.

Today, only block-inspired cooperation in the management of exchange rates exists, even though G-7 countries meet regularly at very high levels to explore possible ways of coordinating economic policy. The most important monetary and economic negotiations are conducted outside the IMF, despite the fact that the Fund is closer than ever to achieving globality of membership. The SDR has become irrelevant as a component of world liquidity. Private markets generate liquid resources for private agents to intervene in the exchange markets, blurring the edges of the traditional definitions of (official) international liquidity. Liquidity distribution is affected through changes in access to and cost of borrowing in the private international markets.

The constellation of exchange rates varies frequently and sharply, and is not anchored: if the price level (properly defined) of all countries increased at the same rate, there would be no change in world exchange rates. And the exchange rate 'system' is, in fact, over-determined: there are more currencies than independent exchange rates.

The asymmetry of adjustment leads to heavy adjustment burdens falling upon deficit non-reserve currency countries, yielding as a result a recessionary, even though relatively small, bias in the world economy. As the efforts of deficit countries to adjust by expanding their exports are not met by equivalent efforts from surplus countries to increase their imports, prices of export products of deficit countries drop, and their terms of trade deteriorate.[6] As a consequence, deficit (non-reserve currency) countries are forced to over-emphasise restrictive macro-policies, overshooting in terms of real interest rate levels, real exchange rate depreciation and unemployment increases.

DIFFERENTIAL EFFECTS ON DEVELOPED AND DEVELOPING COUNTRIES

The asymmetries of intervention and of adjustment pointed out above are a consequence of the characteristics of the system itself, while the asymmetry of liquidity creation is also a by-product of the different economic and financial size of countries. As the European Community and Japan increase in economic importance in the world, their currencies develop as alternative options to the US dollar in its role as reserve and intervention currencies, so that international liquidity is increasingly a multicurrency variable. At the same time, the definition and measurement of exchange rates becomes more complex, and a particular question becomes more and more important: exchange rates *vis-à-vis* what?

Developing countries, facing relatively low price elasticities of supply of exports of primary commodities, and also low price elasticities of demand for imports, require relatively large (percentage) changes in the exchange rate of their currencies in order to produce a given adjustment in their balance of trade. Furthermore, usually such countries do not have developed money markets where coverage against exchange rate fluctuations could be bought at reasonable cost. As a consequence, developing countries, as well as a good number of industrial countries facing similar conditions, need to peg their own currency to that of their main external partner.

In such cases, the main currency determines exchange rate movements of the pegged currencies, movements that may be equilibrating for the main currency, but may quite often be disequilibrating for the pegged ones. In fact, it is to be expected that when the main country is running a substantial surplus, the other countries, in general, will run deficits; a situation like this would call for opposite changes in exchange rates in the two types of countries *vis-à-vis* the rest of the world, while pegging involves changes in the same direction. This would create a disequilibrium, or increase it, in the pegged country instead of reducing it.

So, it is not surprising to find developing countries preferring fixed exchange rate arrangements as a world system, while main currency countries prefer floating rates, as the latter require relatively smaller changes in their exchange rates to achieve a given adjustment in their external accounts.

On the other hand, as private holdings of reserve currencies are several times official holdings, capital movements take increasingly the form of private portfolio adjustments with respect to currency composition. These adjustments, heavily influenced by expectations, produce sharper and more frequent changes in exchange rates than could be explained by variations in fundamentals, transmitting these changes also to LDCs' currencies. All in all, exchange rate changes for the latter currencies (*vis-à-vis*, for example, a trade-weighed composite of main currencies) are sharp and mostly disequilibrating in character in so far they are caused by exchange rate changes among main currencies. This, in turn, introduces unnecessary costs to the opening up of trade and capital movements. It also introduces a measure of erratic variations in international liquidity measured in terms of currencies, over and above the changes brought about by modifications in the external balance of reserve currency countries and by changes in private demand for liquidity in euro-currency markets.

Furthermore, floating exchange rates reduce the demand for official reserves, as rate fluctuations cushion the impact of changes in demand for and supply of foreign exchange on official reserves. But rate fluctuations increase private-sector demand for reserves, as this sector cannot buy or sell foreign exchange at a fixed price from the monetary authorities and is consequently induced to speculate and arbitrate in the market. In order to do so, the private sector naturally accumulates currencies that can be used for such purposes, and not SDRs. In any case, the private sector is not allowed to hold or use SDRs.

So, demand for currencies is enhanced by floating, while demand for SDRs is diminished. As SDRs are allocated on the basis of a formula, while currencies must be earned by non-reserve currency countries, the distribution of the costs and benefits of liquidity creation and distribution is changed according to the way in which liquidity is created. The distribution of the net benefits of liquidity creation is skewed in favour of reserve currency countries when they are responsible for liquidity creation. Such distribution is more even when liquidity is distributed according to reasonable formulas rather than earned by most, developing countries among them, and created by a few.

AN OUTLINE FOR A NEW INTERNATIONAL MONETARY SYSTEM

Three types of problems, obviously interrelated, are to be tackled: adjustment, exchange rates and liquidity.

Symmetrical adjustment incentives are required to distribute adjustment burdens more widely and avoid concentration of the burden on deficit, non-reserve currency countries.

The technical solution here is simple: all countries should settle external payments with assets different from their own currencies; also, assuming 'realistic' exchange rates to start with, external asset accumulation at rates faster than a given benchmark and/or at levels higher than a given ratio with imports or GDP should be taxed through negative interest rates. The 'tax' rate could be progressive, increasing with the discrepancy between the realised and the desired ratio of growth of reserves and/or of reserves to imports or GDP.

A solution of this type would do away with present official sources of liquidity. And this is all to the good, as liquidity ought to be managed by the international community as such, basically through simple rules rather than discretion, which might diminish the probability of large fluctuations in the world economy.

The technical solution to the liquidity problem is thus closely connected to that of the adjustment problem, and opens the ground for the introduction of an internationally agreed-upon instrument of liquidity, internationally issued and internationally managed, like SDRs. SDRs could become the accepted international asset for settlement of imbalances.

Applying positive and negative interest rates on SDR holdings does not create insurmountable technical problems. However, some of the characteristics of SDRs should be revised, particularly those related to SDR valuation and use. In the new system, SDRs should be valued for their role in the system rather than through a rather arbitrary relation with a set of currencies. In this way, SDRs become the asset that performs the role of anchor of the constellation of exchange rates: currencies could establish a 'parity' in relation to SDRs, more flexible than in their original version, allowing for a crawling peg when necessary. 'Exchange rates' of currencies in relation to each other would be a result of their relation with SDRs, and the over-determination problem existing at present would also be out of the way. In fact, this is equivalent to establishing that one SDR equals one SDR: the SDR would then be the centre of the system.

With regard to the use of SDRs, present restrictions should be partially lifted, to allow SDRs to be used at least in inter-bank transactions, a prelude to a wider use when circumstances permitted the existence of a world currency.

A system designed around the general principles indicated above would not be able to withstand private financial markets where liquidity is essentially demand-determined. Two types of regulations of private lending institutions applied at the international level are required: capital adequacy ratios and minimum reserve requirements.[7] The control of these two variables, together with an initial reduction of imbalances in external payments of the major economies would help regulate better the total supply of liquidity, allowing room for supply management.

Some additional safeguards should be considered in at least four areas: adjustment, liquidity creation and distribution, debt, and policy coordination.

The adjustment process often involves unpopular policy measures. In such cases, the effects of positive or negative interest rates on reserves may not be incentive enough to adjust. It might be advisable to consider additional, stronger incentives like freezing a proportion of reserves of a particular country when its surplus or level of reserves exceed the desirable one, or declaring it ineligible for participating in additional allocations of liquidity. In cases of deficit, similar measures could be taken subject to the application of appropriate adjustment policies.

Experience has shown that adjustment is often a medium-to-long-term process, while adjustment financing is basically short-term. This deficiency of the system need to be corrected, both by lengthening the maturity of IMF loans and by working closely with the World Bank.[8]

The recognition of the long-term character of the adjustment process leads immediately to the question of conditionality. Latin America has had a long, varied and traumatic experience with adjustment policies and conditionality in the 1980s and 1990s. In practice, the adjustment policies applied led to lower investment rates, higher unemployment and greater inequality for long periods of time.

Adjustment also led to lower prices for Latin American exports: between 1980 and 1992, the volume of exports from the countries of the region increased 86 per cent, while the value of those exports increased only 42 per cent. That is, more than 50 per cent of the real resource effort to export was lost to the region as a consequence of the fall in prices caused, at least in part, by the fact that the effort to export was undertaken by many countries at the same time. This loss would not have occurred if other countries had expanded their demand for imports by opening up their own economies to international trade.

Conditionality should take into account these 'group effects' and the fact that other countries are not doing their part. This is not to say that conditionality should be lenient; it is to say that it should be different. Conditionality ought to recognize the difficulties, the long-term character and the distributive effects, both domestic and international, of adjustment policies. In a very real sense, this is another way to approach a particular aspect of the problem of asymmetries in adjustment, a problem which is present at both the domestic and the international levels – at the international level, a sharp increase in resources available through the compensatory facility at the IMF, and a revision in the formulas of access to and repayment of borrowings from the facility.

It is now recognised that there are a number of countries where growth and adjustment cannot be achieved within the present resource constraint. These countries, mainly in Africa but also in Latin America, need real transfers of resources without counterpart, that is, need straight subsidies. The international system must be prepared to subsidise in such cases using grants, zero- or low-interest loans, and other forms of subsidies. The International Monetary Fund should not be exempt from this norm.

If the international monetary system is changed in tune with the needs of modern economies, there would not be much use for monetary gold. Gold reserves in the Fund could be sold with the agreement of member countries, and the proceeds could be partially allocated to subsidise operations with least developed countries.

SDR allocations could also be used as a tool to redistribute resources internationally without endangering in any way the liquidity character of the asset. The discussion about different forms of distributing any given allocation of SDRs among countries (the 'direct link') is probably exhausted. A distribution based on IMF quotas, where the quotas of LDCs have a weight double that of other countries, is as good as the present system from the point of view of liquidity, and obviously better from a resource transfer point of view. The same is valid for allocations of SDRs devoted to increasing the lending resources of the World Bank (the 'indirect link'). Furthermore, there is always the possibility of a 'voluntary' link, some countries donating their share to others.[9]

In any monetary system, however perfect it may be, there is always the need to face unexpected developments affecting the agents in the system. From this consideration arises the role of a 'lender of last resort'. In the recent past, private commercial lenders required IMF loans as a prerequisite for their own lending: in a very real sense, the IMF became the 'lender of first resort', a role it is not equipped to play. In the pushing and pulling of the debt crisis, the IMF changed positions several times between last and first resort lender, doing its best to avoid a crisis of the private international financial system. The Fund achieved its purpose, although at the cost of forcing the weaker member countries into a sharp, long recession, which has lasted more than a decade and has exerted a recessionary influence over the world economy.

The lender-of-last-resort function needs strengthening. During the debt crisis, the IMF, the World Bank and the Inter-American Development Bank withdrew funds from Latin America, a few years after the start of the crisis, precisely at the time when they were needed most. It is natural to expect private banks to stop lending at times of stress, but it is contrary to good sense for all financial organisations to do so at the same time. The lender of last resort failed to compensate for the pro-cyclical character of private lending and became itself another pro-cyclical lender. This is a deficiency in the present institutionality that must be addressed, and the capacity to allocate SDRs, together with a more symmetrical adjustment process, provides an opportunity to do so. Perhaps a debt-managing facility, as proposed by many analysts, is also to be considered as part of contingency planning.

In an international system, automaticity is a virtue that saves a lot of political and economic friction. To gain a greater degree of automaticity in the system without endangering stability, it is necessary to introduce indicators that would trigger action in the adjustment, liquidity and exchange rate fields. The use of such indicators would throw light on emergent disequilibria without the need for a formal decision of the Fund; in this way, pressure would be put on member countries, and on the Fund itself, to act. The use of objective indicators was discussed in detail during working sessions of the deceased Committee of Twenty of the IMF.

The publication of the *World Economic Outlook* by the Fund, initially a highly restricted document, was a step, albeit a weak one, in the right direction. The *Outlook* contains information on economic developments in different countries and areas of the world, as well as an evaluation of short-term perspectives and policies. This document, with sharper edges, could be the basis for fruitful discussions, cooperation and coordination of economic policies significant for the world economy.

Policy coordination issues have been widely discussed. Better coordination is implicit in the use of objective indicators. A system of indicators with 'alert' and 'triggering' values would be a very valuable tool.

THE TRANSITION TO A NEW SYSTEM

It does take some imagination to conceive of a world with a monetary system, if one starts from the situation today. Perhaps a first step towards an organised system is to stimulate policy cooperation aimed at the reduction of large imbalances in the external accounts of industrial countries. Under present imbalances, the movement towards a new international monetary system is doomed, as there is no conceivable way to regulate international liquidity and exchange rate changes.

Imbalances on the external accounts of countries have a domestic counterpart: an imbalance in either the public or the private domestic sectors, or in both. The most frequent empirical case is that of the external imbalance being the other side of the coin of a public-sector imbalance. This is probably the case in the United States, where the Clinton administration has already announced the decision to close the US Government deficit.

To avoid negative effects on the world economy as a whole, adjustment in the US should be accompanied by adjustment in the opposite direction in other countries. Japan is probably one of the best candidates, both because of the size of her economy and because of the direction of the adjustment required. However, the fact that adjustment policies in that country should probably aim to increase expenditure by the private sector rather than by the Government complicate the picture. Government expenditure is a policy tool, while private expenditure is the result of other policies. In any case, the Japanese Government has also announced actions generally in the right direction.

If external deficits and surpluses are reduced to manageable proportions, say below 2 per cent of GDP, then it would be useful to think about the accumulated dollar balances (as well as German mark and Japanese yen balances) held outside their issuing country. This particular problem was addressed during the discussions of the Committee of Twenty.

The transitional solution discussed by the Committee was to establish a 'substitution account' in the IMF, available to exchange SDRs for dollars at a fixed rate, to absorb the so-called 'dollar overhang'.[10] The US would undertake to take back its own currency from the account in exchange for SDRs, during a given period, covering the financial cost of the account. As SDRs would be created during the operation, against dollars absorbed by the substitution account, there would be no net increment in liquidity as a consequence of the account. Again, as the US would get back its own currency in exchange for SDRs, the account would finally close with a zero balance.

The whole purpose of the account was to provide time for the US to withdraw dollars from circulation, making room for the new system without requiring unduly, and disturbing, restrictive adjustment policies from that country. Something similar to the substitution account would be required today, except that it should be open to other currencies.

Particular attention during the transition period should be given to banks operating in international markets. A way to ease transition would be to require that their reserve requirements be satisfied with gradually increasing proportions of SDRs, in order to limit their capacity to expand operations. This would, at the same time, increase the demand for SDRs and speed up the implementation of all aspects of the reform.

Common regional currencies, like the Ecu, should pose no particular difficulty for the implementation of a new monetary system. In fact, the type of arrangements and regulations applicable to currencies linked to the ECU could facilitate movement towards a common world currency. Some flexibility is required in the link between individual currencies and the SDR to allow for imperfect policy coordination and unexpected events. But stimulus provided for symmetrical adjustment should minimise the need for exchange rate readjustments. The different aspects of the new system tend to reinforce each other.

Adjustment policies during the transition period might be quite harmful to developing countries. As the priority given to avoid inflation seems to prevail over other policy objectives in most industrialised countries, LDCs may find themselves in a recessionary trap: restrictive adjustment policies of industrial countries in deficit could dominate the world economic picture without counterbalance. LDCs would find that demand for their exports shifts backwards, forcing them to overshoot in their export promotion policies, reinforcing weak tendencies in commodity prices and exerting extra pressure on their environment.

As former socialist countries (FSCs), some of them important commodity producers, fight to restructure their economies, exports from this source could complicate the picture for LDCs. At the same time, FSCs attract the political attention of the West and economic cooperation moves more and more in their direction. Even the IMF has recently established a special facility to assist these countries in their efforts to adjust.[11]

On the other hand, liquidity needs of former socialist countries, together with US efforts to reduce external imbalances, provide an opportunity to reinstate the relative importance of SDRs in the world economy.

It is vital for LDCs that their interest is recognised and taken into account in economic policy negotiations at all levels, within and outside the IMF. G-77 and G-24 working groups have been forcefully presenting LDCs' points of view in different fora. However, institutionality for negotiations usually underestimates the economic and political importance of LDCs. Perhaps a suggestion like the one made by S. Marris, for setting up a Group of the Non-Five,[12] merits serious political consideration.

Even with all the difficulties and risks, LDCs have a lot to gain from a new, organised international monetary system. I am convinced that the technical advantages of a reformed system are many. I am also convinced that several steps can be taken today that would move us closer to a reformed system. The perceived fact that the new system is further away now than in the early seventies is not a sufficiently strong argument to prevent gradual progress.

NOTES

1.   The points of view expressed in this paper are those of the author, and do not necessarily reflect those of the organisations to which he is related. Comments by Ricardo Ffrench-Davis are acknowledged with thanks.

2.   The proposals made, the negotiations and the debate which led to the final agreement are well described in Horsefield, Y. Keith, *The International Monetary Fund 1945–1965* (Washington, DC: International Monetary Fund, 1969).

3. See, for example: Holtrop, M. W. (President of the Netherlansche Bank), 'Method of monetary analysis used by the Netherlanche Bank', in *Recent Developments in Monetary Analysis*, Washington, DC, IMF Staff Papers, Vol. V, no. 3, February 1957. Also, Polak, J. J., 'Monetary analysis of income formation and payments problems', *IMF Staff Papers*, Vol. VI, no. 1, November 1957.

4. See Massad, C., 'Algunas observaciones sobre la crisis monetaria internacional', Santiago, *Cuadernos de Economia*, No. 25, Chile, diciembre 1971, pp. 50–63. Also 'Peligros de la reforma del sistema monetario internacional', New York, *Progreso*, Número especial: banca y finanzas en América Latina, Vol. 5, No 11, diciembre 1972, pp. 26–9, 74. Also 'The revolt of the bankers in the international economy: a world without a monetary system', Santiago, *CEPAL Review* No. 2, Second Semester 1976, Chile, pp. 93–118.

5. Triffin, R. *Europe and the Money Muddle* (New Haven, CT: Yale University Press, 1957), especially pp. 296–9.

6. Massad, C. 'Ajuste recesivo, ajuste expansivo y condicional', conferencia con ocasión del quincuagésimo aniversario del Banco Central de El Salvador, San Salvador, junio, 1984. Also Schmidt-Hebbel, K. y F. Montt, 'Impactos externos, devaluaciones y precios de materias primas', in Eyzaguirre, N. y M. Valdivia (eds), *Políticas macroeconómicas y brecha externa: América Latina en los años ochenta* (LC/G.1532-P), Santiago de Chile, CEPAL, marzo 1989.

7. The suggestion that some form of international regulation of minimum reserve requirements should be established was put forward during the discussion of J. Williamson's paper, 'International monetary reform and the prospect for economic development'. See J. Williamson, op. cit., in Williamson, Griffith-Jones, Sengupta et al., *Fragile Finance*, ed. Jan Joost Teunissen, Forum on Debt and Development, The Hague, November 1992.

8. Ffrench-Davis, R. and P. Meller, 'Structural Adjustment and World Bank Conditionality: A Latin American Perspective', *Notas Técnicas*, CIEPLAN, Nov. 1990. (Prepared for the G-24.)

9. The voluntary form of the link has earned a reference by the Managing Director of the IMF. See IMF *Survey*, Vol. 22, No. 9, 3 May, 1993, pp. 133–4.

10. For an analysis of the substitution account, see Kadam, V. B., 'Implications for Developing Countries of Current Proposals for a Substitution Account', *Report to the Group of Twenty-Four*, UNDP/UNCTAD Project INT/75/015, Studies on International Monetary and Financial Issues for the Developing Countries, 16 August 1979.

11. The 'Systemic Transformation Facility' (STF) has been designed to serve the specific needs of countries moving from a non-market price system to a market price one. See IMF Press Release No. 93/17, 23 April 1993.

12. Marris, S. 'A Proposal to Create the Group of the Non-Five', in WIDER Study Group Series No. 4, *World Economic Summits: The Role of Representative Groups in the Governance of the World Economy*, Appendix A, pp. 34–101, Helsinki, May 1989.

10 On the Modalities of Macroeconomic Policy Coordination[1]

John Williamson

The economic imbalances of the mid-1980s spawned a disillusion with *laissez-faire* in macroeconomic policies, which was reflected in the attempt to correct the dollar exchange rate agreed at the Plaza, the indicators exercise initiated at the Tokyo summit, and the reference ranges adopted at the Louvre. Unfortunately these tentative moves toward macro-economic policy coordination among the G-7 were allowed to atrophy once the initial team that negotiated them (Baker, Miyazawa and Stoltenberg) moved on. The subsequent performance of the world economy, notably the depth and length of the world recession of the early 1990s, does not inspire confidence that the virtual abandonment of policy coordination by the G-7 was a wise non-decision.

Some of my past work has been directed at developing proposals as regards the desirable content of macro-economic policy coordination.[2] The next section of this chapter provides a brief sketch of the nature of those proposals. This is followed by a discussion of whether non-members of the G-7 would have an important stake in the outcome of negotiations on policy coordination. If so, the question arises as to the institutional mechanisms through which their interests could be brought to bear on the decision-making process in an effective way.

THE BLUEPRINT PROPOSALS

The blueprint is conventional in assuming that governments like a high level of activity (implying also a high rate of growth[3] and a high level of employment) and that they dislike inflation, with an intensity that grows progressively as inflation rises. It also assumes that governments have some objective, at least within a range, for their balance of payments on current account. This is not necessarily a zero balance, but at a minimum it must be a range within which any imbalance will not raise questions about the sustainability of financing. Of course, some governments may have well-defined ideas about the desirable level of the country's lending to, or borrowing from, the rest of the world.

Governments cannot in general have everything they would like. Trade-offs must be faced. In particular, lowering inflation generally requires some temporary slack in the economy. Higher activity arising from an expansion in domestic demand tends both to increase inflation and to worsen the current account. A more competitive exchange rate, designed to improve the current account at a given level of activity, tends to increase inflationary pressure.

The blueprint is based on using a medium-term framework to resolve these trade-offs. Each of the participating countries – assumed to be the members of the Group of Seven (G-7) – would be expected to have some notion of the natural rate of unemployment (NAIRU). Their choice should be continuously monitored for realism by whatever international secretariat was charged with responsibility for servicing the policy coordination process. Each country would also select a current account target. Where a government had no precise view on what current account balance was appropriate, one could take the middle of the range that was judged to be sustainable as the provisional target. The secretariat would then have to appraise the mutual consistency of the various targets, taking account of what appears sustainable and acceptable to the rest of the world. If an inconsistency emerged, it would have to be bargained away; the less governments have precise views on current account targets, the less troublesome this should be. Finally, one would need to check that the chosen NAIRUs were consistent with the current balance targets. (Since a more favourable current balance implies a more competitive exchange rate and thus lower real wages, it would tend to raise the NAIRU if wage-earners have a target real wage: see Barrell and Wren-Lewis, 1989.)

Each country would commit itself to a macroeconomic strategy designed to lead to simultaneous 'internal balance' – defined as unemployment at the NAIRU and minimal inflation – and 'external balance' – defined as achieving the target current account balance – in the medium term. Since exchange rates affect trade only with long lags, this implies a commitment to hold the exchange rate close to the level[4] needed to reconcile internal and external balance during the intervening adjustment period. This exchange rate is the 'fundamental equilibrium exchange rate' (FEER), so termed because it is the exchange rate that implies an absence of 'fundamental disequilibrium' in the old Bretton Woods sense (Williamson, 1985). Policy should be directed to keeping exchange rates reasonably close to their FEERs. To say the same thing another way, the exchange rate should be kept within a target zone around its FEER: thus the blueprint incorporates the target zone proposal.[5]

The system needs another intermediate target in addition to the exchange rate, and I have argued that this should be the growth rate of nominal domestic demand. The idea of targeting this is a slight variation on the fairly familiar proposal to seek a constant growth rate of nominal income (see Brittan, 1987; Meade, 1984; McCallum, 1988). It has most of the advantages of a nominal income target, in terms both of providing a constraint on inflation (a 'nominal anchor') while allowing some elasticity to mitigate a supply shock, and of avoiding the shocks that come from a money supply rule when velocity changes.

Unlike most of the proposals for nominal income targeting, the blueprint envisages endogenisation of the target for demand growth. This endogenisation would allow rather more effort to combat a recession and rather more accommodation of an inflationary shock than the traditional proposals for nominal income targeting. There are two reasons for arguing that this modification would be desirable. One is the view that a contra-cyclical policy can be effective in reducing the short-run costs of adverse shocks, provided that confidence in the long-term commitment to price stability is not impaired. The other is the fear that, if governments are asked to subscribe to excessively 'harsh' rules, they are likely to abandon them just at the time when it is most important to reinforce confidence in their resolve to stick to rules that will reestablish price stability in the medium run. The formula incorporated into the blueprint is intended to strike a sensible balance between the need to control inflation and the desirability of limiting recessions.

The other innovation of the blueprint is to require governments to target the growth of *domestic demand* rather than *income*. The difference between the two is the change in the current account balance. The rule calls on a country with an undesirably large current account deficit (surplus) to target a slower (faster) growth of domestic demand than its desired growth of nominal income, so as to promote correction of the trade imbalance.

The final step involves translating the implications of the two intermediate targets into 'rules' to guide monetary and fiscal policy. The blueprint suggests three such rules, subject to two constraints.

Rule 1 says that interest rate differentials among countries should be adjusted when necessary in order to reinforce intervention in the exchange markets in limiting the deviation of exchange rates from their FEERs to target zones. This rule recognises that in the last analysis exchange rate management requires a willingness to devote monetary policy to that end. It does not imply that monetary policy must be devoted exclusively to exchange rate management, because a wide target zone allows substantial scope for monetary policy to be directed to domestic objectives, but it does require that if necessary the authorities give priority to the exchange rate.

Rule 1 only deals with interest differentials and fails to pin down the average interest rate in the system. It raises the question as to which country should adjust if two currencies reach the limits of the target zone: the one with the weak or the one with the strong currency. Rule 2 offers the answer that if aggregate 'world' (or G-7) demand is growing too rapidly the weak-currency country should raise its interest rate, while in the converse case of inadequate growth it should be the strong-currency country that should cut its rate. In other words, the average world interest rate should be adjusted upwards when the aggregate growth of nominal demand is threatening to exceed its target value (the weighted average of the national targets), or downwards when world demand growth is too low. This provides a world rule for aggregate monetary policy to replace the 'dollar standard rule' that the *n*th country (the United States) should seek domestic stability while the other *n*-1 countries follow Rule 1. It is the key to constructing a symmetrical monetary system of the form that will be appropriate for the multipolar world of the twenty-first century.

Rule 3 says that if the monetary policy called for by Rules 1 and 2 threatens to prevent nominal domestic demand growing at close to the target rate, fiscal policy should be adjusted to compensate. This rule calls for the 'Keynesian' use of fiscal policy to ensure that an exchange-rate-oriented monetary policy does not destabilise domestic demand. Such overt use of fiscal policy became unfashionable in the 1980s, but for no good reason: on the contrary, experiences such as the post-1982 expansion in the United States and the post-1987 expansion in Japan demonstrated that fiscal policy had lost none of its power when the conditions implicitly assumed by Keynes (excess capacity and financial confidence) were present.

Constraint 1 says that if fiscal policy is threatening to lead to an unsustainable debt build-up, Rule 3 should be overridden if it calls for an expansionary fiscal policy.

According to Constraint 2, if world real interest rates remain higher than 3 or 4 per cent per year for a sustained period, there should be a concerted global fiscal consolidation.

In retrospect, it is not clear that the combination of a short-run anti-cyclical fiscal 'rule' and two constraints motivated by medium-term sustainability is the best way to have specified rules for the conduct of fiscal policy. It would seem preferable to ask each country to identify the medium-run fiscal stance compatible with its current account target, a sustainable debt position, and a 'normal' real interest rate (say 3 per cent).

Each country would then identify a medium-run (say five-year) path for adjusting its fiscal deficit towards the target position, allowing Rule 3 to be respecified in terms of deviations from this target path. This reformulation would make clear the medium-term link between fiscal policy and the current account deficit that has been emphasised by Boughton (1989).[6]

THE INTERESTS OF NON-G-7 COUNTRIES

In developing these proposals, I always took it for granted that the G-7 countries would decide among themselves on the adoption of the 'rules', which would surely in reality be guidelines rather than hard rules, and on the interpretation of what they imply in specific situations. I justified this by reasoning that the G-7 are less likely to agree on following any rules at all if they have to have them endorsed by third countries or are expected to listen to third countries when deciding how to interpret the rules. I persuaded myself that third countries could only benefit from effective policy coordination among the countries large enough for their policies to have a systemic impact, and hence should not make demands for representation that might prejudice an agreement to implement the blueprint.

On the other hand, it can be argued that developing countries have a very direct interest in the macro-policies of the major industrial countries, and hence that they should be included in any international process that is intended to influence those policies. For example, developing countries have an interest in avoiding excessively deflationary policies being pursued by the industrial countries, since these worsen the former's terms of trade[7] as well as reduce their markets for non-traditional exports. Similarly, US success in badgering Japan into reducing its current account surplus would under some circumstances reduce the savings available for lending to developing countries. Clearly these considerations are also pertinent to industrial countries that are not members of the G-7. Indeed, the marginal excluded industrial countries (Spain and the Netherlands) may resent their exclusion from the decision-making process even more than many developing countries.

There would in fact seem to be at least four grounds on which one could argue that non-members of the G-7 ought to be involved in the management of the policy coordination process:

- Designing, and reviewing over time, the rule that will strike a 'sensible balance between the need to control inflation and the desirability of limiting recessions' is something that affects the interests of all countries and not just the members of the G-7.

- It is not just the design of such a rule but also the way in which it is implemented that will have an impact on the welfare of all countries.[8] Hence all countries have a legitimate interest in monitoring the implementation of the rule.

- I had assumed that in interpreting Rule 2 (requiring a judgement as to whether the growth of 'world demand' was excessive or deficient) it would suffice to take G-7 demand as a proxy for world demand. But according to the PPP-based estimates of world output given in the May 1993 *World Economic Outlook* (Table 33) the G-7 accounts for less than half of world output, rather than almost two-thirds, as the old exchange-rate-based estimates implied. This must increase one's doubts as to whether the G-7 would provide an adequate proxy. If an attempt is to be made to use a more comprehensive measure of demand growth, then it would be necessary to involve other countries in computing target growth rates of demand and estimating actual growth rates.

- The summary in the previous section suggested that 'The secretariat would...have to appraise the mutual consistency of the [G-7's current account] targets, taking account of what appears to be sustainable and acceptable to the rest of the world.' This is too cavalier: if a system of policy coordination involving the assignment of current account targets is to be instituted, other countries have just as much interest as do G-7 members in having an input into the process of choosing their targets. If countries are to be pressured into seeking to achieve such targets, then a process that omitted more than half the world economy would be plainly inadequate, while one that pressured countries into seeking targets that they had not endorsed would be patently unacceptable.

This last point is perhaps the most important. In a world where even 'a senior OECD official [says] policymakers might have to consider actions that they know to be harmful in the long run...[such as] protecting domestic markets to preserve jobs'[9] because of the perceived threat of a loss of jobs to newly industrializing economies, there is an urgent need to provide reassurance to the industrial countries that continued liberal trade with countries poorer than themselves is not a formula for the net destruction of job opportunities. Since there is no reason for any net job-loss to emerge as long as the industrialising economies do not build up current account surpluses, it seems to me clear that the best way of providing such reassurance is for all such countries to adopt internationally agreed current account targets (with agreed policy responses if the targets are missed and, if necessary, sanctions for failure to implement such policy responses).

Thus a search for mutually consistent current account targets now seems to me to have a much broader rationale than that embodied in the blueprint, where it was merely an intermediate step toward the calculation of FEERs. And this broader rationale is one which absolutely demands the participation of at least the major non-G-7 countries.

For these reasons I am persuaded that there is indeed a strong intellectual case for seeking to broaden international control of the policy coordination process. The next section of this chapter considers how that might be accomplished.

ALTERNATIVE WAYS OF BROADENING CONTROL OF POLICY COORDINATION

Such considerations suggest that the sort of discussions on policy coordination hitherto conducted within the confines of the G-7 ought to be relocated to an international forum where all countries can in principle make an input into the decision-making process. The obvious forum is the IMF, with its only visible competitor being a sub-committee of an Economic Security Council based in the UN, which has the critical disadvantage, in my eyes, of being an organisation run by diplomats whereas the IMF, for all its weaknesses, is at least run by economists.

At the same time, there is clearly a case for restricting discussion of sensitive issues of macro-economic policy such as will be essential to achieve effective policy coordination to a small group where participants regard each other as peers and are certain that confidentiality will be respected. As a preliminary to considering how these contradictory objectives can best be reconciled, it is natural to compile a list of alternative possible institutional mechanisms.

At present, policy coordination (such as it is) is undertaken within the context of the G-7 (consisting of the United States, Japan, France, Germany, Italy, the United Kingdom, and Canada). This meets once a year at summit level, but such policy coordination as occurs is undertaken by the Finance Ministers, or more usually their Deputies. The Managing Director of the IMF normally participates in at least the opening part of Ministerial meetings of the G-7, while members of the IMF staff regularly participate in meetings at the Deputy level. Option 1 is to leave these arrangements essentially alone, though preferably with the IMF formally designated as the secretariat for the G-7 exercise and the Managing Director of the Fund included in the whole of the G-7 meetings and invited to represent the interests of non-members.

Option 2 is to increase the size of the G-7 to include other countries. Since the G-7 comprises the seven largest industrial economies, it is natural to consider adding some of the other large economies. Table 10.1 shows World Bank estimates of the PPP-based GDP of the members of the world's 15 largest economies[10] Which of the eight non-G-7 countries included there would be plausible candidates for inclusion in an enlarged G-7 will be discussed below.

Option 3 would again be to enlarge the G-7 but to select the additional members not by virtue of their size but rather on the basis of some claim to represent the non-members of the G-7. If one can assume that the industrial countries excluded from the G-7, and the economies in transition, would forgo any claim to representation, then the country that holds the chair of the G-24[11] or the country that chairs the non-aligned movement would be obvious candidates. If one cannot make that assumption, then it would presumably be necessary for the IMF or some other international body to make arrangements for electing one or more countries to supplement the G-7. One possibility would be to adapt the proposals developed by Stephen Marris (1989) for creating a 'Group of the Non-Five' intended to supplement the G-5 in providing a directorate to manage the world economy.

Another possibility, option 4, would be to use such an election procedure to select not a country (or countries) but rather one or more individuals who would join G-7 meetings to represent the interests of the rest of the world.

Option 5 would be to replace one or more current members of the G-7 by an equal number of non-members, so avoiding any enlargement in the size of the group. (Until recently one might have thought of replacing the four European members by a European Community that was becoming an ever-closer union, but such a reform currently appears unrealistic.) There should be no great difficulty in replacing Canada, since most Canadians seem to regard their place at the top table as a happy anomaly rather than a fundamental right, and Table 10.1 shows that there is indeed a large gap between the size of the Canadian economy and that of all other members of the G-7. The next smallest economy of a current G-7 member is that of Britain, according to the 1991 (though not the 1990) PPP-based measure of GDP, but it would not seem realistic to eliminate the UK, given the role of London as a financial centre. Italy is the other potential candidate for replacement, though it would doubtless resist its ejection strenuously. Hence one might contemplate a reconstitution of the G-7 that would make at least one or at most two places available to countries that are not currently members. The candidates to fill those one or two places would be the same as those considered above under options 2 and 3 to enlarge the G-7.

Table 10.1   Estimates of PPP-based GDP for 15 largest economies

| | GDP, billion dollars | |
	1990	1991
United States	5340	5599
China	2211	1934
Japan	2102	2404
Germany*	1111	1582
Russia**	1086	1033
India	978	978
United Kingdom	853	931
France	851	1051
Italy	844	971
Brazil	717	802
Canada	531	522
Mexico	514	631
Spain	423	494
Indonesia	418	513
Korea	309	358

* 1990 value for FRG is 1026; based on German Embassy statistics for the second half of 1990, GDR GDP=8.3 per cent of FRG GDP; thus total German GDP in 1990 is estimated as $1.083 \times 1026 = 1111$.
Figure for 1991 based on *World Development Report 1993* estimate of per capita GDP and *World Almanac* population estimate for unified Germany.
** The PPP-based weight of the former Soviet Union was estimated at 8.31 per cent of GWP in 1990 (IMF). Russian GDP is estimated to be 55 per cent of the FSU, or 4.57 per cent of GWP. Since US GDP is \$5340 billion, or 22.47 per cent of GWP, then Russian GDP would be \$1086 billion.
1991 Russian GDP based on *World Development Report 1993* figure.
Sources: The World Bank, *World Development Report* (1992 & 1993), estimates based on ICP. IMF, *World Economic Outlook* (May 1993). IMF, *International Financial Statistics. The World Almanac 1993*. German Embassy (personal communication).

Option 6 would be to shift the locus of decision-making on economic policy coordination from the G-7 to the IMF. The Fund's Executive Board currently has 24 members, which between them represent all of the Fund's 178 member countries. Such an option would presumably be conceivable only if the membership of the Executive Board were upgraded, perhaps to the form originally proposed by Keynes where Executive Directors would have been senior officials based in national capitals who came to Washington once a month or so in order to conduct the Fund's major business, which would include policy coordination. Other Board meetings would be conducted by the Washington-based Alternates.

What are the pros and cons of these alternatives?

A first concern relates to the size of the group. One cannot expect that the major countries will consent to engage in a frank discussion of sensitive issues of macro-economic policy within a large group, especially if they believe there to be any chance of leaks. Indeed, it has sometimes been claimed that no serious decision is ever made in a group with more than seven people present. To the extent that this is correct, it argues against options 2, 3, 4, and 6. And if one takes the view that persuading countries to modify their policies in the broad international interest[12] is best done by a country's peers, then it also argues against option 5 and in favour of option 1.

A second consideration is that the G-7 has always been a grouping of *democratic* countries. This is pertinent to deciding which countries might be eligible to join in an enlarged G-7 under options 2 or 3, or to provide the replacement members under option 5. Even if one takes the optimistic view that democracy is, or will soon be, sufficiently consolidated to make Korea, Russia and South Africa (plus, of course, Brazil, India and Spain) eligible for consideration, it certainly excludes China, Indonesia and Mexico. Note that Indonesia claimed that its chairmanship of the non-aligned bloc entitled it to attend the Tokyo summit in 1993; this pinpoints a problem with option 3, since this would require either that the G-7 abandon its democratic principles or that the non-members of the G-7 restrict their choice to countries with democratic credentials.

A third consideration concerns the willingness of the G-7 (G-5) countries to accept the additional (replacement) members. It is unrealistic to imagine that extra participants will be welcomed if their role is seen purely as that of pleading on behalf of countries that would otherwise not be represented. Potential members of a club need to have something to offer as well as something to gain. So the question arises: what could the extra countries contribute to the process that the core members would value? If the Group had a mandate to discuss trade policy as well as macro-coordination, it would clearly be useful to get commitments from non-industrial countries, especially large ones and ones that play an influential role in moulding opinions among the group as a whole. Another answer might be a willingness to negotiate and accept current account targets – something that the core members would presumably value much more if it covered all of the non-G-7 (non-G-5) countries than if it were restricted only to the one or two additional participants. Beyond those two factors, the only extra attraction would be if the particular participants happened to be able to make an intellectual contribution. This would presumably be more likely under option 4 (where individuals would be elected in order to represent the interests of the non-core countries), which would presumably also be the option with the best chance to influence the trade policies or current account targets of the non-G-7 (or non-G-5) as a whole.

If one adds the consideration with which we started, that option 1 excludes many countries from a process that importantly affects their interests, none of the options appears very attractive in its pure form. Hence one is led to consider whether it might be possible to design some synthesis that largely overcomes the problems identified above.

It seems to me that the most promising approach would involve breaking down the decision-making process into a *strategic* phase with wide international participation and a *tactical* stage with a very restricted group of countries involved. The strategic questions should be ones that do not require enormous confidentiality or demand particularly prompt resolution, so as to minimise the disadvantages of a large size of the group.

To be concrete, a revamped IMF Executive Board, as under option 6, might be responsible for agreeing the ground rules and monitoring their implementation *ex post*, including agreeing the formula that would set the appropriate balance between inflation and deflation and assigning a set of current account targets. Imposing sanctions on countries that failed to adjust their policies on the agreed principles when the curent account targets were violated would also be a strategic decision assigned to the Executive Board.

Tactical decisions on when policies need to be adjusted – e.g. when exchange rate intervention is called for, when target zones need to be altered, when fiscal policies ought to be changed, when interest rates should be increased or decreased – will have to be taken in a much smaller group, consisting overwhelmingly of peers, if the major countries are to be persuaded to accept any international input into such decisions at all. Here the options would seem to be number 1 (keeping the G-7 unchanged), number 5 (replacing one or two members of the G-7 by one or two other large countries, presumably chosen from Russia, India, and Brazil), or else replacing one or two members of the G-7 by one or two individuals elected by the countries that are not *ipso facto* members of the group (a slight modification of option 4). My own preference would be the latter, since this would

- allow all countries to have an input into selecting the person(s) that would represent those countries that are not members of the group in their own right;
- increase the chance that the interests of all countries would be taken into account in the decision-making process;
- sidestep the problem of certifying whether countries were sufficiently democratic to be eligible for admission to the inner circle;

- permit the selected person(s) to play a role in negotiating and encouraging the pursuit of current account targets for all the non-core countries;
- make it more likely that persons with an intellectual ability to contribute to the decision-making process would find themselves members of the group.

Of course, such a solution would be workable only if the countries that are not automatic members acted responsibly in selecting a representative(s) who would be intellectually respected and regarded as utterly trustworthy by the G-5/G-6, and it would be aided if they were willing to allow him or her an intermediary role in the negotiation of current account targets. Election of someone regarded as soft on inflation, let alone someone beholden to the ideas of the old New International Economic Order, would be guaranteed to make the group impotent from the start. If it did not kill the prospects for policy coordination entirely, it would ensure that the formal group was marginalised and any real decisions were taken outside it.

None of the proposals discussed in this chapter need involve any change in the the countries that participate in G-7 summit meetings. It would, however, be natural to accompany adoption of a revised mechanism for macro-economic policy coordination by abandonment of the pretence that summits are *economic* events, and admit that they are occasions for the leaders of the most powerful democratic nations to seek mutual understandings on the main *political* issues of the day, which are increasingly unlikely to be primarily economic issues.

NOTES

1. Revised version of a paper presented to a meeting of the North–South Roundtable on 'The UN and the Bretton Woods Institutions: New Challenges for the 21st Century', held at Bretton Woods, New Hampshire, on 1–3 September 1993. The author is indebted to Charles Iceland for competent research assistance and to C. Randall Henning and participants in the North–South Roundtable for helpful comments on a previous draft. Copyright Institute for International Economics: all rights reserved.
2. See Bergsten and Williamson (1983) for the initial development of the target zone proposal, Williamson (1985) for its subsequent elaboration, Williamson and Miller (1987) for elaboration of a 'blueprint' for policy coordination, and Williamson in Johnson (1990) for a concise summary of those proposals.
3. At least, there is a one-to-one correspondence between the level of activity and the growth rate if the growth of supply-side potential is exogenous. This is a reasonable assumption for the short run, but not for the long run.
4. Or, strictly speaking, the trajectory.

5. Because of doubts as to whether the authorities of the major countries would be wise to give overwhelming priority to exchange rate targeting, the proposal allows for wide bands and perhaps, *in extremis*, soft margins. The travails of the ERM in 1992–93 provide a good example of the sort of circumstances in which soft margins could have been useful.

6. The proposal presented here would nonetheless differ from Boughton's policy assignment in retaining exchange rate management. This is needed in order to avoid leaving exchange rates subject to speculative fads and bubbles, with the resultant danger of misalignments.

7. Indeed, it seems that a major part of the mechanism whereby deflation curbs inflation in the developed countries is by reducing commodity prices and thus easing the conflict over income distribution within the industrial countries. See Beckerman (1985).

8. To take a topical example, almost everyone would endorse the Bundesbank's prime objective of implementing a stability-oriented monetary policy, but many of us would challenge its interpretation of what that objective required during 1992–93.

9. Quoted from a Reuters report, 2 June 1993.

10. These estimates show large, inexplicable, and implausible variations from one year to the next, such as a 13 per cent reduction in the size of the rapidly growing Chinese economy and a 42 per cent increase in the size of the German economy in a year when growth was estimated at 3.6 per cent. Despite this, they provide better estimates of the relative size of different national economies than the alternative of a GDP measure based on conversion through the exchange rate.

11. I refer, of course, to the original Group of 24, not the group of 24 OECD countries who hijacked the title to describe their collective for aiding the economies in transition.

12. It is not implied that countries can be expected to make such modifications out of altruism; rather, the bargain is that they submit to a set of international rules that may constrain them at times to do things that are not in their short-run national interests, in the expectation that similar rule observance by other countries will rebound to advance their long-run national interest by more than enough to compensate them for the short-run costs.

REFERENCES

Barrell, Ray, and Simon Wren-Lewis (1989), 'Fundamental Equilibrium Exchange Rates for the G7', CEPR Discussion Paper no. 323.

Beckerman, Wilfred (1985), 'How the Battle Against Inflation was Really Won', *Lloyds Bank Review*, January.

Bergsten, C. Fred, and John Williamson (1983), 'Exchange Rates and Trade Policy', in W. R. Cline (ed.), *Trade Policy in the 1980s* (Washington: Institute for International Economics).

Boughton, James M. (1989), 'Policy Assignment Strategies with Somewhat Flexible Exchange Rates', in B. Eichengreen, M. Miller, and R. Portes (eds), *Blueprints for Exchange Rate Management*, (London: Centre for Economic Policy Research).

Brittan, Samuel (1987), 'The Case for Money GDP' in S. Brittan, *The Role and Limits of Government* (London: Wildwood House), revised edn.

Johnson, Christopher (ed.) (1990), *Lloyds Bank Annual Review, Volume 3: Changing Exchange Rate Systems* (London: Pinter).

Marris, Stephen N. (1989), 'A Proposal to Create the "Group of the Non-Five"', Appendix A to *World Economic Summits: The Role of Representative Groups in the Governance of the World Economy*, WIDER Study Group Series no. 4 (Helsinki: World Institute for Development Economics Research).

McCallum, Bennett T. (1988), 'Robustness Properties of a Rule for Monetary Policy', *Carnegie–Rochester Conference Series on Public Policy*, Autumn.

Meade, James E. (1984), 'A New Keynesian Bretton Woods', *Three Banks Review*, June.

Williamson, John (1985), *The Exchange Rate System* (Washington: Institute for International Economics).

Williamson, John, and Marcus Miller (1987), *Targets and Indicators: A Blueprint for the International Coordination of Economic Policy* (Washington: Institute for International Economics).

Part IV

Priorities for the Twenty-First Century

11 Gender Priorities for the Twenty-First Century

Khadija Haq

It is a matter of grave concern to all women of the world that after three UN conferences on women and two years short of the two decades of UN system-wide efforts to integrate women into development, and to take all appropriate measures to eliminate discrimination against women and to ensure them equal rights with men, for the majority of the world's women the Nairobi statistics are still the reality. Women, though one-half of the world's population, still do two-thirds of its work, earn one-tenth of its income and own one-hundredth of its property. World-wide, one out of every three households is run by a woman. World-wide, one out of every three women work for pay, earning 73 cents to a man's dollar, often in insecure, futureless, health-eroding jobs no man would take. She may work up to 80 hours a week, much of her work unpaid or even unacknowledged. When she falls ill – and in the developing world she often does, due to repeated pregnancy, hard manual labour and undernutrition – two times out of three she will not find a trained health worker to attend her, if the cost of health care, family priorities and cultural practices even allow her to search for one.

At the global level, much has been accomplished during the period in raising consciousness on women's issues through research and advocacy; in setting norms and standards by such means as the Convention of the Elimination of All Forms of Discrimination Against Women; in mobilising countries to set up national machineries; and in mobilising donor resources for women's development activities. But at the national level the concrete improvements in the economic, political, social and legal status of women have been minimal. The UN publication, *World's Women* lists the gender gaps in policy, investment and earnings that prevent women from participating fully in social, economic and political life.

The mainstream strategy chosen by the United Nations, donor agencies and national governments was the integration of women into existing development strategies, structures and institutions. Several studies on women's worsening situation indicate that real and full participation of women requires a transformation of the existing structures. The empowerment of women with knowledge and skills and legal and economic means will set in the transformation process and will eventually lead to full participation of women in the development process. What would such an empowerment concept imply? It calls for a basic change in at least six areas:

(i)   *Human disparities.* The first task is to remove the current disparities in the status of human development between males and females. The UNDP Human Development Reports have documented these gaps which are extremely large in many developing countries. Female literacy rates are generally less than 50 per cent of males in developing countries, and as low as 35 per cent in Nepal and 27 per cent in Sudan. The health and nutritional indicators are distressingly low for females compared to males, with the maternal mortality rate 15 times higher than in industrial countries. Women remain an underdeveloped human resource. What this means is that the national and international targets for human development in the developing countries should become gender-sensitive. A defined time period must be set over which the gender disparities in education, health and other areas should be removed through well-targeted investment programmes and policy adjustments.

(ii) *Invisibility of women's work in national income accounts.* It is time for the national income statistics to take full account of the value of women's work in each country. There are sound economic accounting techniques available to highlight the monetary contributions of women's work, for example, by looking at the opportunity costs of hiring cooks, nannies, maids, accountants, etc. to replace the work performed by women in the households. In a few countries, where such exercises have been carried out, the monetary value of national income accounts goes up by 20–25 per cent. This exercise should become mandatory for all countries. This is important not only to change the stereotype image that man is the only breadwinner in the family but also to share income within the family and to fully appreciate the value of women's work.

(iii) *Legal discrimination.* Despite feminist movements all over the world, serious legal discrimination still persists against women in most societies, including the industrial ones. For instance, in Japan the inheritance rights of women were raised from one-third to one-half of their late husband's property only in 1980. In Switzerland, several cantons denied women the right to vote only a decade ago. But women's pressures are changing these laws in all industrial countries. In developing countries, however, legal discrimination is absolutely stark and remains largely invisible and non-transparent, extending all the way from the denial of voting rights to the denial of permission even to drive cars, from unequal and unfair property rights to legal barriers to hold certain jobs. What is urgently needed is at least a comprehensive documentation of such legal discrimination in each country and international exposure of what is actually going on. This may lead to concrete programmes of action, priority-setting and a timetable to get such legal barriers dismantled through national and global pressures.

(iv) *Market discrimination.* Markets discriminate against women everywhere but this discrimination is far greater in developing societies, with women confined to some low-paid jobs in the informal sector. Human development may be a necessary condition for market participation but it is certainly not a sufficient one, as the experience of some developed countries shows. Women are still the last to be hired and the first to be fired in the marketplace. Affirmative action may be needed in the initial stages to open more market and employment opportunities for women. In the United States, a Department of Labour study shows that women's employment increased by 15 per cent in the companies subject to affirmative action rules compared with only 2 per cent in other companies. In Bangladesh, 10–15 per cent of government jobs are reserved for women. In many international institutions, minimum quotas for hiring women are being established according to new recruitment policies. For example, at the United Nations Secretariat the Secretary General has recently set the target of bringing the gender balance in policy-making levels as close to 50–50 as possible by the 50th anniversary of the United Nations. Of the 21 organisations under the aegis of the UN, 13 have set targets for increasing the number of professional women. These targets range from 30 to 35 per cent to be reached by the mid-1990s. UNICEF and UNHCR have established explicit goals for achieving gender parity by the year 2000. The need to increase the number of women at the professional level is critical at both national and international levels if the issues and specific concerns of women are to be seriously addressed.

(v) *Political discrimination.* One of the strangest spectacles showing lack of empowerment of women is that, despite having over 50 per cent of the vote, women elect less than 10 per cent of their own gender in the world's parliaments. No wonder then that less than 4 per cent of national cabinets are composed of women and, in 1993, only six countries had women as their heads of government. Why should women vote so overwhelmingly for men and not elect more from their own ranks to gain more power and recognition of their rights? This is the current debate in the United States and in several European countries. On the other hand, developing countries are only now making their democratic transition. It was natural to expect power to be wielded by men in uniform under authoritarian regimes: it will no longer be so easily tolerated in the next democratic phase. But full participation of women in the political power structure is still going to remain a long-term process.

(vi) *Social discrimination.* A most disturbing feature of women's treatment as separate and inferior creatures is the cross of life-long social discrimination that they carry, resulting in infanticide to malnutrition within the family, to child abuse, to rape, and to violence. When conflicts erupt, women are the silent victims even when they are only standing on the sidelines – witness the rape of 20 000 women in Bosnia for no fault of their own. Society takes its instinctive revenge against women when it is at odds with itself or with other nations. There is not a single country in the world where violence against women is not a significant problem. For example,

- In India, bridal dowry disputes led husbands and in-laws to kill more than 5000 wives in 1991.
- In Pakistan, for a rapist to receive punishment, four male adults must testify in court that they witnessed the actual rape.
- In Brazil, a man can kill his wife and be acquitted on grounds of honour.
- In Kenya, in 1991 19 schoolgirls suffocated to death trying to escape a gang rape by fellow male students. The teacher testified that the boys did not mean the girls any harm; they only wanted to rape them.

These are not easy matters to comprehend except by women themselves – how they carry deep within themselves the deep scars of centuries of social discrimination.

Women's empowerment is a complex process, challenging all the existing laws, customs and practices; in fact, the whole male-dominated and male-interpreted structures. To change this structure would require a patient, long-term process. But it would also require institutional mechanisms strong enough to withstand powerful pressure groups especially at the national level and to coordinate and reinforce the important work that is going on at the international level.

The UN actions in the seventies and eighties have prepared the stage for women's advancement for the 1990s and beyond. The World Conference of the International Women's Year held in Mexico City in 1975, the World Conference of the United Nations Decade for Women held in Copenhagen in 1980, and the World Conference to Review and Appraise the Achievements of the United Nations Decade for Women held in Nairobi in 1985, were milestones in raising consciousness on women's issues nationally and globally, and in identifying actions to promote gender equality, ensure integration of women in development process and to highlight women's role in fostering world peace. These were the finest hours of the United Nations to stem the tide of inequality and injustice toward one-half of humanity.

The Nairobi Forward-looking Strategies for the Advancement of Women established ambitious objectives for the achievement of equality between men and women by the year 2000. The UN system-wide medium-term plan for women and development adopted in 1987 by the Economic and Social Council of the UN translated the objectives of the Nairobi Strategies into concrete plans for the UN system to implement during 1990–95. The UN Secretariat and the sectoral, functional and the inter-governmental bodies were requested by the General Assembly to help implement the medium-term plan. This led to the establishment of institutional arrangements in over twenty organisations – from a division to a one-person focal point to deal with the different aspects of women's advancement. But there are three UN entities which are concerned exclusively with this issue:

- The Commission on the Status of Women monitors the implementation of the Nairobi Forward-looking Strategies at the intergovernmental level primarily by means of its review of coordination reports on activities for women's advancement by the UN system. The Commission exercises more a moral authority than any executive or operational authority.
- United Nations Development Fund for Women (UNIFEM) serves as a catalyst to ensure integration of women in mainstream development activities and supports innovative and experimental activities directly benefiting women. The total income of UNIFEM to carry on these activities was about $12 million dollars for 1993.
- International Research and Training Institute for the Advancement of Women (INSTRAW) carries on long-term research and training programmes for women at national and international levels.

Other UN agencies such as UNDP, UNICEF, UNFPA and WFP are making significant contributions towards women's advancement at the field level.

The coordination of all these activities for women's advancement by the UN system is the responsibility of the Economic and Social Council. But in view of the involvement of such a large number of agencies, these activities are subject to very inadequate and infrequent intergovernmental reviews.

As the UN system is getting ready for the fourth World Conference on Women, this might be a good moment to ask ourselves: are the existing mechanisms set up for women's advancement adequate? Specifically, do the existing arrangements have the mandate to work for women's advancement in all the areas that touch on women's lives, as UNICEF has for children and UNFPA for population? Does any of the agencies specifically set up for women's advancement, such as UNIFEM or INSTRAW, have enough financial resources to back up its programmes? Do they have the kind of institutional structure that would give them sufficient strength within the UN system to influence national policy-making?

A brief review of the current institutional arrangements for women's advancement suggests that their main characteristics are multiplicity of actors, diffused mandate, limited financial resources and inadequate interaction with national governments. On the eve of a new century, fresh rethinking is needed on the approaches used so far for women's advancement and on the institutional arrangements made to implement the policies. The time has come to ask whether we need to establish a special UN agency for women's advancement with a specific and clear mandate, independent executive board, independent fund-raising ability and institutional arrangements for undertaking projects and programmes in individual countries as well as monitoring progress at national level.

The principal objective of the agency should be to elevate women's advancement and empowerment to the top of national and international policy agendas, to monitor specific achievements and failures in this field on a regular basis and to provide a coordinated policy framework for the ongoing efforts of the international system, including the UN.

Its focus will need to be on policy and strategy formulation and on advocacy. The agency will need to provide some modest financial support to countries in the areas of training, catalytic projects and networking, building, for example, on the current operational activities of UNIFEM and INSTRAW.

The agency can be conceived as an umbrella organisation with some existing facilities and programmes grouped under its jurisdiction so that the agency is established not as a new addition but as an efficient and cost-effective use of existing structures and resources.

The agency should have the explicit responsibility for monitoring gender concerns in policy and actions in all UN agencies.

The challenge for the forthcoming World Conference on Women is to articulate the policy and implementation strategy for women's empowerment at national and international levels. Four years ago, I wrote a paper proposing the establishment of a UN agency for the advancement of women. Since then the proposal has been receiving a lot of support in view of the fact that there is a role for such an organisation if we want to go beyond sensitisation and actually make things happen at national levels.

No one will suggest the establishment of yet another new machinery lightly, especially at a time of aid fatigue and reduced aid budget. But here the real question is whether the existing international, or national arrangements, have gone much beyond tokenism, or beyond the conscience-raising role, and whether real empowerment of women in the twenty-first century will require a different approach.

REFERENCES

1. United Nations, *The World's Women, 1970–1990* (New York: United Nations 1991).
2. NDP, *Human Development Report 1993* (New York: Oxford University Press 1993).
3. *The Washington Post*, 'Third World, Second Class' 14–18 February 1993.
4. Khadija Haq, 'The Role of the UN For the Advancement of Women – A Proposal', SID, Development, 1989:4.
5. UN Economic and Social Council, Development and International Economic Cooperation: Effective Mobilization and Integration of Women in Development, A/48/70, E/1993/16.
6. UN General Assembly, 'Advancement of Women: Note by the Secretary General', A/47/340, 13 August 1992.
7. United Nations Secretariat, 'Special Measures to Improve the Status of Women in the Secretariat', ST/AI/382, 3 March 1993.

12 Biases in Global Markets: Can the Forces of Inequity and Marginalisation be Modified?

Frances Stewart

THE ADVANCE OF THE MARKET

Marketisation was a universal phenomenon in the 1980s – in developed countries under the influence of monetarism and the leadership of Thatcher and Reagan, in the developing countries largely as a result of pressure from the IMF and World Bank, and in Eastern Europe, with the collapse of communism. The advance of markets was both a domestic and an international development. The progressive dominance of domestic markets arose largely as a result of conscious political decisions. While these also influenced global markets, their advance was as much the product of forces outside conscious control – including technology change and especially the communications revolution, migratory forces, and institutional developments. Domestically, marketisation meant reduced state interventions, reduced subsidisation and increased privatisation. Internationally, global markets became increasingly important while systems of regulating these markets were haphazard, biased, non-existent or in retreat.

As well as the advance of the global market, the 1980s saw a marked worsening in world disparities both among and within countries: among developing countries, some areas experienced accelerated progress, notably in much of Asia; but elsewhere – in most of Africa and Latin America – the decade saw a significant decline in average incomes – the first decline of this magnitude and duration since the Second World War. At the same time, worsening inequalities within countries occurred in both North and South.

This essay is concerned with global markets, and with international mechanisms to reduce inequity and marginalisation in this context. Little will be said about the need for domestic institutions to regulate domestic markets and prevent inequities and marginalisation. But it should be noted that domestic measures are at least as important as international ones. Governments may be relatively powerless to steer the course of world markets, but they can protect their own people from the excesses of the market. Conversely, there could be a good international system which protects countries, but if gross inequities emerge within countries, such a system will not succeed in protecting poor people – and since it is people rather than countries with which we should be concerned, domestic measures to control the market and protect the vulnerable are generally more important than international. This is, indeed, just as well, since while it is quite easy to identify changes in the international system which would help prevent international inequities, it is much more difficult to envisage (and even more to bring about) the political conditions in which such changes are plausible.

Global markets include the operation of international financial markets; the actions of transnational corporations, involving flows of technology, finance and management; trade flows; technology flows; and flows of people, both skilled and unskilled.

Each type of global market has increased rapidly over the last two decades; each is becoming increasingly significant, when expressed as a proportion of domestic resources (i.e. resources produced and used in the same country).

International financial markets first expanded on the basis of the recycled earnings of the oil-producing countries in the 1970s. Large surpluses (and deficits) in the world have continued to fuel the markets, while deregulation and technology change led to the effective internationalisation of many of the world's financial markets. Computerised dealings are estimated to transmit more than $300b across national borders each day (UNDP, 1992). Between 1979 and 1989, the share of cross-border equities in total turnover more than doubled from 6 per cent to 14 per cent. Unregulated financial flows can cause severe problems for both developed and developing countries; financial movements can finance growth without adjustment, as in many countries in the 1970s, leading to the accumulation of debt and an unsustainable development path. For many Latin American countries, a major source of problems in the 1980s lay in the excessive bank lending of the 1970s. Speculation on financial markets may lead to sharp exchange rate fluctuations, unjustified depreciation or appreciation, and can cost governments billions of dollars in one day, effectively transferring resources from governments to those (the upper 1 per cent of the world's income earners) who participate in financial markets.[1]

From the point of view of inequity and marginalisation, however, it is the distribution of the capital flows which is the major issue. During the

1970s, flows to developing countries were large, but in the 1980s there was a very substantial net transfer out of developing countries – of $25.4b. in 1990, i.e. a movement from countries of the South to higher income countries in the North. The distribution of private flows among developing countries favoured middle-income countries. Low-income countries, which accounted for nearly three-quarters of developing country population, received 15 per cent of gross disbursements in 1970 and 8.6 per cent or below in the 1980s (Table 12.1). Among low-income countries, Asian economies suffered particularly from a proportionately low share of the lending (and also, as a result, more fortunately, of a lower than proportionate share in the negative flows in the 1980s). Sub-Saharan economies' receipts from the private sector were broadly in line with their population in 1970, but by 1983 they received only 5.6 per cent of the disbursements (compared with a population share of 12 per cent). Developing countries also pay more for borrowing than developed countries. Between 1980 and 1985, average real interest rates among six developed countries were 4.4 per cent, while average interest paid on foreign debt by six developing countries was 16.8 per cent (UNDP 1992, Table 4.2).

Transnational corporations have acquired increasing significance over recent decades. By the early 1980s, trade between the 350 largest TNCs amounted to an estimated 40 per cent of global trade.[2] Global sales of foreign affiliates in host countries are estimated to have grown by 15 per cent p.a., 1985–90,[3] much faster than the growth of output. TNCs dominate interna-

Table 12.1   Financial markets: private sector flows to developing countries

	1970	1980	1983	1990	Population (%) 1991
Gross disbursements					
to all dev. countries ($b.)	4.1	54.8	44.4	34.5	100.0
of which % to					
SSA	12.2	9.5	5.6	4.1	11.9
S. Asia	2.4	1.5	3.6	3.8	27.6
Low-income countries	14.6	8.6	8.6	7.8	73.8
Net Transfers					
to all dev. countries	1.1	12.2	–18.1	–25.4	100.0
SSA	18.2	19.6	15.5	2.0	11.9
S. Asia	–3.6	3.2	1.8	8.7	27.6
Low-income countries	20.0	17.2	14.9	15.4	73.8

Source: World Bank, *World Debt Tables, 1990–91* (World Bank: Washington, DC); World Bank, *World Development Report, 1992* (World Bank: Washington, DC).

tional technology flows: for the US four-fifths of technology receipts are intra-firm, and over 90 per cent for Germany. Even in more arm's length forms of technology transfer, the source of technology supply largely consists in the 'same multinationals which dominate direct foreign investment'.[4]

Developing countries receive only a small proportion of the total financial flows associated with TNCs. Foreign investment in developing countries fell in the 1980s, recovering at the end of the decade. The share of developing countries in global foreign direct investment fell from 31 per cent in 1968 to 25 per cent (1980–84) to 17 per cent (1988–89). In 1980–85, it amounted to an estimated 0.4 per cent of GDP of developing countries.[5] However, the net resource flow (deducting repayments but not dividends) represented by FDI as a proportion of total net external financing for developing countries as a whole fell from 23 per cent in 1984 to 14 per cent in 1986, rising to 20 per cent in 1990.[6] FDI is concentrated in a few mainly middle-income developing countries: three-quarters went to ten countries in the 1980s: Brazil, Singapore and Mexico received over a third of the flows; China, with 10 per cent of the total, is the only low-income country among the 'top ten' recipients.

The dominance of the TNCs contributes to marginalisation in the global economy not only by their concentration on industrialised countries, and among developing countries on middle-income countries, but also by their impact within developing countries – in particular, through the promotion of 'inappropriate' consumer products and often also of inappropriate technology.[7] Their huge size and headstart in terms of R & D and product development, marketing and management skills also makes it difficult for local companies to compete effectively, and thus inhibits the development of local management and technological skills.

The movement of TNCs is inextricably bound up with *the technology market* – as noted above, much technology transfer occurs within the TNC, and the remainder is largely dominated by TNC suppliers. The growth of international technology transfers represents another dimension of globalisation. For the five major industrialised countries, receipts from technology transfer (royalties, fees and technical services) had risen to over $200b. in the mid-1980s, from $27b. in 1973.[8] For the US and UK, about 20 per cent of receipts were from developing countries, with a higher proportion for Japanese technology exports. Although developing country exports of technology have grown, the great majority of transfers are within the North or North–South. This North–South transfer brings with it financial costs, determination of the direction of technology change (often in an inappropriate direction) and loss of local control over decision-making. Technology contracts generally involve strict limitations on action by the recipient, including restrictions of markets and of technology development and transfer.[9]

The global nature of finance and technology markets is to some extent – at least in terms of magnitudes – a new phenomenon. These markets substitute for and also stimulate the more conventional global market – that of *trade in goods*. Substitution occurs as the movement of finance and technology permits relocation of production in consuming areas. Stimulation occurs as the transfer of finance and technology generates imports of capital goods and recurrent inputs in the recipient area, and exports of the output of the new production facilities in a product cycle fashion.[10] International trade has grown faster than production for many decades, partly in response to these forces, partly to reduced transport costs,[11] and partly to trade liberalisation. Export volume grew 1.6 times the rate of world output in the 1980s, 1.25 in the 1970s and 1.4 in the 1960s.[12] In 1990, the total volume of world trade amounted to $3400 billion compared with $130 billion in 1960.

The expansion of world trade presented an opportunity for rapid development for those developing countries able to participate fully, especially in the export of manufactured products. Twelve countries had export growth of over 10 per cent p.a. in 1980–90, and another 11 countries had growth of between 5 and 10 per cent. But over the same period, 21 countries experienced annual falls in exports. The rapid export growth countries were more concentrated among middle-income countries (three-quarters of the over 10 per cent growth and over 70 per cent of the 5–10 per cent growth), while the falls were more concentrated among low-income countries (14 of the 21 countries).[13]

A major problem for many low-income countries was the almost unprecedented fall in commodity prices which occurred over this period. Between 1980 and 1991, a weighted index of 33 commodities (excluding energy) fell by 45 per cent.[14] The deterioration in terms of trade for some commodities was such that countries whose export volume expanded at a respectable pace actually suffered a loss in export earnings. This was the case for cocoa production in Ghana, for example. The counterpart of this deterioration was improvement in the terms of trade of consuming countries (i.e. the North). Within manufactures, also, the terms of trade for products produced by developing countries worsened (although not as sharply as primary products). The gainers were producers of high-technology products.[15]

The unequal benefits conferred by international trade were partly due to the workings of market forces: labour-surplus economies inevitably receive poor terms of trade compared with labour-shortage economies as supplies of exports expand until the labour surplus is absorbed. But the situation was compounded by interventions in the market:

- the patent laws and other ways of protecting returns from new technology deliberately prevent market-determined prices, in the interests of technology producers. These permitted high-technology producers to earn rents not available to low-technology producers.[16]
- trade liberalisation was uneven, with restrictions maintained on many developing country products. Effective rates of protection imposed by industrialised countries against developing country products are higher than those on developed country products, costing developing countries an estimated $40b. p.a. The Multi-Fibre Arrangement is estimated to cost developing countries $24b. p.a. in export earnings. In addition, export-restraint arrangements among GATT members were concentrated on agriculture, steel, electronics, clothing and footwear.[17]
- subsidisation of agriculture by the North hurts net exporters of relevant agricultural products including many developing countries who are actual or potential exporters.
- adjustment policies required by the IMF and World Bank contribute to adverse trade conditions: first, they encourage expansion of primary commodities in a number of countries producing the same commodity, leading to worsening prices. Secondly, they demand import liberalisation of developing countries where they have leverage, but have no leverage over the protection imposed by developed countries. Consequently (aside from the controversial effects of the measures) developing countries are forced to cede a bargaining tool which they might have used to reduce developed-country restrictions. Thirdly, the policies often encourage respect for 'intellectual property rights' – i.e. for practices which permit monopoly rents to be earned on sales of technology to the Third World.

The *labour market* is another sphere where the global market has advanced and developed countries have gains to make, but it has been severely restricted in the area which would most benefit developing countries. Movement of highly skilled workers – from South to North – has been encouraged, but there have been very strict (and increasing) restrictions on the movement of unskilled labour. In the US (itself liberal compared with most Northern countries), skilled workers accounted for 75 per cent of the total migration from developing countries in 1986 compared with 46 per cent twenty years earlier. The brain-drain has had serious costs for developing countries – Africa is estimated to have lost 60 000 managers between 1985 and 1990, for example, while 60 per cent of doctors trained in Ghana have migrated.[18] Restrictions on migration of unskilled labour cost poor countries huge sums in loss of potential remittances (estimated at

$50b. p.a. on conservative assumptions), while they cost poor people even more, since the migrants themselves would gain and those left behind would also gain from remittances and a tightening in the labour market.

This brief account of the advancing global market suggests the following conclusions:

- it has represented an opportunity for some countries, which have used the financial capital and technology transfer to expand production and exports, leading to rapid and sustained economic growth. Malaysia is a good example: economic growth per capita was 4 per cent p.a., 1965–90; export growth was 4.3 per cent p.a., 1965–80 and 10.3 per cent 1980–90; primary commodities fell from 94 per cent of exports in 1965 to 56 per cent in 1990; the investment rate was 34 per cent in 1990 (including a high rate of foreign direct investment), and the savings rate almost as high at 33 per cent; there was also significant progress in human indicators (for example the IMR came down to 15 per thousand). (It is worth noting that Malaysian domestic policies by no means followed the *laisser-faire* market model; with its New Economic Policies designed to improve the position of the Malays it represented a prime example of a 'structured' market.)
- the impact of the global market has been uneven. Some countries were unable to make use of the opportunities, suffered negative resource flows, falling export volumes and worsening terms of trade. An example is Madagascar, with a fall in per capita income of 1.9 per cent p.a., 1965–90; exports rising 0.6 per cent p.a., 1965–80 and falling 1.5 per cent p.a., 1980–90; primary commodities remaining at over 85 per cent of exports throughout the period; the investment rate was only 7 per cent in 1965 but rose to 17 per cent by 1990, with savings rising from 0 to 8 per cent. The IMR in 1991 was 113.
- liberalisation of the global market was biased towards changes favouring the rich countries; liberalised financial markets favoured lenders rather than borrowers; 'liberalisation' of technology markets had inbuilt restrictions favouring technology suppliers; 'liberalisation' of the goods market was uneven, and discriminated against products from developing countries; and restrictions on the labour market were designed in the interests of recipient developed countries.

INEQUITIES AND MARGINALISATION

The advance of the global market had consequences both for inter-country and intra-country income distribution.

Worsening global inter-country income distribution is shown by the 1992 *Human Development Report* – see Table 12.2. The share of the poorest 20 per cent in the world dropped from 2.3 per cent of world income (1960) to 1.4 per cent (1989) and there was a corresponding worsening in the Gini coefficient. The widening regional disparities are shown on Table 12.3. Sub Saharan Africa, South Asia, China and Latin America all showed a deterioration in per capita incomes relative to world averages, while East and South-East Asia, excluding China, Arab states and industrial countries showed an improvement. The least developed country group had the worst performance. By 1989, per capita incomes of this group were just 6 per cent of world average per capita income, while the industrial countries' was 3.7 times the world average.

Table 12.2 Global income disparity among countries

	% of income		
	Poorest 20%	Richest 20%	Gini coefficient
1960	2.3	70.2	0.69
1970	2.3	73.9	0.71
1980	1.7	76.3	0.79
1989	1.4	82.7	0.87

Source: UNDP 1992, Table 3.1.

Table 12.3 Widening disparities: ratio of share of world income to share of world population

	1960	1989	1989 as ratio of 1960
Sub-Saharan Africa	0.27	0.13	0.48
S. Asia	0.16	0.12	0.75
E. & S.E. Asia (ex. China)	0.19	0.29	1.53
China	0.14	0.09	0.64
Arab States	0.38	0.50	1.32
Latin America	0.66	0.52	0.79
All developing countries	0.23	0.20	0.87
Least developed countries	0.15	0.06	0.40
Industrial countries	2.67	3.68	1.38

Source: Derived from UNDP, 1992, Table 3.7.

The evidence on intra-country income distribution is not available for all countries, but the available data show that the trend was towards increasing inequality in most countries. Between the mid-1970s and 1980s, there was evidence of worsening income distribution in each of eight OECD countries[19] and in almost every Latin American country for which there is evidence.[20] There is no evidence for Africa: while some have suggested that policy reforms there may have improved income distribution,[21] there is evidence of rising poverty in large numbers of countries. In Asian countries, income distribution worsened in some countries (e.g. Thailand, Pakistan, Sri Lanka, the Philippines and China), remained unchanged in some (Malaysia, India) and improved in rare cases (Indonesia).

In many countries, the poor suffered from worsening inter-country income distribution, compounded by worsening intra-country income distribution. Both trends are associated with the advance of market forces. Moreover, the same philosophy which promoted marketisation also led to meso policies which favoured the rich and hurt the poor – for example, a move from direct to indirect taxes so as to encourage enterprise and attract foreign investment, cutbacks in public expenditure, including social service expenditure, the introduction of fees on health and education, and reduced food subsidies.

In summary, the advance of the global market was associated with worsening world income distribution and a lesser effort on the part of governments to counter these effects. Internationally also, governments did less to offset adverse primary income distribution as the ratio of aid to developed country GNP fell, while the distribution of aid was broadly anti-poor, more going to richer countries per head than to poor ones.[22]

CAN THE FORCES OF MARGINALISATION AND INEQUITY BE MODIFIED?

The question can be answered at different levels: first, is the issue of whether changes in policy can in principle be devised which would moderate forces making for inequity and counter some of the effects; secondly, there is a more problematic issue of whether, once these changes have been identified, there is any way of getting them put into effect given the politics of the international economy. Contributions to reforming the global system often stop at the first question, but the second is equally important and more difficult to answer.

Action may be taken at the national level, among groupings of countries, or at the global level. Political obstacles to reform increase with the level of decision-making. Thus while it is tempting to devise a new world blueprint, this is probably the least useful activity. All three levels will be considered here.

A. National Action

Nations, individually, have to take the broad framework of the international system as a given, and try to improve their own position (and that of vulnerable groups within the nation) in that context. We may distinguish three broad national strategies:

(i) exploiting the dynamics of the market, while protecting vulnerable groups internally;
(ii) withdrawing from the market;
(iii) using the market selectively, and bargaining for improved conditions.

The last strategy merges into (i) or (ii) depending on the interpretation put on each.

(i) As already noted, some countries – especially in East Asia – were very successful in exploiting the market, as well as protecting their vulnerable groups. Essentially, they succeeded in securing high and sustained growth of manufactured exports, facilitated by high savings and investment rates in physical and human capital, while maintaining a steady performance in agriculture (see Table 12.4). These countries did not simply open their economies to the new market forces, but followed an active policy of development of infrastructure and of human resources, selective import protection together with an interventionist industrial policy, while also adopting policies to protect the weaker members of their society.[23] In this context, they were able to exploit the international markets for technology, goods and finance.

The critical issue is whether other marginalised countries could follow this strategy. One question is the aggregation issue raised by Cline. This does not seem a serious objection to the strategy given that different countries are bound to follow at different paces, while success in some countries will raise world trade and thus possibilities for others.[24] More serious is whether the more marginalised countries have the *preconditions* of infrastructure, human resources and industrial experience to make this a possibility. Each of the successful countries went through quite a long period in which they were building up resources and experience behind protective barriers. They were able to finance this through high levels of savings and foreign investment.

Table 12.4 Some characteristics of successful Asian performers

	Growth in GNP per capita (% p.a.) 1965–90	Literacy rate (%) 1975	1990	GDI (% GDP) 1990	GDS 1980–90	Export Growth (% p.a.) 1965	1980–90
Malaysia	4.0	60	78	34	33	4.6	10.3
Thailand	4.4	82	93	37	34	8.6	13.2
Indonesia	4.5	62	77	36	37	9.6	2.8
China	5.8	n.a.	73	39	43	4.8	11.0
Hong Kong	6.2	90	n.a.	28	33	9.1	6.2
Singapore	6.5	75	n.a.	39	45	4.7	8.6
Korea	7.1	91	>95	37	37	27.2	12.8
All low-income countries	2.9	36	62	31	28	5.1	5.4
Low-income ex. China & India	1.7	36	55	27	20	5.8	1.5
All middle-income countries	2.2	69	65	23	22	3.9	3.8

Source: World Bank, *World Development Report 1992* (Washington, DC: World Bank); World Bank, *World Development Report 1979* (Washington, DC: World Bank).

For most countries in Africa at the moment, many of these preconditions are lacking. Moreover, current pro-market policies are reducing the possibility of realising these preconditions by cutting public expenditure on infrastructure and human resources, and focusing on primary production and removing industrial protection; domestic and foreign finance is deficient.

Adoption of this strategy is feasible for countries close to realising the preconditions – such as India, Bangladesh, Sri Lanka and some Latin American countries. But for African countries still very heavily dependent on primary products, the objective has to be first to realise the preconditions, and this means a partial withdrawal from the market, while the preconditions are developed. Above all, diversification first of production and then of exports is needed from primary production to exports, and the build-up of infrastructure, human resources and experience which will permit this.

(ii) The withdrawal option is neither politically feasible nor economically desirable in the current context. It involves turning away from all the opportunities represented by new technologies, overseas experience, finance and trading opportunities. But it should be recognised that countries that have adopted such a strategy in the past have managed to bring about a fair distribution of income and a high degree of social security – as in Cuba, China in the 1960s and 1970s and Tanzania. But there have been economic costs, which are probably greater today than in the earlier context, as there is less potential external support for such a strategy.

(iii) The selective approach to the global market, however, does offer real benefits compared with a complete opening or a complete withdrawal. Indeed, it could be argued that the successful countries identified under option (i) in fact were practising a selective approach. For example, most adopted some degree of import protection, some industrial intervention, and some limitations on foreign direct investment. Selectivity concerns policies towards both the international and the internal market. As noted in the earlier discussion, selective import protection is essential for countries with very limited manufacturing sectors. Active industrial policies may be needed. Both Japan and Korea also adopted a selective policy towards the import of technology, to help develop domestic technological capacity. The rolling back of the state – including in the social sectors – that currently forms part of the pro-market adjustment packages – also needs to be seriously modified if the vulnerable are to be effectively protected and human resources developed, with health, education and some safety-net mechanisms provided free for low-income groups.

Another aspect of this approach is the use of an active bargaining stance with respect to the international conditions facing the country – including over market access, debt negotiations and resource flows. Large countries have considerable bargaining power on their own – e.g. China has used control over its own market to improve access of its products overseas. But small countries – precisely those most likely to be marginalised – are in a much weaker position. Hence the need for groups of countries to negotiate together.

B. Groupings of Countries

Groupings of countries can improve their position in the world market in two ways – by increasing their bargaining position with the rest of the world, and by undertaking joint activities (e.g. financial, trade, research, marketing activities) jointly, thereby increasing the division of labour and exploiting economies of scale. These joint activities not only have virtues in their own right but also improve the group bargaining power.

(i) *Bargaining*. It is apparent from analysis of the nature and workings of the global market that it is the product not simply of free-market ideology – because if it were the market for unskilled labour would be as free as the market for industrialised country exports – but also of power and interest. Lacking power, developing countries find their interests neglected. Group bargaining can increase countries' power and therefore improve the market conditions they face. What is needed is for countries in the South (one country or a group of countries) to define a change they want and to threaten operational interests in a convincing way until it is achieved. Divergent interests within the South make it unlikely that there is enough in common across the South as a whole for an effective bargaining strategy to be evolved. (Indeed, that was one weakness of the New International Economic Order (NIEO) which tried to cover the whole of the South.) For some purposes the bargain may best be conducted by just one country; for others, small groups of countries; similarly, for some purposes the bargain may best to be struck with one country or a subgroup of Northern countries, not the North as a whole.

Bargaining can be conducted on the basis of different aspects of the international system; for each, different groupings would be appropriate.[25] For example:

- Producer power (as with OPEC) – i.e. the power to withhold supplies;
- Buyer power – the power to remove purchasing power from one market and switch it to another, or withhold it altogether;
- Debtor power – or the power to refuse to make debt servicing payments;
- Political power – or the power to switch alliances;
- Migrants power – or the power to threaten massive migration;
- Environment power – the power to hurt the global environment by national action;
- Nuclear proliferation power – or the power to threaten nuclear proliferation.

There are examples of most of these types of power being exercised effectively. For example, Mrs Gandhi threatened to withhold a major contract from a British company unless the British backed the sixth IDA replenishment, which they subsequently did. Another example is when a British quota on textiles from Indonesia was significantly raised after the Indonesian government cancelled contracts for British machinery and aircraft. Political factors explain the strong support given to Turkey and Pakistan in the cold war years. The potential threat of migration led to

Italian support for Albanian development and is one factor behind NAFTA. The environmental weapon has been used by India and Brazil to improve their conditions in the Uruguay round. The possibility of nuclear proliferation is being used as a threat by China and by the Ukraine, the latter using it to secure more aid as well as political protection.

Bargaining and groupings need not be alternatives to multilateralism. They can be used in order to secure a more satisfactory type of multilateralism. It would appear that this is the current strategy of the US, Japan and Europe in the Uruguay round. As a result, if the Uruguay round comes to a successful conclusion, the interests of these countries are likely to be better incorporated into the agreement than those of less powerful countries. It is noteworthy that a recent analysis of the potential benefits from the Uruguay round found gains for all areas of the world except the weakest, Sub-Saharan Africa, which is expected to suffer a net loss.

The weakest and most marginalised countries also tend to have weak bargaining power. But when they are grouped together, this is not always the case: for example, effective agreements among commodity producers can improve the returns to producers: a spectacular example is the diamond market, where a single private monopolist is able to sustain world prices hugely above 'competitive' prices. The ANDEAN Pact (which broke up for political reasons) was used to improve the conditions of technology transfer to the region, with quite spectacular results. Collectively, poor countries also have strong debtor power; migration potential; and environmental power. Poor marginalised countries may also improve their position by joining groups of more powerful developing countries, who can assist in negotiating skills as well as greatly enhancing the power of the group.

The claims made for the NIEO by the Third World in the 1970s in some ways did a disservice to developing countries by suggesting that they could negotiate as a group – an impossible aim, given divergent interests. The NIEO also made the mistake of appealing to the goodwill of the North, rather than using a bargaining approach. A group approach has also been undermined by the prevalent market ideology – enforced and reinforced by the IMF and World Bank who always negotiate country by country and make it clear that any group approach by developing countries would result in a seriously second-best solution which departs from the market ideal, and who have also invariably disparaged any attempts to present group solutions (e.g. the ECA Plan of Action) as intellectually flawed. The agenda has been presented as *either* a perfect market *or* groups, bilateralism and second-best solutions. Yet the true agenda is *either* a biased market *or* groups and more equity in the global market.

(ii) *Economic groupings of countries.* There are many arguments favouring the creation of groupings of developing countries to increase trade, ease financial flows, enhance transport links and conduct joint activities subject to economies of scale. Low-income countries would benefit from trade arrangements which permit them to combine more competition and more division of labour and economies of scale, while retaining some protection from competition from much more advanced countries. These groupings would also ease joint bargaining. Despite a quite high failure rate, there have been successes in developing such groupings – e.g. CARICOM (for the Caribbean), ECOWAS (West Africa) and ASEAN (South-East Asia).

C. Global Solutions

A blueprint for world institutions to prevent or offset inequities and marginalisation might contain the following ten elements.

I. Institutions to ensure satisfactory global economic management, eliminate large economic fluctuations with high unemployment rates, prevent huge surpluses/deficits arising which disrupt other countries, and speculative capital movements leading to excessive exchange rate fluctuations. These were precisely the functions Keynes intended in Bretton Woods in 1944. But then and after, the institutions that were created at Bretton Woods have become corrupted so that they do not in almost any way fulfil the intended role.

● they play no role in providing resources (e.g. through credit creation) when world demand is inadequate. Indeed, by constant stress on the importance of controlling inflation, and exclusive focus on conditionality of deficit countries, the IMF has a deflationary impact on the world economy.
● the 'scarce currency' clause was never invoked, thereby eliminating any control over surplus countries.
● since the move to floating exchange rates, world economic institutions have done nothing to prevent exchange rate fluctuations.
● they have played only a marginal role in recycling surpluses.

Any attempts to coordinate the world economy and promote its prosperity take place outside the Bretton Woods institutions – in the G-7, or Europe and in bilateral meetings. The result is they are rather sporadic, there is no body responsible for briefings and analysis of what is needed, and no one responsible for seeing that decisions are followed up. All action takes place at the national level. International institutions have nothing to contribute.

World economic growth is at least as important for the 'marginalised' countries as for others – since commodity prices and market access depend on it. It follows that an essential aspect of the blueprint will be an international institution, responsible for analysis and decision-making, whose objectives are to maintain steady growth of world output, prevent massive imbalances emerging, recycle surpluses and avoid large exchange rate fluctuations. Two options arc possible: one is a world security council, with appropriate staffing, whose decisions are binding on member countries; the other is a true world bank, which can create currency and spend it, pronounce currencies to be scarce, intervene in currrency markets, etc. Technically, the second would be a neater solution; politically, the first would appear to be more likely, given the history of the deviation of IMF and World Bank from the founders' intentions.

II.   International mechanisms to support commodity prices. An International Commodity Office (ICO) – possibly part of an International Trade Organisation as proposed at Bretton Woods – would determine – after research and negotiations – an initial minimum price for each commodity and a range below this for permitted price falls. The ICO would investigate options for maintaining prices for different commodities, including taxation of production by producing countries, international stockbuying (to be resold if prices rose above the minimum), national production quotas, etc. Ideally, the scheme would be financed by a tax on importers of those commodities, which varied inversely with the price of the commodity. A more ambitious scheme would finance the purchase of the commodities by newly-created SDRs, thereby adding to world demand at a time when it was deficient.[26]

III.   A true GATT in which developing-country products were treated on a par with developed countries, i.e. extending GATT rules to textiles, agriculture etc. A new scheme of special preferences – to apply only to the least developed – would give special access (where access remains restricted) and reduced tariffs for all products, primary and manufactures, emanating from least developed economies.

IV. A TNC Regulatory Mechanism (TRM): in the new global economy, there are almost no mechanisms for regulating TNCs. The United Nations special agency for TNCs has recently been abolished, while UNCTAD, which did much useful work in documenting developments in this area and developing a Code of Conduct, has been diverted from this area. While national companies are subject to national taxation and regulation, and anti-monopoly legislation, the much more powerful multinational companies can avoid much national taxation and are subject to no international regulations of their behaviour with respect to accounts, taxation, monopolistic behaviour, etc. Countries compete to attract TNCs, reducing wages and labour protection and giving generous tax incentives.[27] This is one element behind the shift to indirect taxation. The weaker the country, the more they offer and the less regulation they provide. The TRM would define a Code of Conduct for TNCs, ensure that they pay fair taxation in each country, disallowing special incentive schemes, regulate conditions of technology transfer, including restrictions imposed on recipients, lay down minimum labour conditions and investigate oligopolistic or monopolistic behaviour. The Code might also include environmental clauses. Penalties for non-observance of the code could take the form of internationally imposed fines, or of reference to national courts.

V.   A new approach to intellectual 'property', recognising that legal systems which protect such property represent a departure from competitive ideals, developing a system of fair prices and protection which (a) will incorporate the need for less developed countries to have conditions which encourage the development of local technological capacity; and (b) gives differential favourable treatment to the less developed countries.

VI. Reform of the distribution of aid resources so that aid is allocated according to three criteria: (i) in inverse proportion to development levels, as indicated by a combined index of per capita GNP (three-quarters weight) and growth in per capita GNP (one-quarter) over the past decade; (ii) in inverse proportion to access to private sources of finance (including borrowing and FDI); and (iii) in proportion to the human priority ratio.[28] Distribution of aid through multilateral channels should take into account the known distribution of bilateral aid.

VII.   An increase in levels of aid. Write-off of debt (official and private) of the least developed.

VIII.   A world social charter which defines social rights for all people in all countries, with associated mechanisms for their enforcement. Such social rights are already agreed in a general way in the International Covenant on Economic, Social and Cultural Rights (1976) and the Declaration of the Rights to Development (1986). The first requirement would be careful work defining the rights at each level of development. Minimal social rights would be common throughout the world, but above a defined minimum, social rights would vary according to income level. Once defined they should form part of the conditionality of aid donors, while deviation from them would be regarded as a justification for trade and other embargoes.

IX. Reform of conditionality towards a focus on social goals and economic growth. The current package focuses on stabilisation and marketisation. These would form part of the reformed package only in so far they can be shown to be necessary aspects of the achievement of social goals and economic growth. The new conditionality would need new (or radically reformed) institutions to enforce it, since the expertise, ideology and governance of the IMF and World Bank all support existing style of conditionality, and would have difficulty with the proposed new conditionality. Independent commissions, composed of government representatives, members of UN agencies responsible for social programmes and human development, and independent experts, could draw up proposed social and economic strategies incorporating the new conditionality.[29]

X. Finally, major reforms are needed in treatment of countries at war – to speed up and improve the distribution of relief, and to support human and economic development for countries at war.[30] Countries at war are in general the most marginalised of all.

Political Feasibility

The political feasibility of most elements in the blueprint does not seem high. The imaginative structure at Bretton Woods, and the Marshall Plan which followed and supported it, arose from the interests of the dominant economic power – the US – with the outcome of the plan – a more stable and prosperous world economy. As far as the Marshall Plan was concerned, US industry was the direct recipient of resulting trade, and without the Plan the US would have suffered. Today there is a more complex world economy, with three major sources of economic power, and also more complex politics. The present leadership of the US might have the imagination to support a new world order, but it lacks the economic surpluses to pay for it. Europe is lacking leadership and cohesion. Japan could take on the erstwhile role of the US, but shows no signs of wanting to: moreover, even if it did introduce a new Marshall Plan as a way of distributing the balance of payments surplus and of generating employment at home, the likely recipients would not be the 'marginalised' countries discussed in this chapter, but Russia, other members of the former Soviet Union and Eastern European countries. Trade negotiations are carried out in the interests of the three major economic powers, not those of the least developed.

The critical problem for those marginalised by the global market is that their marginalisation is not just a matter of economics but also of politics and, because of this, they cannot expect that a new system will be introduced which offsets the negative effects of the market. At most they can hope for marginal improvements in the world system – e.g. some reform in aid distribution and minor changes in conditionality. This is why the earlier discussion of what countries can do for themselves – including bargaining for better treatment by the international system – is of greater relevance than the more utopian discussion about a new international system.

NOTES

1. On 'Black Wednesday', 16 September, 1992, the British government lost around $3b.
2. Oman quoted in Ghai (1993).
3. United Nations (1992) quoted in Ghai.
4. Lall (1987).
5. Data from UNDP (1992).
6. Data from IMF (1992).
7. For example, Langdon shows how TNC investment in the soap industry in Kenya was larger-scale, with more capital-intensive technology, more expenditure on product promotion, more packaged and standardised products than local competitors. The latter were forced in the same direction by loss of market to foreign investors.
8. United Nations Centre on Transnationals (1987).
9. These were documented by UNCTAD in the 1970s – see UNCTAD (1976).
10. See Vernon (1966), Hirsch (1967).
11. World Bank (1992b).
12. GATT (1990).
13. Data from World Bank (1982a).
14. UNDP (1992).
15. UNDP (1992) estimates that nominal prices of manufactures produced by industrialised countries rose by 35 per cent over the 1980s while those produced by developing countries rose by 12 per cent.
16. See Krugman (1979).
17. UNDP (1992).
18. UNDP (1992).
19. Boltho (1992).
20. Cardoso and Helwege (1992); Stewart (1992).
21. E.g. Dorosh and Sahn (1993) – but no hard evidence is available.
22. White and McGillivray (1991).
23. See Wade (1990); Amsden (1989); UNDP (1990).
24. See Ranis's reply to Cline – Ranis (1982).
25. Streeten (1975) was among the first to analyse different types of bargaining power accessible to poor countries, exploring difficulties involved in exercising bargaining power and ways of overcoming these difficulties.
26. This is similar to the scheme of Hart, Kaldor and Tinbergen (1964).
27. Singapore, for example, has recently reduced the Corporation Tax rate and increased investment incentives, specifically 'to maintain Singapore's

competitiveness as an investment location'. *The Financial Times*, 27 February 1993.
28. Government expenditure on human priorities expressed as a proportion of GDP. 'Human priority expenditures' are those expenditures which provide basic goods and services most likely to contribute to human development. A minimal definition includes primary health care, primary and secondary education, and basic water services. For further elaboration, see UNDP (1992).
29. As proposed by Ranis (1989).
30. See discussion in Stewart (1993).

REFERENCES:

Amsden, A., *Asia's Next Giant: South Korea and Late Industrialisation* (New York: Oxford University Press, 1989).
Boltho, A., 'Growth, income distribution and household welfare in the industrialised countries since the first oil shock', Innocenti Occasional Papers (Florence: UNICEF, 1990).
Cardoso, E. and Al. Helwege, 'Below the line: poverty in Latin America' *World Development*, 20, 1, 1992.
Cline, W., 'Can the East Asian model be generalised?', *World Development*, 1982.
Dorosh, P. and D. Sahn, 'A general equilibrium analysis of the effect of macroeconomic adjustment on poverty in Africa' processed (Washington, DC: Cornell University Food and Nutrition Policy Program, 1993).
GATT, *General Agreement on Tariffs and Trade: What It Is Is, What It Does* (Geneva: GATT, 1990).
Ghai, D., 'Structural adjustment, global integration and social democracy' in D. Prendergast and F. Stewart (eds), *Market Forces and World Development* (London: Macmillan 1993).
Hart, A., N. Kaldor and J. Tinbergen, 'The case for an international commodity reserve currency', in N. Kaldor, *Essays on Economic Policy, II* (London: Duckworth 1964).
Hirsch, S., *Location of Industry and International Competitiveness* (Oxford: Clarendon Press, 1967).
IMF, *World Economic Outlook* (Washington, DC: IMF October 1992).
Krugman, P., 'A model of innovation, technology transfer and the world distribution of income', *Journal of Political Economy*, 87, 253–63, 1979.
Lall, S., 'Technology transfer, foreign investment and indigenous capabilities', mimeo (Institute of Economics and Statistics, Oxford University, 1987).
Langdon, S., 'Multinational corporations' taste transfer and underdevelopment' *Review of African Political Economy*, 1975.
Oman, C., 'Trends in global FDI and Latin America', paper presented at the Inter-American Dialog meeting, 1991.
Ranis, G., 'Adjustment, growth and debt fatigue: can the case-by-case and global approaches be combined?', Occasional Paper (San Francisco: International Center for Economic Growth, 1989).
Ranis, G., 'A reply to Cline', *World Development*, 1982.

Stewart, F., 'War and underdevelopment: can economic analysis help reduce the costs?' *Journal of International Development*, 5, 4, 357–80, 1993.

Stewart, F., 'Protecting the poor during adjustment in Latin America and the Caribbean: how adequate was the World Bank response?', L.D'A and QEH Development Studies Working Papers (Oxford: Queen Elizabeth House, 1992).

Streeten, P., 'Dynamics of the New Poor Power' in G. K. Helleiner (ed.), *A World Divided: the Less Developed Countries in the International Economy* (Cambridge, Cambridge University Press, 1975).

UNCTAD, 'Technological dependence: the nature, consequences and policy implications', in *Proceedings of the United Nations Conference on Trade and Development*, Fourth session, Vol. III, *Basic documents*, TD/190, 1976.

UNDP, *Human Development Report 1992* (New York: United Nations, 1992).

UNDP, *Human Development Report 1990* (New York: United Nations, 1990).

United Nations, *World Investment Report: Transnational Corporations as Engines of Growth* (New York: United Nations, 1992).

Vernon, R., 'International Investment and International Trade in the Product Cycle', *Quarterly Journal of Economics*, 53, 190–207, 1966.

Wade, R. *Governing the Market* (Princeton: Princeton University Press, 1990).

White, H. and M. McGillivray, 'Descriptive Measures of the Allocation of Development Aid', processed (The Hague: Institute of Social Studies, 1991).

World Bank, *World Development Report* 1992 (Washington, DC: World Bank, 1992a).

World Bank, 'Global economic prospects and the developing countries' (Washington, DC: World Bank, 1992b).

13 Poverty Eradication and Human Development: Issues for the Twenty-First Century

Richard Jolly

> Our age is the first generation since the dawn of history in which mankind dared to believe it practical to make the benefits of civilization available to the whole human race.
>
> Arnold Toynbee

VISION AND GOALS

When Toynbee wrote these lines in about 1947, the world was still a world of empires, wide gaps between developed and what were then called 'under-developed countries', school-enrolment ratios were mostly low, smallpox was endemic and infant mortality rates were three times present levels. Few developing countries had experienced sustained and rapid economic development, or the impressive advance in basic human indicators we have seen over the postwar decades.

Toynbee's vision was all the more impressive given any lack of hard experience to rest it upon. It serves as a reminder of the vision of many of the post-Second World War thinkers – and of the need for vision today. If today, we are to look ahead with creativity to the challenges of the next century, we also will need to build beyond the solid base of past experience. We will need the intellectual courage shown by the drafters of the UN Charter and the founders of the Bretton Woods organisations, who rose above the painful events of the Second World War and of the prewar failures to look beyond to the world needing creation.

The architects of change were also bold at that time in considering international actions needed to achieve national economic and social objectives. One example was the 1949 UN report, *National and International Measures towards Full Employment*.

Today, we may look ahead boldly to the eradication of absolute poverty. We have a number of solid experiences to build upon, notably:

- the considerable progress made over the postwar decades, socially and economically, in both developed and developing countries;
- the new recognition that government has an important role to play, nationally and internationally, in place of the widespread scepticism about government in the 1980s;
- with the end of the cold war, the new opportunities and a growing willingness to use the UN and international agencies as a catalytic force for international action.

There are already, in the early 1990s, more specific openings available on which to build towards Toynbee's vision.

1.   Goals have been defined and agreed. Among the most relevant are the goals of *Agenda 21* for humanitarian and sustainable development agreed at the United Nations Conference for Environment and Development in Rio in June 1992. *Agenda 21* looks to the progressive alleviation of the various aspects of absolute poverty, as a central element in sustainable development. The specific goals of *Agenda 21* drew on goals and commitments from a variety of earlier conferences and meetings: the Amsterdam Declaration on Population and Development; the Jomtien Conference on Education for All by Year 2000; the World Health Assembly, which defined specific targets within the broader goal of HFA-2000, Health for All by the Year 2000; the World Summit for Children which brought these and other goals together in a political commitment for the 1990s.

Agreement on international goals is hardly new: the novel element in the cases of the two Summits is the commitment to prepare national plans of action, as a means of adopting and adapting the global goals to the specifics of individual countries. At the time of writing, over 90 countries have prepared national plans of action to implement goals for health, nutrition, water and sanitation, and education, usually including family planning and reduction of gender disparities; another 50 to 60 countries have such national plans of action in the process of preparation.

2.   Proven strategies now exist. For all the difficulties of the 1980s, decisive progress towards poverty eradication and human development has been and is being achieved, in a growing and impressive number of countries throughout the world. Countries in South-East Asia first showed it was possible, desirable and cost-effective to combine rapid economic development with clear advances in human development, usually with investments in education leading to economic investment and rapid

economic advance. But broader elements of human development have also been combined with economic advance. Thailand, for example, reduced serious and moderate malnutrition from 15 to 1.5 per cent over the 1980s; Korea established universal access to a national health system between 1977 and 1989; Indonesia reduced its under-5 mortality rate from 131 to 86 between 1980 and 1991. East and South-East Asia's practical experience of combining rapid economic development with impressive advance in basic human indicators provides models which are increasingly attracting attention in other countries.

But the success stories are by no means confined to South-East Asia, let alone to countries which have achieved rapid rates of economic growth. UNDP's Human Development Report shows that South–North gaps have narrowed over the last two or three decades in *all six* Third World regions with respect to life expectancy, under-5 mortality, adult literacy and access to safe water. Calorie supply has also increased, except in Sub-Saharan Africa and parts of Latin America and the Caribbean. In all continents, there is a core of countries which have shown clear human advance over a wide field of human indicators – and many countries which have shown that rapid progress is possible in targeted areas. No less than 72 countries expanded immunisation and achieved the target of 80 per cent coverage by 1990, mostly beginning from low levels in the 1980s, but now saving the lives of at least three million children each year and helping set the stage for actions which will further reduce fertility and population growth. Under-5 mortality rates are now below 70 in 41 developing countries and another 31 smaller countries with more than a million population – a level not attained by most industrial countries until after the Second World War.

There has also been a dramatic reduction in deaths from natural disasters. Famine, if not eliminated entirely, has been sharply reduced in all parts of the world, except in areas of severe conflict: all of South-East Asia, most of Asia (excluding Afghanistan), almost all of Latin America and the Middle East, and also – it appears after 1991–92 – much of southern Africa.

3.   Positive experiences exist to demonstrate that rapid progress in human development is possible on a regional and global scale worldwide. Over the 1980s, 1.3 billion gained access to clean water, slightly more than the total number who had access in 1980. In all Third World regions except sub-Saharan Africa, malnutrition was reduced in all categories of malnutrition save anaemia among women. Access to primary health care increased and, as mentioned, immunisation and use of oral rehydration accelerated greatly. Contraceptive use increased to 49 per cent in developing countries as a whole and fertility fell further to 3.9 children per family in 1990,

compared with 6.3 in 1960. Thus the gap required to reduce fertility to replace population levels has more than halved in the years after 1960.

There are considerable differences between regions and countries underlining this broad pattern of success. In several respects, progress in the 1980s was slower than in the previous two decades. Most important, for the least developed countries and for sub-Saharan Africa as a whole, progress was more limited than elsewhere and, in many respects, the 1980s were years of decline rather than advance.

4. Popular support for human development is strong. Sample surveys of public opinion in most of the industrial countries consistently show popular support for international assistance to poorer countries providing such assistance is directed to poor people and is broadly cost-effective. Indeed, many such surveys show that a majority of the population of industrial countries would support an *increase* in aid if they are assured of these conditions. Aid-weariness and aid-pessimism by these tests is often exaggerated – and is mostly associated with the use of aid for other purposes, such as trade promotion or political advantage.

These four elements all provide a firm basis of opportunities on which to build towards Toynbee's vision: goals, proven strategies, positive experiences and popular support are all there. What is needed is decisive action to build positively on this base of opportunities.

SEVEN CRITICAL STEPS

Seven steps are needed in the mid-1990s to accelerate and sustain action over the short-to-medium term – essential to achieve the goals of the Year 2000.

- First, clear political commitment and serious mobilisation, nationally and internationally;
- Second, identification of a limited agenda of practical goals, building progressively from mid-decade goals to more ambitious goals for the year 2000. Already goals agreed internationally and nationally provide a starting-point for this. Such goals need to be adopted and adapted at local level and planned year by year to provide a steady build-up of action and achievement;
- Third, participation at district and local level in developing countries, in support of national action focused on priorities that match local needs and local capacity in areas where national and international support are forthcoming;

- Fourth, mobilisation of the media with their unprecedented outreach and capacity to influence and energise. The media need to be engaged for the task of mobilising awareness and action – and sustaining interest and commitment by reporting on results. The media's potential for education is still grotesquely under-used, especially in developing countries.
- Fifth, a macro framework is needed to combine poverty reduction and accelerated action to meet basic human needs. Such framework is needed within each country. Such a framework should also guide each aid donor; action on both tracks is required to meet the goals in a comprehensive and sustainable fashion.
- Sixth, adequate resources should be mobilised nationally and internationally, primarily by restructuring and better prioritising existing expenditures. Only a country-by-country analysis can establish precisely what is needed. But in most countries, restructuring of existing government budgets can provide most and often all the resources needed, providing serious weight is given to priority social sectors and reasonable cutbacks are made in lower priority areas, especially in military expenditure and unnecessary subsidies. In countries where public expenditure forms a low share of total GNP, some increase in taxation may be needed. All such restructuring will be made easier if undertaken in the context of reasonable rates of economic growth along the lines set out twenty years ago in strategies for *Redistribution with Growth*.

Among aid donors, the need to restructure aid towards priority social sectors is long overdue. A doubling or trebling of the share of aid going to priority social sectors is the challenge – but a reasonable one, especially at a time when aid expenditures in total are unlikely to increase. A restructuring of aid towards human development would accord with popular thinking, with rates of economic return and with many public declarations that this is a desirable change in aid policy. Although figures are somewhat uncertain, it still seems that most donors allocate less than 10 per cent of their aid to such priority sectors.

- Finally, monitoring systems need to be built up nationally and internationally. Without this progress towards the mid-decade and year 2000 goals will not be possible. Monitoring is obviously a requirement for technical and administrative assessments of progress. But monitoring is also needed as an important mechanism of political mobilisation, to provide popular evidence of progress and a stimulus to everyone to take the next steps.

These seven steps are vital if countries and communities are to move from the rhetoric of poverty-reduction and human development to its reality. They are also needed to avoid the build-up of negative coalitions of scepticism and disbelief, which too often in the past have undermined action for serious progress. Amartya Sen has stressed this point in arguing that the world could abolish deaths from famine within a few years if only the objective were taken seriously. But, instead, he says, 'One of the problems that makes the task of the prevention of famines and hunger particularly difficult is the general sense of pessimism and defeatism that characterizes so much of the discussion on poverty and hunger in the modern world. While pictures of misery and starvation arouse sympathy and pity across the world, it is often taken for granted that nothing much can be done to remedy these desperate situations, at least in the short run.'

There is, in fact, little factual basis for such pessimism and no grounds at all for assuming the immutability of hunger and deprivation. Yet those unreasoned feelings dominate a good deal of public reaction to misery in the world today. He adds, '....famines are nearly always avoidable, even after gigantic natural disasters. Sensible public action, including appropriate legislation, can systematically eradicate large-scale starvation altogether'.[1]

INTERNATIONAL SUPPORT

In financial terms, $25 billion has been estimated as the total resources required to meet the basic goals in the areas of health, nutrition, water sanitation, family planning and basic education.[2] Roughly one-third of this is needed to be mobilised internationally by industrialised countries, the remaining two-thirds within developing countries. Regionally, Africa is estimated to require relatively more support from outside. Half of the $9 billion required in total for sub-Saharan Africa would need to come from abroad, the remaining half from internal resources.

As important as resource mobilisation, is a clear restructuring of national and international priorities. Internationally, the World Bank and the IMF have critical roles to play, in close partnership with agencies of the United Nations. The policy framework papers and the sectoral policy papers generally prepared by developing countries with the World Bank need to reinforce and focus more clearly on the poverty objectives; so also should Consultative Groups and Round Tables. Thus many of the mechanisms already exist. The challenge is to use these mechanisms to direct and monitor accelerated advance, country by country, towards poverty eradication and human development.

At country level, the country strategy notes, being developed by the UN as a coordinating mechanism for inter-agency support, can be used to ensure coordinated action by the United Nations system towards the goals of poverty eradication and human development.

The World Social Summit planned in April 1995 provides an excellent opportunity for building further these commitments. Action should not wait until the Summit but rather the Summit should be used as a target-date by which to have many of these building-blocks in place. The Summit can then be used to assess what is needed to take these commitments further on a broader and more effective basis.

Finally, the development of compacts between individual countries and a core of supportive donors would serve as a catalyst for accelerating action and as a mechanism for sustaining it over the inevitable fluctuations year by year. The need for such compacts has increasingly been discussed in the last few years. Support for poverty eradication and human development might be the appropriate focus for their introduction, perhaps initially on an experimental basis in a dozen or so countries.

AN AGENDA FOR THE TWENTY-FIRST CENTURY

All the above provides a double agenda for the years until the end of the decade. But what of the agenda beyond, of the challenges of the next century and the next millennium?

Without doubt, international economic decision-making for the next century will require much broader vision and longer-run goals. *Agenda 21* contains some glimpses of the issues which must be addressed – issues of environment and sustainability, life-styles and consumption patterns, technological change and a more integrated approach to management of science and economic development. All of these raise complex and controversial questions, which experience in the United Nations Conference on Environment and Development in Rio shows are difficult to tackle at present. They become matters for the long-run agenda for which more thought, more research, more analysis of experience and more debate are needed before agreement can be reached.

Three particular issues must be put high on the long-run international agenda. First, is the need to go beyond issues of poverty reduction and human development to issues of greater global equity in life-styles in both developing and industrial countries. The present gap between the richest and poorest groups globally is of the order of 150-to-one, exceeding many times the 26-to-one gap in Brazil, which is itself the largest inequality observed today between upper and lower social groups within any one country, and raises and complex issues of ethics, equity and political feasibility. Such gaps will be unsustainable.

Second, is the need to achieve reasonable standards of living and consumption, life-styles of happiness and fulfilment while consuming much lower levels of resources than typically found in the industrial countries today. This will be one way to moderate the ever-growing levels of inequality between the most industrialised countries and most of the developing countries. The very fact that the gaps in human welfare between developed and developing countries are so much less than the gaps in resource use is an indication of the economic inefficiency which needs to be tackled.

Third, is the need to move to different patterns of growth and development, nationally and internationally. This in turn will require different mechanisms to influence and underpin this growth. The international institutions will need to devise ways to influence these patterns, using the price mechanism, certainly but often going beyond it. Even now, both the United Nations and the Bretton Woods Organisations ought to set up working groups to explore these issues.

At present, inadequacies in all three areas have led to a pattern of global growth and resource use which will be unsustainable in the longer run. The World Banks's 1992 *World Development Report*, on 'Development and the Environment' stated that 'the key is not to produce less, but to produce differently'. This report went on to estimate that by the year 2030, world GDP may have grown to almost $70 trillion in real terms, three-and-a-half times what it was in 1990 – $20 trillion. Though this will have enabled a three-fold income in average incomes of developing countries as a whole, income gaps between the higher-income countries and most of the developing countries will have grown even further; and substantial regional differences will persist.

Equally important, though not mentioned in the Report, income gaps within many developing countries are likely to have grown absolutely, with the elites aspiring to higher life-styles still largely defined by those of the high-income countries, with average incomes of over $40,000.

These are issues which urgently need to be explored, with at least as much zeal as the industrial countries currently accord to issues of population growth. In terms of potential pressure on global resources, these issues of unequal consumption patterns have thirty to fifty times more impact on resource use than inequalities in population growth.

Fundamental questions should be raised. Are such widening gaps politically sustainable? Already barriers against far migration are being strengthened – even as the human injustice of such barriers becomes ever more evident. In a world of instant communications, universal access to television, growing tourism and travel to education, for how long will it remain possible to sustain ever-widening gaps? Will the frontiers between these gaps remain defensible when immigrants meet (or avoid) the immigration police, when tourists meet (or avoid) frustrated slum-dwellers, when Third World students challenge those materially much better off, by virtue of nothing other than country of their birth?

There are no certain answers to such questions. Pessimists will answer that inequalities have persisted within countries for hundreds of years. A moderate use of force and decisive action against the leading trouble-makers has usually proved sufficient to keep protest in check. Even popular education, over the last century, has often helped to nurture attitudes and beliefs for working within the system rather than challenging it – both in capitalist and in non-capitalist countries.

The question is not only whether such systems are sustainable, but whether they are desirable. One must ask, are the present patterns of growth and ever-increasing levels of consumption, necessary and cost-effective for happiness and human welfare? Paul Wachtel, a social psychologist, provided a devastating critique of US growth from 1950 to 1980, during which production soared three times and consumption per head roughly doubled. If the evidence of increases to happiness and welfare are so shaky, how robust is this growth pattern as a desirable model for the future for all the world?

INTERNATIONAL ROLES IN SUPPORT OF THIS AGENDA

What are the roles and comparative advantages of the various multilateral organisations in support of this agenda, both in its more immediate and its long-run elements? In particular, what are the roles of the Bretton Woods Institutions, the Regional Development Banks and the UN specialised and operating agencies?

At present there is in the industrial countries a tendency to underestimate the value and role of the UN agencies in contributing to economic policy-making and to direct support of development in developing countries. The Bretton Woods institutions possess much more resources, provide each year more capital and more technical assistance to developing countries and generally produce analyses of higher economic quality. By virtue of these characteristics (and of the voting control which the industrial countries possess) over them, the Bretton Woods institutions also wield much more economic influence. Notwithstanding this, the UN organisations also have important characteristics: much stronger field presence, a style of interaction with recipient governments given more by solidarity and political impartiality, and an approach to analysis which is, at its best, more technical and multidisciplinary. It is often forgotten that at least six Nobel prizewinners in economics have worked for the United Nations and that many of the basic innovations in Bretton Woods practices have grown out of analysis and recommendations first put forward by the United Nations and only later adopted by the World Bank or IMF, often after a period of initial opposition.

Even in terms of resource flows, the United Nations operational agencies may be relatively more significant in relation to the World Bank and IMF than is often realised. In recent years, the net transfers to Africa by the United Nations have exceeded those of the World Bank and IMF together, and they have been made on grant terms rather than as loans.

The basic point is that forceful committed support is needed from all parts of the multilateral system if the goals of human development and poverty eradication are to be achieved. All four pillars of the system must play their part, fully and together, if the goals of poverty eradication and more balanced global development are to be realised – and realised within a time horizon which is politically and economically acceptable.

Basic leadership must be taken by each country. But supportive actions by the multilateral community will often be critical – in resources, in exchange of experience, in help with monitoring and, perhaps above all, in encouragement and focused catalytic support. Conditionality will be less important than assurances of a long-term commitment and the avoidance of approaches or measures that may undercut on one hand what is being encouraged in poverty reduction and human development on the other.

At country level, the main mechanisms of coordination should be used to ensure strong and mutually reinforcing support: consultative groups and Round Tables, the resident coordinators and country sectoral teams. The new country strategy notes could play a strategic role in focusing multilateral support in each country on human development and poverty eradication. Catherine Gwin's analysis of the comparative advantage of the key multilateral partners makes clear that there are roles for all.

With this as background, one can move to a final point: the need to provide strong and collaborative support, but not necessarily in total bureaucratic coordination. There is strength in diversity, especially of views and approaches in situations where it is not entirely clear what is needed to be done in the longer run. Recognition of the need for *diversity* would legitimise a measure of international debate on uncertain or controversial elements. This will be critical if the multilateral system is adequately to look forward and probe the longer-run actions required for further progress towards poverty reduction and human development in the twenty-first century.

NOTES

1.   A. K. Sen, 'Public Action to Remedy Hunger', The Fourth Arturo Tanco Memorial Lecture, The Hunger Project, 1990.
2.   UNICEF and UNDP calculations summarised in *State of the World's Children Report, 1993.*

14 Role of the Multilateral Agencies after the Earth Summit

Maurice Williams

REDIRECTING DEVELOPMENT TO PROTECT THE ENVIRONMENT

The 1992 Earth Summit provided a vision of the seriously threatening environmental problems which the world would face if it continued on its current path of conventional economic development. The Conference highlighted a range of adverse effects that economic activities have had on local ecosystems – from loss of forests and plant and animal species to the pollution of air and water and land. Also alarming is the danger that increasing emissions of carbon dioxide and other 'greenhouse' gases could produce significant and possibly catastrophic changes in the global climate.

Both industrialisation and poverty are factors in environmental degradation. The developed countries have contributed disproportionately to worldwide emissions of carbon dioxide and they consume the lion's share of the world's natural resources. Developing countries have contributed a lesser share of greenhouse emissions, although this will change as their accelerating development efforts place increasing demands on finite resources to provide for their expanding populations. Overly-affluent consumption in the rich countries and the pressures of poverty and increasing populations on natural resource depletion in the poor countries combine to create an ominous threat to world ecosystems.

The Earth Summit concluded that what is urgently needed is a change in the nature of economic development in order to deal with the ever-widening scope of environmental degradations. In an increasingly global economy, the goal of environmentally sustainable economic growth recasts North–South relations in the context of interdependence and mutual responsibilities.

The Earth Summit agreed on a far-reaching Plan of Action to provide comprehensive guidance for fully integrating the environmental and economic dimensions into the development programmes of governments and development agencies. Parallel negotiations produced two framework conventions, on climate change and biological diversity. The main product of the Earth Summit, however, was the *Agenda 21* Plan of Action to protect the environment and promote sustainable growth into the twenty-first century

Agenda 21 created the conceptual and programmatic framework for a global partnership based on a mutuality of interests which all countries share in the need for policy reforms at the national level. For developing countries this task focuses on the importance of development assistance, both in terms of its volume and more effective use.

The industrial countries have not been forthcoming with increased financial assistance, in part due to recognition that developing countries cannot effectively mount expanded sustainable development programmes without a good deal of retooling of existing policies and programmes, reforms which *Agenda 21* strongly emphasised.

It also has been clear that under existing conditions of global economic recession and budgetary stringency a substantial portion of new funding must be obtained from redeployment of existing resources, in both developed and developing countries, as well as the reshaping of current policies and fiscal practices to provide incentives for investment in sustainable development from private as well as public sources.

The new emphasis on sustainable development coincides with current broad social movements that aim to increase popular participation in national economic and political life.

Agenda 21 gave major emphasis to human and institutional capacity-building as a basis for redirecting current development efforts and for new investment activity. A lead role for helping developing nations with capacity-building was assigned by *Agenda 21* to the multilateral agencies and specifically to the 'United National Development Programme, the World Bank and regional multilateral development banks, drawing on the expertise of the United Nations Environment Programme...'.[1]

ESSENTIAL MULTILATERAL FRAMEWORK FOR SUSTAINABLE DEVELOPMENT

Agenda 21 recommended a UN Commission on Sustainable Development (CSD), by means of which governments could review progress toward the goals of the Earth Summit and formulate an integrated approach to economic and environmental policy-making. The General Assembly established the CSD as a 53-member state body meeting annually and reporting to the General Assembly through the Economic and Social Council.

It was also agreed at the Earth Summit to restructure the Global Environment Facility (GEF), a pilot project set up in 1990 – with joint management of $1.3 billion over three years by the World Bank, the UN Development Programme (UNDP), and the UN Environment Programme (UNEP). The GEF funds projects that address global warming, destruction of biodiversity, pollution of international waters, and ozone depletion. Negotiations began at Rio to restructure the decision-making of the GEF centred on a proposed 'Participants Assembly' that could open policy-making to a majority of states.

Institution-building of the GEF and the Commission for Sustainable Development are fostering closer collaboration between the UNDP and UNEP and the World Bank which together constitute the key multilateral components for helping nations achieve environmentally prudent development.

- UNDP is the lead agency for technical assistance to help developing countries build capacities for sustainable development;
- UNEP is the agency charged with monitoring and assessing the critical state of global and regional environmental problems;
- The World Bank is the lead institution for policy advice, and for appraisal of global and national investment requirements and mobilising the means for meeting them.

Although the multilateral agencies only provide about 20 per cent of total official aid and have been slow to incorporate environmental criteria in their programme, they are looked to by major countries to lend coherence to the overall global effort of development assistance. There is need to clarify roles, strengthen capacities and assure that relationships among the agencies is mutually reinforcing.

This chapter reviews the strengths and weaknesses of each of the key institutions in terms of their respective responsibilities for implementing *Agenda 21* and the means to improve their performance.

UNDP AND THE TRANSITION TO SUSTAINABLE DEVELOPMENT

UNDP is at the centre of the United Nations development system for funding technical cooperation (TC). About half of TC activities of the UN system is funded by voluntary contributions through UNDP; the other half is provided by donors directly to the trust funds of the specialised agencies.

UNDP, as the central funding mechanism, is at the hub of the UN system for TC activities and, through its offices in 124 countries, exercises a pervasive influence on the system's relations with governments at the field level. For each TC recipient country, UNDP operates a system of aid programming which identifies aid requirements.

It is in this coordination role that UNDP convenes aid-donor Round Tables for the poorest countries to help them in the mobilisation of assistance. This parallels similar activity by World Bank Consultative Groups for developing countries with relatively large capital programmes. The Bank looks to UNDP to report on TC requirements.

The effectiveness of UNDP in fulfilling the role of adviser and coordinator of TC activities depends heavily on the experience of its country resident representatives. UNDP's annual funding is relatively small – about a billion dollars annually for an average of 1300 new project starts in 150 countries with an ongoing portfolio of some 6000 projects. UNDP professional staff are generally well-informed on developing country conditions.

Despite these assets and experience, UNDP's role in TC and its coordination has been a declining one. The decrease in UNDP funding has limited its effectiveness. Also the quality of its resident representatives is uneven. UN TC activities are often criticised for poor quality and inadequate funding of an overly-diffused number of small projects lacking central programme focus and adequate attention to building the skills and institution capacities of recipient countries – a critique which UNDP itself has acknowledged and seeks to remedy.

UNDP has reduced its dependence on UN specialised agencies for project design and execution, which currently only accounts for 30 per cent of its project funding. Hence, UNDP is neither an effective funding-coordinator of the system nor has it succeeded in becoming an autonomously effective development agency in its own right.

UNDP has sought to redefine its role and focus its programme mainly on the strengthening of developing country capacities to manage all aspects of the development process. As part of enhancing the management capacity of developing countries, UNDP has been expanding recipient execution of projects, in sharp contrast with past practice of favouring external executing agents.

And UNDP's Human Development Reports have gained worldwide recognition and focused attention on human and institutional assistance. A number of governments see UNDP as the lead agency for carrying out a principle objective of *Agenda 21*, namely the building of developing-country capacities for sustainable development.

At the Earth Summit, UNDP launched a Capacity 21 fund with a target of $100 million 'to help developing countries formulate economic, social and environmental plans, programmes and policies that lead to sustainable development'. Indications are that a total of about $30 million may be made available.

Despite this promising initiative, UNDP has not been fully effective in follow-up implementation, because of a budget crunch due to decline in donor contributions. The funding problem is symptomatic of a more serious underlying crisis given the uncertainties about reform of the UN and its role in development. UNDP is at a crossroads. It is no longer the central funding mechanism for the UN system and it lacks the staff for sustainable project design to provide content for Capacity 21.

UNDP looks to its field representatives, together with developing-country officials, to formulate the projects for Capacity 21. The need to strengthen field staffs is clear. Generally, 'CAPACITY 21 is a catalytic fund which will be used to facilitate environmental considerations in all programmes and to strengthen sustainable aspects of the programme'.[2]

UNDP has still to face the more fundamental changes required if it is truly to become the lead agency for technical cooperation and capacity-building in support of sustainable development, including the following recommendations:

● UNDP needs to strengthen further its professional staff capability for design, review and evaluation of capacity building projects. A central TC design and review centre for this purpose should be constituted to advise and service the TC operational activities of the UN system as a whole.
● Measures should be agreed to ensure that the TC activities of the system meet standards of excellence. It is not common funding but assurance of common standards of excellence which are essential to improve the performance of UN agencies.
● UNDP's core programme should be reviewed to ensure integrated concentration on capacity-building for sustainable development.
● UNDP, in consultation with developing country officials, should complete a comprehensive review of what needs to be done for early completion of sustainable development strategies for review by donors.
● UNDP experience on human and institutional capacity building should to be assessed as a guide to best practice and to avoid the mistakes of the past.

UNEP AND THE UNITED NATIONS ENVIRONMENTAL EFFORT

The 1972 United Nations Conference on Human Environment in Stockholm concluded that a special entity was required to ensure follow-up of a programme of environmental assessments and management, and to serve as a 'central catalyzing, coordinating and stimulating body on environment within the United Nations system'. In response, the United Nations Environment Programme (UNEP) was established in Nairobi.

With a relatively small secretariat and limited budget, UNEP has made good progress in laying the foundation for a global monitoring network and development of environmental law and policy, but it largely failed in environmental coordination with the United Nations. Governments recognised the need for a stronger coordination agency by establishing the Commission for Sustainable Development discussed above. Generally, however, governments have endorsed UNEP's ongoing programmes and reinforced its existing role, with some changes in emphasis.

UNEP has stressed that a key to dealing with environmental problems is generating scientifically reliable information and assessments. UNEP's annual reviews on key conditions and environmental trends are largely drawn from 'Earthwatch', a loose affiliation of programmes incorporating the research and monitoring efforts of the United Nations system.

However, the Earthwatch database is of variable quality, and much needs to be done to strengthen the collaboration of the agencies and programmes contributing to Earthwatch and to ensure that countries are able to use the information that is available. There is a particular lack of information about the environment in developing regions. In most sectors, the data also is not adequate on regional trends as a basis for policy evaluation.

To promote technical and programmatic contributions by scientific and other professional communities, UNEP – in collaboration with other UN agencies – commissioned independent experts to foster consensus on controversial policy matters. These have included programmes involving experts on marine pollution, desertification and climate change. The programmes receive inputs from operating agencies of the UN and their counterparts in national governments in cooperation with the scientific community.

UNEP encouraged START (Global Change System for Analysis, Research and Training) being developed by the International Council of Scientific Unions. The aim of START is to promote inter-disciplinary studies in 13 regional ecosystems to strengthen research capabilities in global change science and encourage their application by developing countries.

UNEP plays an important role in promoting international environmental law and policy. Early initiatives by UNEP led to the proposed 'Action Plan to Protect Stratospheric Ozone' which laid the basis for the Vienna Convention in 1985 and the subsequent agreement for the total phaseout of CFC production under the 1987 Montreal Protocol.[3]

Related work by UNEP, in collaboration with the WMO, led to intergovernmental negotiations on the Framework Convention on Climate Control. And it was UNEP which provided the impetus for negotiation of the Convention on Biological Diversity. UNEP initiatives also contributed to other important agreements on transboundary movements of hazardous wastes and protection of regional seas.

Less successful have been the combined efforts of UNEP, FAO and UNESCO to deal with the problems of degraded natural resources, such as desertification and loss of forests, where to date monitoring and assessment efforts have not led to significant international management programmes. *Agenda 21* highlighted the importance of future efforts on desertification and tropical forests.

Overall, UNEP has been engaged in helping governments with the environmental policies, practices, conventions and regulations which have emerged to form a growing body of international environment law. *Agenda 21* reiterated the major role of UNEP in further development of international environment law, and the importance of UNEP assistance to enhance national legal and institutional frameworks.

However, UNEP's efforts to introduce systematic environmental management practices into the UN system were largely frustrated. UNEP, with its small staff and limited funds,was largely marginalised by the major UN agencies. UNEP was able to encourage periodic discussions of specific issues and a report of environmentally related activities underway throughout the UN system – an exercise which had little effect on the programmes of the agencies or governments.

To summarise, UNEP has led in development of important monitoring and evaluation networks, and it has played a key role in extending international environmental law as well as adoption of methodologies for management of global environment problems.

Recommendations to further strengthen UNEP follow:

- UNEP should concentrate its activities in areas of its established comparative advantage, namely as the centre of expertise within the UN for monitoring and assessment and for expert advice on major environmental problems.
- Governments should substantially increase assistance in support of UNEP's monitoring and assessment of environmental problems at regional and global level. This would strengthen UNEP's important role in identifying emerging environmental risks and impending natural disasters.
- UNEP's work in environmental law and expert advice to governments should be strengthened.

- UNEP's expert advice should be readily available for periodic reviews of sustainable development progress and needs. At the global level UNEP substantive assessments will be essential to the work of the UN Commission on Sustainable Development. UNEP also should be appropriately staffed to assist the UN regional commissions in assessment of progress and programmes.

WORLD BANK RESPONSE TO THE ENVIRONMENTAL IMPERATIVE

The Bank was the first of the financing agencies to subject its project appraisals to environmental criteria, but their application has been quite uneven.

Only in 1986–87, during the presidency of Barber Conable, did the World Bank begin to take environment considerations seriously, and that was after a series of hearings by the US Congress which illuminated the flawed environmental practices of the World Bank. American NGOs were prime movers in mobilising public and Congressional attention to the failure to pursue sound environmental practices, citing many examples of poorly-conceived World Bank projects with adverse environmental effects.

During the Earth Summit preparations, the World Bank engaged in intensive efforts for integrating environmental protection into its decision-making processes by expanding its environmental research and adopting comprehensive procedures and methodologies for environmental assessments, and augmenting resources and staffs, including a new Vice-President for Environmentally Sustainable Development.

Responsibility for integrating environment concerns into the operation of the Bank rests with the regional bureaus. Each of the six regional vice-presidents has a regional environment division (RED) and there is a growing number of environment staffs within country departments.

The environment impact assessment (EIA) of prospective projects is central to the Bank's approach for integrating the objectives of environment protection into its lending programme. While it has been routine for the Bank to identify which prospective projects should undergo an environment assessment, in 1991 for the first time all Bank/IDA loans were given an environment assessment rating. Also in 1991 the World Bank issued a new and enhanced Environment Assessment Operation Directive.

Clearly the World Bank has adopted exemplary environmental directives and procedures which should help to guard against the major environmental mistakes of the past. Still, the problem of the Bank's environmental performance cannot entirely be met by directives. More fundamental are the operating assumptions of the Bank's country departments in appraising projects.

The operating assumption of Bank officials has been that there is a direct trade-off between economic growth and environment protection and that rather than dealing with the initial cause of environmental degradation, one means to mitigate its effects. However, there is no objective standard for determining how much environmental damage is acceptable and the usual compromise by Bank officials has been to seek assurances from developing-country recipients that they will undertake mitigating measures – assurances which often arc not fulfilled. The process facilitates approval of projects but the environmental costs are sometimes high.

This approach by the Bank has been severely criticised by some environmentalists, who would have the Bank apply more stringent environmental standards. Distrustful that the Bank's new directions are other than cosmetic, environmental NGOs continue to seek a more transparent information policy by the Bank, and an independent review process with mandatory power to block environmental abuses in Bank projects.

The elements of the Bank's new environmental strategy was outlined in the Bank's 1992 World Development Report, *Development and the Environment*.[4] The Report, drawing on the research work of the Bank rather than its operational experience, conveys the important conceptual conclusion that in most cases environmental protection and economic growth are compatible, given an appropriate policy framework.

Policies that are good for both environment and development include removal of subsidies on natural resources, clarification of property rights, and investing in education and family planning programmes, agricultural research and extension, and water and sanitation infrastructure. The appropriate policy involves correcting past market failures and distortions by price adjustments. These are the so-called 'win-win' policies of the Report. Different policies are required when there are negative links between growth and environment, based on assessing the relative costs and benefits of intervention and designing means to reduce environmental excess – such as pollution and deforestation. Policies are the key in either case.

The new environmental strategy proposes reformed market-oriented policies and more purposeful institutional reforms. The emphasis on institutional strengthening furthers the Bank's involvement in this area, since policies are only as effective as the capacity of institutions to execute them. Consequently, the new environmental strategy sees the Bank's role in both policy reform and institutional strengthening as being as important as its lending programme.

Given the scale and range of World Bank commitments – $21.7 billion for 222 Bank and IDA projects and programmes in FY 1992 – it is possible for the Bank to demonstrate activity in most of the 40 chapters of *Agenda 21*. By the Bank's own accounting, in FY 1992, 19 loans totalling $1.9 billion were *primarily* for environmental purposes (defined as projects with at least 10 per cent financing or estimated benefits for the environment). An additional 43 projects had a 10 per cent environmental component and are classified as environmentally *significant*. The criteria for such classification is highly judgemental in nature.

In line with *Agenda 21*, the Bank's overall programme emphasises the complementarity between poverty and environmental degradation and includes commitments to expand poverty reduction programmes. Under a new system of classifying projects with specific interventions for reaching the poor, or involving a measure of their participation, about 20 per cent of overall Bank lending in FY 1993 incorporated such interventions.

The Bank and Institutional Capacity Building

The World Bank has increasingly expanded the scope of its technical cooperation activities. For example, it has assumed an increasing role in the preparation of national environment studies and environment action plans (EAPs), appropriate regulatory frameworks, and in assistance to strengthening environmental institutions, technical training and monitoring regimes.

The Bank now requires all borrowers to prepare EAPs and has expanded their scope in line with the broader national sustainable development strategies initiated by UNDP. In each case, the country planning approach seeks to engage the participation of the local people concerned. The plans also seek to engage the donor community, both for their aid to country capacity building and as a means for donor coordination.

In summary, the Bank now sees institutional strengthening and capacity-building as an integral and highly cost-effective component of its new environment strategy. For only by strengthening the institutional capacity of developing countries will it be possible to achieve a balanced and effective mix of policies and investments.

Critique of the World Bank

While the Bank clearly has made great strides in its effort to integrate the goals of environment and development, there remain several questions about the efficacy of its approach. The first is whether the Bank's project appraisal and review process is now fully adequate as a safety-net against approval of environmentally flawed projects. The second is concern that the new environment strategy is overly economic in its approach and difficult in application for most developing countries without a good deal of training and on-the-ground adaption. And the third is whether the Bank is appropriately equipped to carry out the institutional capacity building required by its new strategic approach.

Effective change-over to the new strategy naturally will take time, both in terms of rolling over the Bank's portfolio to the new-style projects and retreading operating officials in the country departments to the new approach.

The Bank's new environmental strategy, as laid out in the *World Development Report 1992*, represents advanced conceptual thinking on the application of market-based policy reforms and environmental management. Pricing reform is the fundamental proposal for environmental sustainability in virtually all sectors of the economy. Application of the economic policies proposed by WDR 92 has been fairly limited. In fact, they are well in advance of current practice in most advanced industrial economies which have, for the most part, practised command-driven regulatory policies in their environmental programmes.

Application of the Bank's new environmental strategy will require adaptation to developing country experience, and institutional strengthening is the principal means envisioned for adaptation to the new policies, as well as conditionality linked to environmental targets.

Increased demands on the Bank in the area of environmental performance come in a period when the Bank is already heavily committed to a multiplicity of development tasks and increasingly criticised for an overly-directive style of dictating developing country policies and projects and, generally, seeking to impose its views by multiple conditionalities on its lending. The result is that developing-country recipients tend to accept conditioned lending more from necessity than conviction and increasingly ignore Bank-imposed conditions.

This situation explains, in part, the deterioration in the quality of the World Bank's loan portfolio as reported by former Bank Vice-President Wapenhans in a special 1991 *Report on Portfolio Management*. Measured by such key indicators as economic rates of return and not in compliance with loan conditions, the Report indicates that project performance by the World Bank Group was satisfactory up to 1973, somewhat irregular up to 1982, and declined sharply thereafter. In particular, borrower compliance was 'only 22% of the financial covenants in loan/credits agreements'.[5]

A group of developing country officials concluded that more Bank-financed projects would prove satisfactory if project selection and related policy options should be determined by them as borrowers rather than being dictated by Bank staff on a 'take it or leave it basis'.[6]

Given this experience, the Bank obviously will need to link appropriate institutional and policy capacity-building measures with the new-style environmentally sustainable projects. Since institutional strengthening for effective environmental development policy formation must be tailored to the specific circumstances of individual developing countries, and requires a close type of follow-up implementation support, the World Bank is not currently well-equipped for the task.

The Bank is a highly centralised organisation, with 6000 employees concentrated in headquarters and only some 100 posted in the field. With the high degree of centralisation in the control of operations from Washington, its generally low priority for technical assistance relative to capital lending, and the cost to its borrowers of loan-financed TC compared to the grant aid of the UN, the Bank labours under built-in constraints in using TC for institutional capacity-building.

Further, the Bank staff is more oriented to preparation of projects than their supervision. As the Wapenhans Report observes, the inbred organisational culture of the Bank primarily focuses on and rewards effectiveness in the headquarters process of loan project design oriented mainly towards gaining approval of the Bank's Governors. There is little incentive for the Bank staff to focus on the problems or successes of implementation, although this may be changing.

While the Bank is well equipped to handle traditional infrastructure and policy-based lending with its central staff, the Bank is not set up for effective technical assistance in areas related to environmental and social institutional development.

Recommendations for the World Bank

First, the Bank should appoint a full-time independent ombudsman responsible to the Bank's Board of Governors for on-going surveillance and review of adherence to Bank policies and procedures in project preparation, appraisal and follow-up execution. Such a watchdog function would assist in the transition to effective application of its recent new policies for poverty eradication and sustainable development, recognizing that the extensive new directives in these areas are well ahead of current practices within the Bank in many cases.

Second, the Bank generally should pursue a policy of transparency on the availability of public information concerning the environmental effects of the projects its finances. The Bank is already moving to implement a policy of providing prior information to people directly affected by projects it anticipates financing, which means insisting on full disclosure by the concerned member government.

Third, the Bank-sponsored Environmental Action Plans should be comparable with UNDP-sponsored National Sustainable Development Strategies. The Bank and UNDP should cooperate closely in assuring the timely preparation of these country sustainable development plans for funding reviews.

Fourth, the World Bank should limit its application of 'green conditionality' on its financing of development projects, stressing instead compliance by developing countries through well-formulated packages of related training and institutional strengthening to ensure that recipients have the capacity for compliance with the desirable performance standards.

Fifth, the Bank should join in the work of the proposed TC project design and review in UNDP, recommended above, and in the application of best experience in the formulation of TC capacity building packages for sustainable development for both project and free-standing sector development. Grant funding of essential TC packages for Bank-financed sustainable development projects should be available from UNDP-sponsored Capacity 21 as well as from bilateral donors.

CONCLUSION

The Earth Summit dramatised the necessity of shifting from conventional development strategies which seek to repair environmental damage to integrated strategies which prevent or at least minimise environmental degradation. And *Agenda 21* provides an action plan for redirecting development on an environmentally sustainable basis.

Since the Earth Summit, most nations are undertaking to change conventional patterns of production and consumption because of concerns that environmental degradation is becoming an increasingly serious constraint on development objectives and may actually reach irreversible thresholds which damage the earth's ecosystems. Developing countries face a particularly difficult task and require the best possible advice and assistance in their transition to sustainable development.

In general, the goals of environmentally sustainable development must be pursued in the ongoing investment and development programmes and by the national and international institutions directly involved. In this context the roles of the World Bank, UNDP and UNEP assume special importance.

The World Bank is well advanced in strengthening staff capabilities and adopting appropriate policies and procedures for incorporating sustainable development in its operations, but their fully effective application is still in progress. UNDP is at an early stage of building and redirecting its institutional capabilities for environmental development assistance. UNEP has achieved a sound programmatic foundation for environmental assessment and advice, one which now requires substantial improvement and expansion.

The close collaboration of these three key institutions has assumed increased importance, for sustainable development is inherently a process which demands an integrated application of functional inputs – capital investment, technical capacity building, and scientifically sound assessments. Each of the three multilateral institutions is dependent, in part, on the work of the other two for assuring the best results in fulfilment of its role.

NOTES

1. United Nations Conference on Environment and Development, Rio Declaration (New York, 1992).
2. UNDP Governing Council paper, 'The Follow-up to UNCED', May 1993.
3. Peter S. Thacher, *Global Security and Risk Management,* World Federation of United Nations Associations (Geneva, 1991), p. 17.
4. World Bank, *World Development Report 1992*, 'Development and the Environment' (New York: Oxford University Press, 1992).
5. Willi A. Wapenhans *et al., Report of the Portfolio Management Task Force* (internal World Bank document, 1 July 1992), p. 1.
6. 'Summary Proceedings of Conference with Borrowers', Annex B, *Report of the World Bank Task Force on Portfolio Management.*

15 New Challenges for Regulation of Global Financial Markets

Stephany Griffith-Jones

INTRODUCTION

This chapter starts by describing recent trends in private financial markets, both globally and in developing countries. Then it analyses the structural changes that have occurred in global private financial markets – particularly resulting from deregulation and liberalisation – and attempts to evaluate their benefits and costs. Based on this analysis, it attempts to define the increase – and change in the nature of – risk, particularly of a systemic type. Special reference is made to risks as they affect LDCs. The chapter then reviews some of the main aspects of the supervisory and regulatory response to the changes in financial flows and, above all, to changes in perceived risk which they generate. Finally, conclusions are drawn and policy recommendations made, the latter going from those which are fairly widely accepted (but not implemented) to those which would be more innovative.

RECENT TRENDS IN PRIVATE FINANCIAL MARKETS AND IN FLOWS TO DEVELOPING COUNTRIES

Globally, in 1992 borrowing on international capital markets continued its rapid increase for the second year in a row; in 1991, there had been a rapid increase (of 20.7 per cent) in the aggregate volume of international capital flows; in 1992, there was a further increase of 16.2 per cent (see Table 15.1). In fact, in 1992, global borrowing was at a level 54 per cent above its 1987 level.

Though borrowing on international capital markets by developing countries continued its increase, in 1992 to their highest level since the early 1980s, the growth (at 2.3 per cent) was negligible in real terms according to OECD estimates; it was also *far lower* than growth in 1991, when develop-

Table 15.1   Borrowing on international capital markets (US$b) (Borrower composition)

Borrower	1987	1988	1989	1990	1991	1992
OECD countries	349.6	413.8	426.5	384.4	457.9	535.7
Developing countries	26.3	22.5	21.8	28.6	46.2	47.3
Eastern Europe	3.7	4.6	4.7	4.6	1.8	1.5
Others	13.3	12.6	13.5	17.3	19.0	25.2
Total	392.9	453.5	466.5	434.9	524.9	609.7
Year-on-year per cent increase		15.7	2.8	−6.8	20.7	16.2

Source: OECD, *Financial Market Trends,* Vol. 54, February 1993, p. 7.

ing countries were reported to have had an increase of *62 per cent* in the volume of borrowing on international capital markets, from $28.6 billion to $46.2 billion (see again Table 15.1). In comparing with the 1987 level, developing countries' borrowing was at a level 80 per cent above its 1987 level. Thus, growth of lending to LDCs has been faster over the 1987–1992 period than that for global flows.

If we examine the share of developing countries' borrowing in the global total, this share first fell from 6.6 per cent in 1987 to 4.7 per cent in 1989, increased to 6.6 per cent in 1990, increased further to about 9 per cent in 1991, but declined somewhat in 1992.

Indeed, it was growth in OECD countries' borrowing which accounted for practically all the rapid growth of global borrowing in 1992, whereas in 1991 LDC borrowing had contributed fairly significantly to that growth.

As in previous years, the main dynamism globally in 1992 did not come from syndicated loans (which remained at approximately the same level as in 1991), but came from growth of securities and non-underwritten facilities (see Table 15.2).

As can be seen from comparing Tables 15.3 and 15.2, developing countries seem to follow similar trends to global ones, with declining importance of syndicated loans, (especially marked in 1992) and with sharp increases in securities (particularly important in 1992 in bonds, but also reflecting a continued large increase in equities). It is also noteworthy that non-underwritten facilities (which include Euro-commercial paper) have increased a great deal in 1992, reaching then the same level as equities.

It is worth noting that, according to other sources, such as the World Bank,[1] which have made major efforts to have complete coverage of these new flows to developing countries, the figures for private portfolio flows to

Table 15.2   Borrowing of the international capital markets (US$b; %)

	1988	1989	1990	1991	1992
Securities	234.8	263.8	237.2	321.0	357.2
Loans	125.5	121.1	124.5	116.0	117.9
Committed back-up facilities	16.6	8.4	7.0	7.7	6.7
Non-underwritten facilities[1]	76.6	73.2	66.2	80.2	127.9
Total	453.5	466.5	434.9	524.9	609.7
Memorandum item: Year-on-year percentage change	+15.4	+2.8	–6.8	+20.7	+16.2

1. Including Euro-commercial paper.
Source: *Financial Market Trends*, Vol. 54, February 1993, p. 87.

LDCs are somewhat higher. Thus, according to World Bank recent estimates (World Bank, op. cit.), *gross private portfolio flows to developing countries* grew explosively since 1989; indeed, these flows which averaged *under $6 billion a year* in the 1982–88 period, were estimated by the World Bank to have grown to an estimated $34 billion in 1992.

The increase has reportedly gone largely to a few countries in Latin America, where gross equity flows have grown more than tenfold in four years, (mainly via ADRs and GDRs) from $434 million in 1989 to an estimated $5.6 billion, and where bond financing increased almost fifteenfold, from $833 million in 1989 to $11.7 billion in 1992 (see Table 15.4).

Table 15.3   Borrowing by developing countries (OECD definition) ($b)

Instruments	1987	1988	1989	1990	1991	1992
Bonds	3.1	4.2	2.6	4.5	8.3	14.0
Equities	0.0	0.3	0.1	1.0	5.0	7.2
Syndicated loans	20.1	17.4	16.2	19.8	26.7	16.5
Committed borrowing facilities	1.3	1.3	0.9	2.1	4.5	1.3
Non-underwritten facilities[1]	1.8	1.2	2.0	1.2	1.7	7.9
Total	26.3	22.5	21.8	28.6	46.2	47.3

1. Same as in Table 2.
Source: OECD, *Financial Market Trends* Vol. 54, February 1993, Statistical Annex.

Table 15.4   Portfolio Investment in Latin America, 1989–92
(millions of US$)

Type of Investment	1989	1990	1991	1992[1]
Equity investment from abroad	434	1 099	6 228	5 570
of which				
Closed-end funds	416	575	771	293
ADRs/GDRs	–	98	4,697	4 377
Direct equity investment	18	426	760	900
Bonds	833	2 673	6 848	11 732
Commercial paper	127	0	1 212	840
Certificates of deposit	0	0	670	1 100
Total	1 394	3 772	14 958	19 243

– Not available.
1. Estimated.
Source: World Bank staff estimates.

Though the increase in securities flows to developing countries (and especially to Latin America) has been impressive, some analysts argue that these levels could be sustained or even increased, at least till the end of the century.[2] These kinds of 'optimistic' estimates are based on very aggregate projections and draw on facts such as: total of assets of pension funds, life insurance funds, mutual funds and others reach as much as $14 trillion; the share of their assets invested in developing-country stock markets is on average less than 5 per cent of foreign equity holdings, and *less than a quarter per cent of their total assets*; an increase in the share of industrial countries' institutional funds assets going to emerging markets from, for example, a quarter per cent to half a per cent could imply large increases of investments in those markets; similarly, it is also stressed that as emerging stock market capitalisation represented 6 per cent of world share of equity markets in 1991 (double its 1987 share), a share which is likely to increase, however, in coming years, there is considerable scope for international equity flows to LDCs if industrial country investors hold developing country stocks in proportion to the LDC markets' share in the global total.

Finally, though we will concentrate in this chapter on borrowing, it is interesting to stress that FDI flows to developing countries are estimated[3] to have increased significantly in recent years, both in value (from $9.8 billion in 1986 to $35.9 billion in 1991) and as a share of global FDI (from 13 per cent in 1986 to 22 per cent in 1991).

Though there may be specific causes encouraging FDI and lending flows to LDCs, the fact that both FDI and lending flows to LDCs are increasing in parallel, and roughly concentrating on the same region, would seem to imply that similar underlying common causes (such as improved growth prospects in certain LDCs, recession in industrial countries) are also very important in explaining all these flows.

STRUCTURAL CHANGES IN GLOBAL PRIVATE FINANCIAL MARKETS

Deregulation and Financial Innovation

During the last ten years, the size and the structure of financial markets has undergone profound changes.

The process of structural change is very complex (largely because it is not homogeneous across countries), and is therefore difficult to understand at a global level. There are, however, many common features in the direction and key features of the changes, practically in all countries.

The dominant initial force explaining these changes is deregulation, which considerably enhanced the role of free market forces in determining choices open to economic agents. By the beginning of the 1980s, many of the restrictions which previously limited competition (e.g. by restrictions on lines of business, geographical operation, quantitative restrictions on credit, interest rate and price restrictions, controls on foreign-exchange transactions and international capital flows) had either been removed or else been undermined by market developments. As we shall discuss further below, in this context of much greater freedom, strengthening of capital adequacy standards became the main regulatory constraint on bank portfolio choices.

As a result four trends seem to have clearly emerged. Firstly, financial markets have become increasingly globalised and integrated. Domestic markets became progressively more integrated with each other and with off-shore ones. Capital flows across borders intensified and the number of institutions operating in foreign centres increased. Furthermore, the global interlocking of national financial markets has far exceeded the global inter-locking of national productive structures, as the very rapid growth of international financial flows was far quicker than the growth of trade and direct investment.

Secondly, the size and the influence of markets in finance has increased markedly throughout all countries. Again, here there is a contrast with the past, as till the end of the seventies the importance of financial markets was more an Anglo-Saxon peculiarity. Indeed, the fundamental changes in the regulatory and technological environment increased competitive pressures and – in a broadly favourable macro-economic environment – led to rapid growth in financial activity and trading. The major expansion of the financial industry world-wide (as illustrated in Table 15.5) is reflected, for example, in a massive increase in turnover on all the major securities markets and in the explosion of the value of payments over the last decade; indeed, according to BIS (op. cit.) estimates, the ratio of annual value of financial transactions (measured as payments through the main interbank fund transfers system) to GNP in the three countries with the largest financial markets in the world grew dramatically and systematically, from less than 10 per cent in 1970 to over 75 per cent in 1990, for the US, from just over 10 per cent in 1970 to over 110 per cent in Japan and from around 10 per cent in 1970 to over 40 per cent in the United Kingdom.

Thirdly, there has been an important trend for dissolution (where it existed, e.g. in the United Kingdom) of functional boundaries, particularly between banking and securities activities. This has led to the creation of increasingly complex institutions, which integrate both types of activities.[4] In those countries (like the United States and Japan) where barriers remain, banks are however free to combine banking and securities abroad, and are increasingly finding ways round the law in their home markets. Banks had been weakened during the last decade by a decline of underlying profitability; partly this is due – on the asset side – because they have lost some of

Table 15.5   Indicators of growth in the financial industry

	Share in value added[1]		
Countries	*1970*	*1979*	*1989*
USA	4.1	4.5	5.7
Japan	4.5	4.9	5.6
United Kingdom	12.5	14.8	20.0
Switzerland	4.6	5.8	10.1
Germany	3.1	4.2	5.0
France	3.3	3.5	4.7
Spain	3.5	5.7	6.5
Australia[2]	8.5	9.0	12.1

1. GNP/GDP, plus imputed bank service charge, at current prices.
2. Includes real estate and business services.
Source: Based on data in BIS *62nd Annual Report*, Basle, June 1992.

their most profitable and safest business, as securitisation reduced the
demand for bank loans from prime borrowers, as commercial paper,
corporate bonds and other types of direct financing displaced bank lending;
it is also due – on the liabilities side – to the fact that banks have lost part of
their core interest free retail deposits, and are forced to bid for funds
against each other, which has implied an increasing use of more expensive
and less stable wholesale markets and a decline in the proportion of interest
free deposits. More broadly, as the cost of processing information fell, borrowers and lenders found it more feasible to deal with each other directly,
and by-pass the banks. Partly to compensate for this decline in banks'
profitability, banks, bank regulators and governments have started to break
down remaining barriers between banking and securities markets, greatly
enlarging banks' involvement in securities business. Though this integration of banking and securities generates economics of scope (and therefore
benefits to the consumer, both due to lower costs based on joint 'production
and marketing', and due to greater convenience of purchasing different
financial services from a single firm) it seems likely that it will increase the
risks to the financial system as a whole, because securities provide additional risk-taking opportunities by aggressively managed banking institutions. This is particularly so because there is empirical evidence (quoted
in Dale, op. cit.) that the securities business is riskier than any other financial activity, and because securities activities are less heavily regulated than
banking activities. The integration of banking and securities' firms (even in
countries with separate firms) could lead to conditions in which a shock
coming from the securities market could spread through the banks and
return (amplified) to the securities markets. The internationalisation of both
markets could make such a potential crisis international. Furthermore,
because the pace of product innovation in securities markets is so rapid,
risks in this area are increasingly difficult to assess, both by market actors
and by regulators.

Though deregulation was broadly more limited in insurance, by the early
1990s a few countries (especially in Europe) had eased restrictions on the
combination of insurance with banking business.

These changes have favoured the creation of complex conglomerate
structures, (often across national borders), which combine traditional banking services with various types of securities and – more recently, with the
provision of insurance. In the case of 'simple' banks, also a greater proportion of their credit and liquidity exposures was incurred off-balance-sheet.

Fourthly, as hinted at above, there has been a vast expansion of available
financial instruments, which was facilitated by the explosion of information technology. Many of these instruments (e.g. futures, options, swaps)

are very sophisticated, and the exact level of risk they generate is as yet unclear. As the range of financial instruments grew, a higher proportion became marketable. In the US, even bank loans and company receivables have become marketable.

Fifthly, there was a greater institutionalisation of savings, which provided a base for the expansion and greater sophistication of the securities markets. Their push towards international diversification was an important factor behind the internationalisation and integration of markets.

Evaluation of Structural Changes in Financial Markets

Deregulation was driven by the perception that constraints on financial activity were ineffective or caused important inefficiencies in the allocation of capital and operation of monetary policy. Then deregulation acquired its own momentum, as elimination of restrictions in some areas led to pressures for their relaxation elsewhere. A third reason for deregulation grew from differences in regulatory treatment.

(a) Benefits

Deregulation has delivered important benefits.[5] Thus, both original suppliers and final users of funds are able to obtain better terms, via a richer and higher-yield range of financial assets and easier as well as cheaper access to external finance. Securitisation is seen not only to allow for lower costs, but also for longer maturities, which is crucial for the market viability of certain types of activities, that only become profitable in the long term. The abolition of foreign exchange controls, and the broader process of globalisation widened the international choice, both in terms of diversification of portfolios and sources of finance. At one level, the wider range of available financial instruments allows for better distribution and management of risk. Furthermore, the fall in transaction costs has increased the liquidity of securities markets. Finally, capital can flow more freely towards higher returns.

As regards developing countries, the potential benefits of deregulation and globalisation are particularly high, as capital is relatively scarce, and thus the prospect of *larger inflows* via, for example, securities (particularly at a time when bank credit flows are far less likely to come in than in the past) and lower costs are especially attractive. It seems that certain instruments have been particularly beneficial in lowering the equity cost of capital in developing countries. Thus, international stock trading (through for example American Depository Receipts – ADRs) has proved to be a valuable mechanism for lowering LDC companies' cost of capital decline. Furthermore, the issuing of

ADRs is reported[6] to not only lower costs for individual firms but also to do so for other domestic firms via important spillover effects.

(b)   Costs

The issue that needs to be addressed is of the costs which deregulation has brought about, and of the measures that need to be taken (both nationally and internationally) to minimise those costs. Indeed, the changes brought about by deregulation and the freeing of market forces in the financial sector are creating new regulatory needs (such as capital adequacy requirements on financial institutions), which probably would not have existed had markets not been deregulated. It is argued in this chapter that these new regulatory challenges have only partly been met, and that urgent tasks (nationally, regionally and internationally) still need to be accomplished. This is largely because on the whole the development of regulation of markets tends to lag behind the changes that deregulation brought in the structure of the financial system. Particularly if the benefits of deregulation are valued, it is important to take measures that minimise costs, especially those that could disrupt in a major way the proper functioning of those markets, and have significant negative macro-economic effects.

The costs of financial innovation relate to greater financial instability and fragility, reflected in the form of very large fluctuations in asset prices and/or distress among financial institutions. Both asset prices and exchange rates have gone through periods of sharp fluctuations in the last decade. As the BIS (op. cit), correctly points out, the main source of concern is not short-term volatility (which if not extreme is relatively harmless), but longer-term volatility, especially when prices seem misaligned from their apparent sustainable levels, which lead to both misallocation of resources and the risk of large and disorderly changes.

One particular aspect of recent changes which may be important in contributing to explain capital market volatility is institutionalisation of savings.[7] Indeed, some US commentators blamed fund managers' portfolio strategies for causing volatility at the time of the 1987 Crash. More generally, the rise of global asset allocation as a tool of fund management, and the development of markets such as stock index futures stimulated and facilitated massive growth in short-term cross-border equity flows. Though the investors wish to reduce risk by such strategies, the focus of funds on a small number of leveraged instruments often destabilises markets and leads to sharp swings in asset prices; there is also evidence that switches of resources by large fund managers affect exchange rate developments.

More generally, the greater internationalisation and integration of the financial industry meant that shocks are more easily transmitted across borders, as well as from one market to another. This is particularly well illustrated by the global nature of the stock market crashes of 1987 and 1989.

Furthermore, regular performance checks against the market (as frequent as monthly in the US but less in the UK) may induce 'herding' among funds to avoid performing worse than the median fund, again with destabilising effects on the prices of assets.

The problems of rapid switches between markets are likely to be of importance in an international context as well as in national markets. There is evidence that this is likely to have greater incidence on volatility the smaller the market (as is the case for developing countries) and the greater the role played by foreign investors in it.

This is a special source of concern for developing countries, as traditionally the capital markets of LDCs show far greater volatility than those of industrialised economies. As can be seen in Table 15.6, the standard deviation of monthly percentage changes in share prices on the emerging markets were significantly higher than those of the US, UK or Japanese stockmarkets. This was particularly true for the case of Latin American markets.

Table 15.6   Standard deviation of LDC and DC share price indexes
(five years ending December 1989)

Market	Number of months	Standard deviation
Latin America		
Argentina	60	37
Brazil	60	21
Chile	60	8
Colombia	60	6
Mexico	60	16
Venezuela	60	12
Asia		
Korea	60	8
Taiwan	60	15
Turkey		24
IFC Regional Indexes		
Composite	60	7
Latin America	60	14
Asia	60	8
Developed Markets		
US (S&P 500)	60	5
UK (F.T. 100)	60	6
Japan (Nikkei)	60	5

Source: IFC.

A second main reflection of increased financial instability and fragility is the fact that in the 1970s and especially the 1980s there have been several episodes of financial distress among financial enterprises.

Episodes of financial distress include:

● the dollar overvaluation of the mid-1980s;
● the global stock market crash of October 1987, and the mini-crash two years later;
● property market crisis (Japan, UK);
● extended banking crisis (the secondary banking crisis in UK, the savings and loans disaster in the US, the collapse of the Nordic banking system);
● bankruptcies of large individual banks (Continental Illinois), or financial conglomerates (BCCI, Maxwell);
● crisis in the inter-bank market by spillovers of individual failure (Drexell Burnham Lambert, Herstatt);
● accidents in the payment systems (Bank of New York).

It is important to emphasise that, increasingly, instability in asset prices and institutional financial distress are related, as financial intermediaries hold – or lend against – the value of assets. As discussed above, banks have, in many countries, increased their securities business; they have also increased their exposure to real estate. As a consequence, their earnings – and their financial strength – became more sensitive to price fluctuations, of both shares and real estate. Both losses in securities markets and, especially, the weakness of real estate prices have been significant in the recent problems faced by many banks.

INCREASES, AND CHANGES IN THE NATURE OF, RISKS

As a result of the changes in the structure and workings of the financial system, the nature and transmission of systemic risk changed significantly, and possibly increased.

Systemic risk is defined by the BIS as 'the risk that the collapse or insolvency of one market will be transmitted to another participant'. It is a macro-economic phenomenon linking together different sources of financial instability, and is the unintentional outcome of externalities between decisions and conducts of individual agents under uncertainty.

A first major source of these externalities, that pose a potential for systemic risk, is the payment and settlements system; this has always been the main channel for the propagation of systemic crisis, triggered usually by the inability of one or more institutions to settle their obligations. However, the explosion of the volume of financial transactions flows over the last decade has dramatically changed the scale of risks involved. These are concentrated in the inter-bank wholesale transfer systems. Banks participating in these systems incur now extremely large intraday liquidity and credit exposures, possibly larger than the exposures traditionally captured in their balance sheets and frequently less closely monitored by regulators. This increases the vulnerability of the system to a participant's default or to technical failure, heightening the risk of a domino effect. These risks have been illustrated by the international ramifications of Herstatt's bankruptcy, by the technical failure of the Bank of New York and the unwinding of Drexel.

Beside being the channel through which counterparty risk (the risk that the counterparty to a financial contract will not meet the terms of the contract) is channelled, settlement arrangements can be an independent source of systemic risk, due to computer breakdown, concentration of risk in a clearing house inadequate to sustain it in a crisis, or because incompatibility between timetables and legal obligations in different markets increases the strain as turnover rises at a time of market disturbance; indeed, strains that could begin as a liquidity problem could become a solvency one.

As an OECD study[8] points out, organised settlement systems offer the opportunity to reduce or redistribute risks in a way providing better protection for market participants and for the system as a whole.

Several recent reports have made various recommendations to improve and accelerate settlement arrangements, for example within and between national securities markets. These goals may take a long time to reach, due to legal problems, as well as technological and cost factors. It seems that the greatest contribution to the management of risk can potentially come from achievement of delivery versus payment, shortening of settlement periods and the construction of legally valid systems of netting.

A second major source of systemic risk is increased exposure of institutions to market risks (the risk of losses in on-and-off balance sheet positions – stemming from movements in market prices, including interest rates, exchange rates and equity values); this has happened because of the rapid development of securities and derivative markets, as well as foreign exchange contracts. Large variations in the market price of assets (e.g. shares) are a very important source and channel of transmission of potential shocks. As positions are increasingly taken across a large number of markets, problems in one part of the market can quickly be transmitted to the others. As the BIS (op. cit.), points out, the stock market crash of 1987 clearly illustrated how very different operating arrangements in different markets for highly substitutable instruments can have destabilising effects because they result in differing price reaction speeds and uncoordinated stoppages.

The underlying force is that the deflation of asset prices destroys financial wealth. Because banks hold a large and increasing part of tradeable assets in their portfolios (due to the liberalisation of banks' permitted range of activities and the rapid development of financial markets), or because they lent heavily to asset holders, the quality of bank assets can decline rapidly in such a situation.

The integration of market segments (and particularly that of banks and securities) thus increases the transmission of disturbances in financial markets. So do developments in information technology. The main potential channel for such transmission of disturbances is now the seizing-up of funds in the wholesale markets or unwillingness for counterparties to enter into transaction with institutions whose soundness is in doubt, and not – as in the past – a generalised withdrawal of deposits.

This shows that, somewhat paradoxically given increased marketability of assets, the provision of liquidity has become more important in the new financial environment. Indeed, in a situation of slump of asset prices, a key risk is that the liquidity of some market makers can be threatened, which provides a channel to spread instability between underlying and derivative markets. Because of the key importance of liquidity, banks continue to be at the heart of financial activity, even though their share of financial intermediation has fallen in several countries. Indeed, the 1987 stock market crash highlighted the need to keep open credit lines to securities and derivative market operators precisely to avoid systemic instability.

Special concerns with banks' exposure to market risks have very recently (April 1993) led the Basle Committee on Banking Supervision to produce a consultative proposal on the Supervisory Treatment of Market Risks. This proposal suggests that specific capital charges are applied to open positions in debt and equity securities in banks' trading portfolios and in foreign exchange; these capital charges should constitute a minimum prudential standard relative to the potential for losses that might occur for a given portfolio; these would complement the capital adequacy rules approved already by the BIS referring to banks' credit risks, which began to be implemented on 1 January 1993. Secondly, the proposed capital charges for each type of instruments would be roughly equivalent in economic terms, to avoid creating artificial incentives favouring some instruments.

However, as we will discuss in the next section, regulation of banks' market risk (once implemented), though a positive development, will create problems of asymmetry with the regulation of securities' market risk, as coordination between banks' and securities' regulators (and among securities' regulators of different countries) has not yet been agreed.

Indeed, as we will develop more in the next section, it would seem that large variations between different national regulations of financial firms (and especially securities) as well as fundamentally different approaches to regulation amongst banking and securities' regulators may themselves be, at least for a time, a third source of potential increase in systemic risk. Indeed, the OECD document quoted above implicitly recognises this, when it argues that: 'this diversity in regulatory coverage causes international systemic concern because it encourages regulatory arbitrage, leaves some significant risk-taking activities by intermediaries outside the supervisory net, fails to deliver a comprehensive supervisory oversight of conglomerates, and complicates the task of international cooperation among supervisory authorities'. All this is a particularly important source for concern, because as the Federal Reserve Bank of New York put it in its 1985 Annual Report:[9] 'A shock that starts in one market may spread quickly along this network of linkages until it finds a weakness in some seemingly unrelated place. In fact *there is a growing tendency to build financial links along regulatory fault lines where the responsibility for supervisory oversight is weak, divided or clouded.*'

The issue of possible systemic risks arising from differences among supervisors, as well as supervisory gaps in certain markets and countries, is made more serious because financial markets have become more opaque, both for supervisors and market actors, in spite of efforts carried out. This opaqueness relates to instruments, relationships across instruments and markets, as well as the organisational structure of institutions. Indeed, the growing complexity of organisational structures, for example international financial conglomerates, clouds the evaluation of the soundness of institution. As the UK Bingham Report shows, the trend towards opaque corporate structures – and the problem it poses to regulators – are well illustrated by the BCCI case.

An important question to ask, which seems to have been insufficiently addressed in the existing literature and by policy-makers, is the extent to which the systemic risks associated with globalisation and securitisation are the same or different for flows going to developing countries. This important issue can be tackled at three different levels. One is at the level of investor protection; the second is at the level of global effects of possibly additional risks from flows to developing countries; a third level refers to the additional sources of potential macro-economic instability generated for developing countries by these new types of flows. We will focus here on the third level (which is of particular interest to LDCs) as the first two seem far less of a source of concern, given that the share of institutions' total investments going to developing countries is at present very low, and therefore problems in LDCs would affect their total assets only marginally; furthermore, as regards global effects of potential instability in LDCs, these would not seem on the whole to be that different from other global effects of financial instability discussed above. However, this matter may require further study.

As regards the potential additional sources of macro-economic instability generated for LDCs by the new type of flows, the main one would seem to relate to balance-of-payments funding risk. To the extent that securities' flows (and in particular international investment in equities) are potentially far more liquid than bank lending, then if a balance-of-payments crisis or the prospect of a major devaluation threatened in an LDC, foreign equity investors could move out very quickly. This would occur, to the extent that – as is the case in many LDCs, and particularly in those LDCs experiencing large portfolio flows at present – there are no or very scarce relevant foreign exchange controls (see Table 15.7), and to the extent that the foreign equity investors would sell their shares to nationals of the LDC, and not to other foreigners. Naturally new foreign investment in such equities would also cease at that time. The result would be additional pressure on the balance-of-payments and on the exchange rate, possibly contributing either to a major balance-of-payments crisis and/or to a large devaluation. Both would have undesirable effects on the LDC economy's levels of output and of inflation. Therefore in a pre-balance-of-payments or exchange-rate crisis situation, large international equity outflows (in relation to the domestic economy) could seriously magnify problems arising from other sources.

Naturally, this is not just related to international equity flows, nor is it a purely LDC problem, as is clearly illustrated by the effect of private financial flows in September 1992 on several currencies in the ERM. Indeed, there have been reports that some of the investors who were involved in the 'speculative' flows that so seriously affected some of the then ERM currencies, are now 'going into Latin America'.[10] However, the scale of the impact could be larger for LDCs, given the smaller size of their economies and *their greater fragility*, and the special features of their securities' markets.

Furthermore, as discussed above, price volatility of LDC stock markets is in general higher than that for developed countries. Therefore, the impact of potentially large sales by foreign investors (or nationals with 'trans-

Table 15.7   Entering and exiting emerging markets: a summary of investment
regulations (as of 31 March 1992)

Are listed stocks freely available to foreign investors?	Repatriation of: Income	Capital
Free entry		
Argentina	Free	Free
Brazil	Free	Free
Colombia	Free	Free
Jordan	Free	Free
Malaysia	Free	Free
Pakistan	Free	Free
Peru	Free	Free
Portugal	Free	Free
Turkey	Free	Free
Relatively free entry		
Bangladesh	Some restrictions	Some restrictions
Chile	Free	After 1 year
Costa Rica	Some restrictions	Some restrictions
Greece	Some restrictions	Some restrictions
Indonesia	Some restrictions	Some restrictions
Jamaica	Some restrictions	Some restrictions
Kenya	Some restrictions	Some restrictions
Mexico	Free	Free
Sri Lanka	Some restrictions	Some restrictions
Thailand	Free	Free
Trinidad & Tobago	Relatively free	Relatively free
Venezuela	Some restrictions	Some restrictions
Special classes of shares		
China	Some restrictions	Some restrictions
Korea	Free	Free
Philippines	Free	Free
Zimbabwe	Restricted	Restricted
Authorised investors only		
India	Some restrictions	Some restrictions
Taiwan, China	Free	Free
Closed		
Nigeria	Some restrictions	Some restrictions

Note
The industries in some countries are considered strategic and are not available to
foreign/non-resident investors, and the level of foreign investment in other cases
may be limited by national law or corporate policy to minority positions not to
aggregate more than 49 per cent of voting stock. The summaries above refer to 'new
money' investment by foreign institutions; other regulations may apply to capital
invested through debt conversion schemes or other sources.

Table 15.7 *cont.*

Key to Access
Free entry – No significant restrictions to pruchasing stocks.
Relatively free entry – Some registration procedures required to ensure repatriation rights.
Special classes – Foreigners restricted to certain classes of stock, designated for foreign investors.
Authorised investors only – Only approved foreign investors may buy stocks.
Closed – closed, or access severely restricted (e.g. for non-resident nationals only).
Key to Repatriation
Income – Dividends, interest, and realised capital gains.
Capital – Initial capital invested
Some restrictions – Typically, requires some registration with or permission of Central Bank, Ministry of Finance, or an Office of Exchange Controls that may restrict the timing of exchange release
Free – Repatriation done routinely

Source: *Emerging Stock Markets Factbook, 1992*, International Finance Corporation.

national' mentality) would be to depress particularly significantly the prices of shares. This could, via a wealth effect, contribute to a decline in aggregate demand and/or lead to other forms of financial instability. This latter would especially be the case to the extent that in the particular LDC there was strong integration of banking and securities, development of financial conglomerates, etc.

Other special features of LDC stock exchanges also increase their potential for generating negative effects in other parts of the economy. These relate for example, in some countries to inaccurate and slow settlements procedures. As discussed above, this increases instability in the stock exchanges, that can spill over to other sectors. Furthermore, the LDC stock markets tend to suffer from a shortage of good-quality, large capital-isation shares. This can result in quick overheating (that is, rapid increases in prices) when domestic and international interest is generated in these markets, due to some positive shock of expectations, and in quick 'over-cooling' (that is, rapid falls in prices), due to some negative shock of expectations, as discussed above.

Though on the whole foreign direct investment flows are far more stable and long-term, it has been reported[11] that international companies often do play the 'leads and lag game', with some of their funds, for example in anticipation of a devaluation, and that this 'speculative' behaviour can be an additional, though probably a more limited, sources of exchange rate instability.

As regards bonds, held by foreign investors, two problems could arise. Firstly, if investors saw the risk of a crunch coming, there could be fears that the seniority of bonds (which has been an important factor in attracting bond finance to LDCs) could be reversed; this fear will be increased, to the extent that bonds become a high proportion of the LDCs debt. Secondly, as the bonds and their interest are denominated in foreign exchange, if there are fears of a large devaluation, then the foreign investor would fear an increase in his credit risk. For both reasons, investors in bonds might want to sell if a balance-of-payments or exchange-rate crisis was foreseen. To the extent that these bonds could be sold to nationals of the LDC (which seems more difficult than in the case of shares), then this would have a balance-of-payment funding and/or an exchange-rate effect.

Last, but certainly not least, as regards inflows to LDCs, and especially to Latin America, there is a fairly high proportion of those inflows that specifically come in for a very short period, e.g. three months, mainly attracted by interest rate differential. Naturally, these flows are highly volatile, and in the case of a threat of a balance of payments or exchange rate crisis, would leave very rapidly, and with destabilising effects.

Finally, it should be stressed that such major and rapid outflows of capital from an LDC as have been discussed above is far more likely to occur if there is a large macro-economic imbalance in that economy. Therefore, in the current world of globalisation and free capital flows, the importance of prudent macro-economic policies is paramount. With prudent macro-management, large, sudden outflows that are particularly destabilising are far less likely, though they cannot be completely ruled out. Indeed, the recent G-10 Dini Report acknowledges, that even for the case of developed countries, 'a country can experience downward pressure on its currency despite the fact that its macro-economic policy and performance have been sound'.

EXISTING SUPERVISION AND REGULATION; SOME LIMITATIONS

The changing nature and possible increase of systemic risk implies a number of major challenges and issues for governments. The first one (on which we will concentrate here) is to improve prudential regulation and supervision of individual institutions, so as to curb excessive risk-taking at source.

One issue that needs clarifying is that *of coverage of* regulation and supervision; this should cover all those financial companies whose collapse would trigger systemic turmoil. Though there is considerable consensus (see, for example BIS (op. cit.)) that supervisory coverage limited to banks may well not be enough, a number of major supervisory gaps still exist; probably the most obvious is one that allows some securities houses to carry out certain activities via unsupervised affiliates.

Above all, there are important differences in the extent to which and the form in which similar institutions are regulated in different jurisdictions, as well as different institutions are regulated both in the same and in different jurisdictions, a subject to which we will return below.

An important issue in this context is whether institutions should be supervised on a consolidated basis. The question is whether, if legal and economic separation of, for example, banking and securities can be achieved (which is in itself very complex), and 'firewalls' established to limit transfer of capital between them, this will be sufficient to separate the market perception of the credit standing of both institutions, and therefore isolate one unit from the other in a period of distress. As the Drexel case illustrated, funding seems to be withdrawn from institutions that are sound, due to associations in the public mind with problems arising in affiliates. Therefore, failure to consolidate can result in serious supervisory gaps. Though consolidation is a standard practice in banking supervision (following in particular the problems caused by Banco Ambrosiano), it is not yet generally accepted in the supervision of securities and insurance.

Consolidation of supervision between different types of activities is made difficult by conceptual difference among their regulators, based on key differences in the nature of their business.

The most fundamental difference between securities and banks is that the former have a far shorter commercial time horizon than banks. Banks typically hold loans on their balance sheets until maturity, while securities firms experience rapid asset turnover.

Because the bulk of securities firms' assets are marketable, they are therefore subject to severe pressures in periods of market downturn (which leads therefore to market risk), and to a similar decline in the firm's net worth. Because firms need to meet losses quickly, securities regulators emphasise liquidity, treating illiquid assets consecutively and often allowing certain forms of short-term subordinated financing to be counted as capital. As the key concern is that securities firms should be able to run themselves down in a very short period and meet their liabilities, so that their clients/counterparties will not incur losses, the key supervisory test is that of net liquid assets. Thus, a firm should have liquid assets (valued at current price) which – after allowance for possible reductions in the value of the assets before they could be sold, exceed total liabilities. In contrast, a major proportion of bank assets are traditionally non-marketable; as a result the main risk for banks is credit risk. Differently from securities' houses, banks are not expected to respond to financial problems by going out of business, as their assets could only be sold at a heavy discount, implying losses for creditors and depositors. Therefore, the main objective of bank regulators is to sustain banks as going concerns, especially because bank failures involve risks to the financial system as a whole. Therefore bank supervisors tend to focus far less on liquidity and short-run changes in asset values, and more on the long-run viability of the bank. Therefore, the regulatory definition of capital only included financing instruments of a more permanent nature (excluding, for example, subordinated debt from primary capital).

Regulatory differences extend also to the role of deposit insurance and lender of last resort, which are important for banks, but are on the whole unavailable for securities.

The above differences in the regulation of banks and securities firms have for example led to difficulties for EEC policy-makers in their attempts to establish an appropriate regulatory framework for the single European financial market. The EEC's Directive on the Capital Adequacy of Investment Firms and Credit Institutions (known as CAD) allows alternative definitions of capital for the supervisors of non-bank investment firms and for banks undertaking securities activities. As Dale (op. cit.), points out, these alternative definitions of capital are mainly intended to meet the policy objective of ensuring a 'level playing-field', between banks and non-bank investment firms. However, there is a concern that these capital rules are *not* justified on prudential grounds.

In particular, though the appropriate regulatory goal defined by the EEC for bank supervisors is solvency, for securities, the EEC regulatory objective is more limited: to protect investors and counterparties without necessarily ensuring solvency, a goal that can be achieved by more liberal use of subordinated debt. But, as we discussed above, given the way that securities markets developed and the Drexel episode led to a crisis of confidence in the investment firms, the EEC's objectives seem inappropriate or at least insufficient to deal with systemic risk.

Thus, the main problem with the EEC CAD directive seems to be its focus on establishing a level playing-field between banks and non-bank investment firms, while failing to address the following more fundamental policy dilemma. This is that increasingly in non-banking financial markets similar systemic risks can be created as occurred previously only in narrower banking systems; if the official safety net were extended by national authorities to activities like securities, then the problem of subsidised – and thus excessive – risk-taking could be extended from banks to securities.

Indeed, the EEC approach seems to accentuate these problems, as it allows banks to dilute their capital, while allowing the risk of cross-infection from securities activities to increase.

Besides the problems of new regulations in the EEC, there is the issue that the EEC and the US seem to be moving in opposite directions in the key issue of risk segregation. Thus, in the EEC it is increasingly assumed that a bank would always stand behind a related securities firm; in the US, the new holding company and firewall structure is designed explicitly so that a securities firm in problem is *not* supported by its bank affiliate. This may imply that in Europe the lender of last resort function could be extended (directly or indirectly) to bank related securities firms. In contrast, the US scheme (which assumes that firewalls, and other mechanisms, can separate effectively risks between banking and their securities branches) would tend to restrict the official safety-net only to banking.

The coexistence of these sharply opposed structures could be particularly problematic in times of global financial stress. Thus, in the EEC, the temptation could arise, for lenders to move their exposure from independent to bank-related securities, as the latter are more likely to get official support. Furthermore, in those circumstances, there would be a strong incentive for lenders to withdraw their exposure from US securities in favour of securities firms that are affiliates of European banks. Such large moves could accentuate financial distress in the US, and globally.

Indeed, it is differences in the perception of securities' regulators (and particularly between those of the US and of the rest of the countries) that have impeded a global agreement on capital requirements of securities' firms (which would have done for securities what the Basle accord has done for banking). An attempt to reach such an agreement was made, after much preparatory work, at the 1992 IOSCO (International Organization of Securities' Commissions) Annual Conference; unfortunately, this attempt failed.[12] It should however be mentioned that IOSCO did reach some important agreements, such as the approval of principles for regulation of financial conglomerates.[13]

Perhaps equally serious is the fact that had IOSCO been able to agree on common risk measures and capital adequacy rules for securities, this would have served as a basis for a joint framework (to be elaborated by the BIS and IOSCO) for commercial banks, investment banks and securities houses. As a result of this inability to reach agreement within IOSCO, the Basle Committee has launched its own suggestions (discussed above) to limit market and other related risks for securities activities carried out by banks, by setting capital requirements on them. If approved, this will cover an important supervisory gap, but will still leave a very large gap in the regulation of non-bank securities.

As a result, supervision and regulation globally is patchy as regards certain aspects, and very uneven. Indeed, as can be clearly seen in Table 15.8, while securities firms and financial conglomerates outside the EEC will *not* in the next few years *have to adhere to any international guidelines, banks inside the EEC will have to meet three different sets of rules for measuring market risks and for capital requirements to cover those risks* (the BIS ones, the EC Directives and possibly some national ones). The issue is made more complex by the fact that Basle rules are stricter than the EC's Directive, for example as regards capital requirements on foreign exchange risk.

Indeed, as can be seen in Table 15.8, banks are regulated by up to three sets of regulators in an EEC country like the UK; they are regulated internationally by the 1988 Basle Accord and will probably be regulated by Basle on their securities activities; banks are also regulated in a country like the UK by its own national regulations and by the EEC capital adequacy directive. On the other hand, neither securities nor financial conglomerates outside the EEC have any form of international regulation, though there are national regulations for securities; for the EEC countries, there are special EC regulations approved or in the process of approval for securities and financial conglomerates.

Table 15.8   Regulatory frameworks of financial institutions

	International	*EC*[3]	*USA*	*UK*
Banks	x[1]	xx	x	xxx
Securities	–	x	x	xx
Financial conglomerates	–[2]	x	x[4]	x

1. Includes both the 1988 Accord and the regulation of securities activities of banks, the latter proposed in 1993 and to be implemented by 1997 at the earliest.
2. There is an IOSCO proposal for principles on which to regulate financial conglomerates, but no formal regulatory agreement.
3. EC directives to be enacted by 1996.
4. Till recently, US regulation of non-bank securities' houses, within major financial groups, was practically non-existent.

Source: Table prepared by the author, on the basis of interview material, BIS and IOSCO documents, Dale, op. cit.

It would seem, that unless special efforts are made to overcome this asymmetry, it is likely to remain for quite a number of years. This relates not only to the conceptual differences between regulators discussed above (which originate largely in the diversity between different financial institutions and their differences among individual countries), but also due to institutional differences, for example between BIS and IOSCO. The BIS is a long-established G-10 institution, which carries a lot of weight, as it provides the basis for a 'central bank of central banks'. Its members, the G-10 central banks, also are the lenders of last resort of their own banking systems. Its work on international harmonisation of supervisory standards has gone on for around 20 years. Therefore it seems to find it easier to reach agreements than IOSCO, which is a far newer institution; though created in 1974, mainly by Latin American institutions, it became international only in 1987. Its work on harmonisation of international regulations is thus far more recent than that of the BIS. It represents bodies from 51 countries, which in itself makes it more difficult to reach agreement than in a G-10 institution. Furthermore, the bodies whose activities it coordinates (the securities commissions) themselves tend to be fairly young, and do not have special lender-of-last-resort powers domestically. For these reasons it may also well continue to be more difficult to reach agreements on common regulations, and to enforce those agreements, in securities than it is in banking-related activities. EEC directives, once formally approved, which tends to imply a long process, do have enforceable sanctions as they follow a legal process (unlike both the BIS and IOSCO).

Though all this is understandable, it does pose serious additional risks to the financial system originated in regulations' asymmetries.

There can be problems even in cases where regulations are integrated, for example due to the fact that contract law exists at a national level and therefore cannot be integrated. This is particularly an issue in so far as there is growth of transactions whose settlement is at a future date.

The differences of laws amongst countries can affect, for example, liquidation proceedings of collapsed financial institutions, to favour one group of national creditors against the rest.[14] It therefore not only creates inequalities internationally, but also imposes additional pressures on settling situations of financial failure. The promotion of international treaties, e.g. via the UN, the GATT or other bodies, though complex to achieve, would need to play an important role to help overcome these types of problems internationally, whereas in the context of the EEC these problems would decrease as integration progresses.

Besides the general issues relating to supervision and regulation in the new financial environment, it seems important to emphasise that there may be specific issues posed by the new types of risk generated by the impact of these new trends specifically related to LDCs. Though for example, national securities' regulators do have special treatment for firms investing in LDCs (which for example in the UK case discriminates somewhat between different types of LDCs, mainly related to the quality of regulations of the countries' stock exchange),[15] the focus on LDCs seems somewhat limited, as for example it does not seem to take any account of macro-economic developments in those countries even in the context of its possible impact on investor protection.

On the broader issue of the effects of financial flows on macro-economic performance of countries (and specifically LDCs), this is explicitly *not* a matter of concern to any of the regulatory bodies, unless it affects the potential solvency of the financial institutions which they regulate.[16] This poses the need for other international institutions (e.g. the IMF), possibly for regional bodies, and/or last but certainly not least for the national recipient governments to closely monitor the impact of such flows on current and future macro-economic trends in the LDCs, and possibly to define specific regulations to influence the level and composition of such flows.

CONCLUSION AND POLICY RECOMMENDATIONS

There is a growing consensus that global financial deregulation and liberalisation, though having many positive effects, have also resulted both in greater risks for the global financial system and for individual investors. As R. Breuer,[17] Member of the Board of Managing Directors, Deutsche Bank, succinctly put it: 'This leads to a need for re-regulation and harmonisation of supervisory legislation.' This does on the whole clearly not mean a return to the types of regulations that existed in the 1970s, but to types of regulations appropriate for the needs of the new financial system of the 1990s, resulting largely from deregulation.

Though it may seem somewhat paradoxical, the more free-enterprise-oriented a country is, the greater the role of official supervision of financial institutions will be in such a country. This is due to the fact that in a truly market-oriented economy, the danger of business failures will be high, leading to greater risk to the balance sheets of the financial institutions lending to the business sector. Especially if governments and central banks wish not to bail out financial institutions, then deregulation needs to be supported by close and well-coordinated supervision of financial institutions.

From our analysis above, we can see that, to achieve close and coordinated supervision of financial institutions globally, several important tasks need to be accomplished. These pose an important and difficult challenge to governments and especially to regulators.

Firstly, the issue of appropriate and coordinated supervision of securities needs to be dealt with far quicker than in recent years. Though the recent Basle consultative proposal makes a valuable effort in dealing with the complex issues of regulating capital adequacy for banks' securities activities, no equivalent basis exists yet for non-banks' securities. This is an important regulatory gap that needs to be filled fairly urgently. As discussed briefly above, this will need, as a pre-condition, to overcome the differences in regulatory approach to risks in securities, between the US and other countries, and in particular the EEC.

Furthermore, to achieve a more closely integrated system of supervision of internationally active intermediaries in securities markets, this would probably require securities regulators to develop their equivalent of the Basle Concordat for banking supervisors, defining the responsibilities of a lead regulator in the home country in relation to host countries.

Secondly, more generally, a serious effort needs to be made to extend regulatory coverage to financial institutions that are now effectively unregulated, such as financial conglomerates. This requires closer coordination between banking and securities' supervisors. If this is not done, competitive realities will continue to lead to a shift of business away from more regulated to less regulated entities, increasing the risks to the safety and soundness of the financial system.

Thirdly, though agreements on capital requirements for banks – and, one hopes, in the near future for their securitised activities – in the context of Basle provide a key regulatory input, there also needs to be a large effort to reach agreements on standards, e.g. accounting standards and disclosure standards. These agreements need to be reached first globally within each financial industry's regulators (e.g. banking, securities and insurance) and then agreements to coordinate such standards need to be met. Particular emphasis needs to be placed on integrating LDC representatives into these efforts, as their standards may often be lower or particularly different from those of the developed countries.

Fourthly, additional work needs to be done to improve in specific aspects, such as crucially the organisation of settlements systems for securities, so as to avoid them acting as an independent source of systemic risk. Organised settlement systems offer the opportunity to reduce or redistribute risks in a way that provides better protection both for participants in markets and the system as a whole. Among the measures necessary to improve and accelerate settlements arrangements within and between national securities markets are: shorten settlements periods, links between settlement arrangements in home and host countries and, especially, the achievement of simultaneous good delivery of securities against payment for them.

Fifth, as discussed above, there may be an increasing need to achieve greater global integration of contract law, so that contracts can be challenged internationally, and regulators can carry out liquidation proceedings that are internationally equitable. Such legal integration would both facilitate further global financial integration and aid the task of regulators in effectively and equitably enforcing their regulations. Naturally this task poses difficult issues relating to the promotion of international treaties.

Sixth, the issues raised above – and others raised by globalisation and increased complexity of finance – seem to require creation of a strong and ongoing institutional capacity, at the international level. At a minimum, this would require in particular a substantial strengthening of IOSCO and a closer integration of all countries into the Basle Accord. A more ambitious approach – both far more difficult to implement and far more satisfactory – would be to create a global board of regulators,[18] with central banks and other regulatory representatives, and possibly with members drawn from the private sector. Such a body could set mutually acceptable minimum capital requirements for all major financial institutions, establish uniform trading, reporting and disclosure standards and monitor the performance of markets and financial institutions.

One of the virtues of such an approach is that it would increasingly achieve a truly global perspective on regulation, integrating both different national and functional perspectives; at present such global perspectives are difficult to achieve as regulators respond to their constituencies and their conceptual frameworks (both at a national level and at a functional level). This is clearly a more long-term task.

Besides the above-described initiatives at a regulatory level, two initiatives can be suggested, one that specifically focuses on LDCs and the second, on a proposal for an international tax. There is a specific need to fairly urgently monitor precisely the scale and composition of capital inflows into developing countries. Due to the rapid pace of innovations, and to other factors, this is no easy task. Important efforts are being carried out in this area by the World Bank and the IMF. Beyond monitoring, there seems to be a need to assess at least the present and likely future macroeconomic impact of such flows on the LDCs. There may be fears that the scale and/or composition of the flows is having important undesirable effects, for example on overvaluing exchange rates via a 'financial Dutch disease phenomenon' which will discourage export growth; or there may be related fears that a dramatic reversal of large flows could have negative future effects, on output or inflation, as occurred in the debt crises of the 1980s (though the mechanisms would be slightly different). In such situations, there may be a case for measures to be taken to discourage excessive inflows, especially of certain types of flows (e.g. shorter-term ones).

An important issue is – institutionally – who should take the initiative. Clearly the first level is that of national LDC governments; thus, the

Chilean, Mexican and Brazilian governments have taken such measures in recent years. Secondly, regional institutions (e.g. CEPAL in Latin America) and/or regional development banks (e.g. IDB) can take an interest. Thirdly, global institutions, such as particularly the IMF and the World Bank need to take an interest, and exert influence, especially to the extent that insufficient action takes place at the national level (the recent dispute between the Argentine government and the IMF on the need for reserve requirements on capital inflows provides a good example).

Such actions need above all to be guided by the principle that the capital inflows to LDCs should contribute to countries' long-term growth and development on a sustained basis, and that future debt or major foreign exchange crises need to be avoided. The last LDC debt crisis is such a recent phenomenon, that we can all remember the 'sins of omission' by different key actors and extract relevant lessons for the management of the new type of private flows of the nineties, so that their long-term effect is more beneficial and sustained.

Finally, a measure that may deserve attention is Tobin's proposal to levy an international uniform tax on spot transactions in foreign exchange.[19] Tobin's proposal is for a 0.25 per cent tax on currency transactions. The aim would be to slow down speculative, short-term capital flows (which would be more affected as by definition they cross borders often, and would be taxed every time), while having only a marginal effect on long-term flows. This would somewhat increase the autonomy of national authorities for monetary and macro-economic policy, with a bit more independence from the effects of international money markets. Such an autonomy would be particularly valuable for LDCs, to the extent that their economies adapt less easily to external shocks and because their thinner financial markets are more vulnerable to the impact of external capital inflows and outflows. The proposal would be particularly attractive to LDCs if the proceeds of it were to go, as Tobin suggested, to the World Bank.

This proposal is different from the other seven listed above, in that it may seem more radical. However, there is a widespread feeling, even in private circles, that financial liberalisation may have proceeded too far or at least too fast, and that financial liberalisation carried to the extreme may even risk damaging the far more important trade liberalisation, whose benefits are far more universally recognised. Furthermore, a new tax would be attractive to fiscally constrained governments.

Therefore, a small tax on financial flows – which particularly discourages short-term flows – could be a welcome development. It could be introduced on a temporary basis for a fixed period, e.g. five years. This would be consistent with the fairly widespread perception that financial fragility and systemic risk are particularly high in the current stage, of 'transition' from regulated to deregulated financial markets.

The tax would have an additional advantage. It could greatly facilitate monitoring of international financial flows, by providing centralised data basis on such flows. This could be particularly valuable for innovative flows and flows going to LDCs, where particular information gaps exist.

Doubtless technical problems would need to be overcome. An institution like the IMF would be very competent to deal with them. More seriously, probably, would be the opposition of certain parts of the financial community, which would lobby against such a proposal. However, the attractiveness of the idea, and an apparent increase in support for that type of initiative, could lead to such an innovative measure to be taken globally.

NOTES

1. See, for example, World Bank, *Global Economic Prospects and the Developing Countries*, 1993, pp. 35–6.
2. See, World Bank, op. cit.; WIDER, *Foreign Portfolio Investment in Emerging Equity Markets*, Study Group Series No. 5, Helsinki; S. Gooptu, *Portfolio Investment Flows to Emerging Markets*, World Bank Working Paper, March 1993, WP51117, Washington, DC.
3. World Bank, op. cit.
4. For a detailed analysis of this trend, see R. Dale, *International Banking Deregulation, the Great Banking Experiment* (Oxford: Blackwell, 1992).
5. See, for example, BIS, op. cit.; also, R. O'Brien, *Global Financial Integration: The End of Geography* (London: Pinter, 1992).
6. See, World Bank, op. cit.
7. See, for example, E. P. Davis, 'The Structure, Regulation and Performance of Pension Funds in Nine Industrial Countries', mimeo, Bank of England, 1992; also, Howell, M. and Cozzini, A. (1991) *Games without Frontiers; Global Equity Markets in the 1990's*, (London: Salomon, 1991).
8. OECD, 'Systemic Risks in Securities Markets', *Financial Market Trends*, No. 49, June 1991, Paris.
9. E. Frydl, 'The challenges of financial change', Federal Reserve Bank of New York, *Annual Report* (1985).
10. Interview material.
11. Interview material.
12. Interview material; see also, *The Economist*, 31 October, 1992, 'Capital spat' and *The Financial Times*, 4 May 1993, 'Tough time making a level playing field'.
13. See, IOSCO, Final Communiqué of the XVII Annual Conference, London, 1992.
14. Interview material.

15. Interview material.
16. Interview material.
17. R. Breuer, 'Financial Integration – The End of Geography', IOSCO XVII Annual Conference, London, October 1992.
18. H. Kaufmann, at the 1992 IOSCO Conference, suggested the creation of such a body, and called it 'Board of Overseers of Major International Institutions and Markets'.
19. J. Tobin, 'Tax the speculators', *The Financial Times*, 22 December 1992.

16 A New Framework for Development Cooperation

Mahbub ul Haq

The end of the cold war opens up some new opportunities for reallocation of aid to improve its quality and effectiveness. In fact, a major improvement in the quality of aid could serve as the most powerful argument for an increase in its quantity.

Presently, there is no clear link between aid and several global objectives which are normally mentioned as the avowed goals of donors. This is because aid still carries the scars of the cold war:

- high military spenders among developing countries receive about twice as much ODA per capita as more moderate military spenders.
- El Salvador gets more total aid than Bangladesh, even though Bangladesh has 24 times more population and it is five times poorer.
- Of the $21 billion that the US provides in foreign assistance, about one-half is still in the form of military assistance.

The present link of aid with the global objective of poverty alleviation is fairly weak and tenuous:

- only one-quarter of official development assistance is earmarked for three-quarters of the world's poor.
- India, containing 34 per cent of the world's absolute poor, receives only 3.5 per cent of total ODA.
- Egypt receives $370 per poor person, India receives only $4.
- The richest 40 per cent of the developing world population receives twice as much per capita ODA as the poorest 40 per cent.
- The much poorer South Asia currently receives $5 ODA per capita; the much richer Middle East receives $55 per capita.
- According to an ODC study, the US provides $250 per capita to high-income developing countries and only $1 per capita to low-income countries.

There is no strong link between the present allocations of ODA and the global objective of supporting priority human development goals:

239

- While the education sector received around one-tenth of bilateral aid in the 1980s, only 7 per cent of these funds were earmarked for primary education.
- Of the total ODA that was channelled to the health sector, only 27 per cent was given for primary health care.
- The share of rural areas in the total aid earmarked for water supply and sanitation was only 19 per cent.
- Only 6.5 per cent of total bilateral assistance is currently earmarked for human priority concerns – viz., basic education, primary health care, rural water supply, nutrition programmes, and family planning services.
- Of the total aid given to low-income countries, only 2 per cent is presently earmarked for primary health care and 1 per cent for population assistance. In sub-Saharan Africa, during the 1980s, only $1 of assistance was provided per primary pupil, $11 per secondary pupil and $575 per university pupil.

These priorities reflect, of course, the priorities of the developing countries themselves. But the main point is that many donors do not try to influence or correct these distorted priorities but often go along with them willingly in view of their own commercial interest in brick-and-mortar projects.

There is also no clearly-established link of aid with human rights at present, despite considerable shrill rhetoric on this subject:

- Recent studies by US scholars have established a perverse correlation between US aid and human rights violations during the 1980s: this was because strategic alliances in the cold war era took precedence over human rights considerations.
- The recent experience of Bangladesh, Pakistan and the Philippines demonstrates that their per capita ODA allocation went down, not up, after martial law was lifted in these countries. Donors often like political stability and economic management policies under martial law regimes, despite their protests to the contrary.

There has also been no link between aid and decentralised governance. In fact, according to the analysis carried out in the 1993 *Human Development Report*, aid has had a very centralising impact. Almost all aid is negotiated with the central governments. While it is not necessary that it should also be spent by the central authorities, in practice this is what has happened. Very few developing countries are keen to pass on aid funds to local bodies after having guaranteed their repayment at the central level. And only a few donors have insisted on a more decentralised implementation of their aided projects, through local authorities or NGOs.

There is also very little link discernible between technical assistance and national capacity-building – though capacity-building has been the sacred mantra for technical cooperation. After 40 years of technical assistance, 95 per cent of these funds (over $12 billion a year by now) are still being spent on foreign consultants, despite the fact that outstanding national expertise is available from within these countries. Africa receives around $6 billion of technical assistance, and yet its human development indicators are the lowest in the world and it has perhaps received more bad advice per capita than any other continent. There is no other form of assistance which deserves as radical a surgery as technical assistance today.

The above analysis is not offered as an indictment of aid but as an opportunity for a considerable improvement in aid-allocation priorities. There have been significant successes of development cooperation: but what is also obvious is the considerable further mileage that we can squeeze out of existing funds. It is in this spirit that a determined attempt must be made to improve the quality of assistance and to design a new framework of development cooperation to fit the post-cold war realities. The following proposals are offered as a contribution towards this objective.

First, we need a new motivation for development cooperation, based on fighting the growing threat of global poverty rather than the receding threat of the cold war. Can the rich nations convince their people that while their security may no longer be threatened today by the prospect of a nuclear holocaust, it is certainly threatened by the travel of global poverty across international frontiers without even a passport in the form of drugs, AIDS, pollution, illegal migration and terrorism? While the chances of a global nuclear suicide were always very small, the chances of every family being affected by these new threats are very great. I recognise that we would all love to base the new edifice of development cooperation on some firm moral foundations – and we must – but let us also not forget that fear has been one of the most motivating forces in human history. And let us, by all means, couple this fear about common survival with the great potential for common prosperity through rising global interdependence.

If we are to create a new motivation for aid, let us also put aside around 2 per cent of existing ODA budgets (or about $1 billion a year) for cultivating the new constituencies of change – half of it to be spent bilaterally, and half through international channels. We live in an age of communications, where powerful vested interests exploit the resources of the media for their own narrow ends. Why should we hesitate to use the same channels to promote a new framework of development cooperation to safeguard global human security?

Second, let us persuade the nations of the world that the cold war must be phased out of the Third World as well. Let us candidly recognise that the cold war is not over yet. The job is only half-done. We have phased out the cold war in East–West relations. But we have forgotten to phase it out in the Third World.

Let us clearly recognise that many Third World countries are still:

- spending two to three times as much on arms as on the education and health of their people.
- maintaining eight times more soldiers than doctors.
- increasing their military expenditure (particularly in the poorest regions of sub-Saharan Africa and South Asia) at a time when global military expenditures have been declining since 1987.

We must persuade the developing countries to at least freeze, or even reduce, their current military spending levels. And we should persuade the rich nations to fix a timetable (say, the next three years) within which they:

- close down all existing military bases.
- convert all existing military aid into economic aid.
- stop the existing arms shipments of over $35 billion a year to make huge profits from poor nations that cannot even feed their people.
- eliminate subsidies to arms exporters and retrain their workers for jobs in civilian industries.

Third, let us demonstrate to our sceptical public opinion that we can finance the essential human development agenda even by reallocating priorities in our existing budgets. Let us design a new 20-20 vision. Let us persuade the developing countries to commit an average of 20 per cent of their budgets to human priority concerns instead of the present 10 per cent – by reducing military expenditures, by privatising inefficient public enterprises and by eliminating low-priority development expenditure. And let us persuade the rich nations to raise their human priority allocations from the existing 7 per cent to around 20 per cent. This new global human compact can be financed entirely by recasting our existing allocation priorities. It requires no new resources. What it requires is courage and skill. And it would yield $30 to $40 billion of additional allocations for urgent human development agenda in the poor nations, two-thirds through their own courageous decisions and one-third from the international community. If such a compact is implemented, look at the human pay-off: within the next ten years, all children will be in school, primary health care and clean drinking water will be available to all the people, family planning services will be provided to all willing couples, and severe child malnutrition will be eliminated.

We have constructed many grand designs in the past based on an elusive additionality of aid. Isn't it time that we became realistic and demonstrated to the world what we can accomplish even out of existing resources? Isn't it time to design such a new 20-20 compact and present it to the forthcoming World Social Summit in March 1995? Won't it be the best strategy to convince our reluctant legislatures and sceptical public opinion that they must support additional aid by demonstrating to them what mileage we can get even out of existing resources – by showing, for once, the doable, the possible, the achievable?

Fourth, let us redress the growing imbalance between short-term emergency assistance and long-term development support. While the UN spent less than $4 billion on peace-keeping missions during the first 48 years of its existence, it is likely to spend over $4 billion on such missions in 1993 alone. And to deliver every dollar of humanitarian assistance, it is now costing about ten times as much on soldiers. It is time to review this strange and disturbing imbalance. And it is time that we all recognised that if there are diminished funds for socio-economic development, there are likely to be many more emergencies in the future.

This has at least two policy implications. One, we must persuade the donors that allocations for UN peace-keeping operations should come out of their defence budgets, not out of their limited ODA budgets. After all, peace-keeping operations are an extension of their security requirements, not a gift to the poor nations. Two, the developmental role of the UN must be strengthened. The Agenda for Peace must be complemented by an Agenda for Development. Without peace, there will never be a stable framework for development. And without development, peace will always be at risk. In the final analysis, this means that the UN must be given the mandate for sustainable human development, it must be provided more assured sources of development financing, and it must have a forum for global economic decisions at the highest level in the form of an Economic Security Council.

Fifth, let us search for a more innovative model of development cooperation which is based on the new insights into human security, not on outmoded ideas of charity. Such a new model will require tremendous courage and it must embrace three new mechanisms:

● We must create a new mechanism to facilitate payments by one country to another for services rendered. These are mutually beneficial services which by their very nature cannot be mediated by markets. Examples include payments for environmental services, payments for control of narcotic drugs, and payments for the control of contagious diseases (like AIDS).

- We must create a new mechanism to facilitate compensation for damages when one country inflicts an economic injury on another. Compensation can be thought of as fines payable by countries which depart from internationally agreed rules of good conduct. Some of the examples may include: encouragement of the brain drain from poor nations, restrictions on the migration of low-skilled labour in search of international economic opportunities, trade restrictions on exports from poor countries. These compensations are in a sense voluntary since they can be avoided by refraining from engaging in objectionable behaviour.
- We must create a new mechanism of automatic resource mobilisation for global objectives which embrace common human survival on this fragile planet. This should be seen essentially as a shared price for shared human existence. It will particularly apply to environmental protection where the huge sums needed may have to be raised through tradeable permits for carbon emissions, or through an international carbon tax, or through other such measures, which make the matter of human survival an automatic decision, not subject to national legislative approval.

Sixth, let us broaden the concept of development cooperation to include trade, investment, technology and labour flows. And let us keep our accounts on that basis so that we can keep monitoring that what is given with one hand is not taken away with the other, and that the real focus of all our efforts continues to be on opening up global market opportunities. Let us not forget the startling conclusion of the 1992 *Human Development Report*: developing countries are being denied $500 billion of global market opportunities every year while they receive a mere $50 billion in aid.

Seventh, we need a new aid policy dialogue, linked with the new issues of reduced military spending, improved national governance, more emphasis on sustainable human development. I am personally in favour of persuasion rather than coercion; constructive alliances for change with domestic policy-makers rather than outside intervention; an enlightened policy dialogue rather than an inflexible conditionality; a two-way compact rather than one-way pressure. What is more important, however, is to change the *substance* of the policy dialogue. I have a lurking suspicion that aid has been unpopular at both ends because policy dialogue is entirely between governments rather than between people. No discernible objectives are defined or served – and certainly it is very difficult to sell the message of aid to suspicious public opinions unless its link with global objectives is clearly spelt out and monitored regularly. I hope that greater transparency can be introduced in the data concerning aid. It is impossible today to monitor aid on the basis of its link with various laudable global objectives: the limited illustrations I gave at the start were collected after tremendous research. And it is certainly impossible to get any data today on military assistance, military debts, military bases, or subsidies to arms exporters. It is time to give DAC the mandate to collect and publish such data. This will certainly make their annual reports a significant international event.

These are controversial issues. They are not easy to agree on, but an honest dialogue must begin around these issues. After all, the heresies of yesterday have already become the conventional wisdom of today.

Index